Understanding Computers

Understanding Computers:

What Managers and Users Need to Know

MYLES E. WALSH

Director, Information Systems Planning
CBS, Inc.

A WILEY-INTERSCIENCE PUBLICATION

JOHN WILEY & SONS, New York • Chichester • Brisbane • Toronto • Singapore

Library of Congress Cataloging in Publication Data:

Walsh, Myles E
    Understanding computers.

    "A Wiley-Interscience publication."
    Includes index.
    1. Electronic digital computers.   I.   Title.
QA76.5.W285   001.64′2   80-20547
ISBN 0-471-08191-4 (CLOTH)
ISBN 0-471-87417-5 (PAPER)

Printed in the United States of America

10 9 8 7

to Diana

Preface

For over twenty years, I have worked in the field of electronic data processing. I've worked as a control clerk, as a tab operator, as a computer operator, as a computer operations supervisor, as an application programmer, as an operations and facilities coordinator, as a manager of systems and programming, as a director of computer systems and operations, as an information systems consultant and most recently as a director of data base systems. During these last twenty years, I have been exposed to virtually every aspect of commercial data processing. In writing this book, I am attempting to share with you the benefits of my experience. If I have done well, you will have a foundation, a beginning, from which you may commence further study. At the very least, you will have an understanding of the fundamentals of commercial data processing.

The book is in three parts: the first deals with computer basics, the second with more sophisticated concepts, and the third with commercial data processing and management information systems. In the first part there are five chapters. The first describes a computer in functional terms. Chapter 2 examines peripheral or auxiliary storage devices, the equipment which holds the large volumes of data that are processed by a computer. A description of the equipment used for getting data into and out of a computer configuration is also found in chapter two. Chapter 3 looks at data and how they are grouped. Computer programs, that is, the sets of instructions that tell a computer how to solve a particular problem, are also discussed in chapter three. Groups of programs, sometimes referred to as systems, receive attention in chapter 4. Some of the more advanced computer technology are also introduced. Chapter 5 describes computers in a little more detail. The basic components of a computer are explained in such a way as to give you a working knowledge of components such as transistors and fabrications such as semiconductors.

The second part also contains five chapters. They deal with computer systems software. Software is a combination of computer programs and sets of data that enable computers to perform complex chores. Chapter 6 examines operating systems, those collections of computer programs and sets of data that enable a computer to execute a number of programs concurrently. Data bases and their management, that is, complex arrangements of sets of data on auxiliary storage devices and their management receive attention in chapter 7. Chapter 8 explains how data base elements are stored and retrieved from files and data bases. Descriptions of teleprocessing and distributed processing are found in chapter 9. Teleprocessing involves computer processing with input and output devices that are remotely located and physically connected to the computer by means of telephone lines. Distributed processing involves computer processing where two or more computers share work and are connected to each other locally or over telephone lines. Teleprocessing and distributed processing are becoming known as computer networking. Moving data around these networks is the subject of chapter 10.

The third part of the book deals with commercial data processing and information systems. Chapter 11 traces the evolution of commercial data processing. The process of getting an application "onto the computer," is the subject of chapter 12. Chapter 13 deals with some contemporary electronic data processing developments, while chapter 14 attempts to briefly take a look at the computer situation at the beginning of the decade of the 1980s.

The appendices are included to enhance the text. Appendix A describes a broadcasting network's election system. In it, there are elements of nearly everything described in the first two parts of the book. The glossary strives to explain some terms that are sometimes a source of confusion. Other more common terms found in other glossaries and explained well there are not found in this book's glossary. There's no sense trying to redo what has been done well elsewhere.

This book thus attempts to take a functional look at computers and several aspects of commercial data processing; it is, for managers and users, a place to begin.

MYLES E. WALSH

New York, New York
October 1980

Acknowledgments

This book was developed to provide a simple, easy-to-understand overview of computers and their application in a commercial environment. My objective in this work is to describe computers in a working or operational sense. Other, more definitive, works on computers go into greater detail than is necessary for those wishing an overview. The person wishing to go further would lose little if he read this book first. Most of my 20 years' experience has been with IBM computers and peripheral devices. Consequently, it may appear that I am biased in favor of IBM equipment. This bias is unintentional and to some degree unavoidable. However, it is not the purpose of this book to pass judgment on the merits of one manufacturer's computers and peripheral devices relative to another's. IBM's equipment is most familiar to me, but as far as I am concerned, Burroughs, Univac, CDC, Honeywell, DEC, Data General, and others, have similar equipment, equivalent to IBM's.

Several individuals were instrumental in getting this book published. Jim Andrews of the Association of System Management, himself a publisher, encouraged me to "hang in there." Stephen Kippur introduced me to Jerry Papke, who decided to publish the book. Julia Van Duyn's editing imposed the discipline necessary to transform the work from a spotty and somewhat disorganized manuscript into a book worthy of publication.

All authors owe thanks to many individuals. I am no exception. First, foremost, I thank my wife Diana for motivating me. I am also grateful to the professionals in the computer field at CBS, where I have worked in several capacities for 15 years. CBS is an above-average corporation as far as talent is concerned, and this includes those in the computer or MIS groups. My association with them was instrumental in prompting me first to write this book and secondly to persevere in getting it published. At the risk of missing a few, I mention several individuals who provided me with particular motivation. John Hurley, a director of systems for the Columbia House Division of CBS, put up with me in my first managerial position. Max Pinkerton, a vice-president in the same division, provided a model of professional competence. David Allen and Jim Walsh, CBS corporate vice-presidents of MIS at different times, Pete Schementi, and John Lalli, MIS directors, taught me things not found in managerial text books. The list could go on for pages; Ray Vail, Mike McSweeney, Richard Silverman, Warren Mitofsky, Bob Chandler, all helped or inspired me to this work. I am also in debt to Dianne Bowman and Carol Resta, who typed and retyped until a completed manuscript was produced. Dick Pierce, Babe Lanzetta, Bob Syvarth, Betsy Meehan, and Ed Leary are peers who read parts of the manuscript and made helpful suggestions. There is also another group including Joan Chalk and Ron and Janet Proudley, with special gifts, who were instrumental in getting this book into production. To all of them, I am grateful.

M.E.W.

Contents

Understanding Computers

introduction

Within the past several years, an ever-increasing number of individuals have been somewhat intimately involved with computers. Along with this intimacy there is a degree of intimidation. Several half-truths or misconceptions are the root cause of the intimidation that individuals feel when confronted by computers or computer people. The first is that a computer is a mysterious "black box" understandable only by the wizards of the computer industry. This is a half-truth. Although the specific technology for building computers and making them do things can be quite complex, understanding the basic concepts of a computer is significantly less difficult. The wizardry is a myth. Manufacturing computers is a sophisticated process, but it is done by human beings, not wizards. Making them do things (computer programming) can be sophisticated, but it is also done by humans, not wizards, and in some cases it is being done by near or total incompetents.

Another misconception is that computers are used mostly for performing monumental mathematical calculations impossible for men to do. This is also a half-truth. Computers do perform complex computations otherwise virtually impossible for men, but this represents only a fraction of their use. Computers, or more accurately, computers and computer peripheral equipment,* are used more often for applications that are somewhat mundane in contrast to large computational tasks. These applications include: payroll processing, order entry, inventory, accounts payable, and accounts receivable, keeping track of student records in schools, the printing of previously typed text, and a host of other applications that do not require large computations.

Another serious misconception is the idea that computers can develop solutions to problems. Individuals and organizations that have believed this have run into severe difficulties when implementing computer systems. A computer is merely a machine that can do exactly

---

Computer peripheral equipment is those devices such as printers, magnetic tape and disk-storage devices and cathode-ray tubes (CRTs) that are entities separate from a computer, but electronically connected to a computer. These devices receive detailed attention within this book.

what it is told and do it with phenomenal rapidity. If a well-thought-out method or problem solution is programmed into a computer system, the results will almost always be satisfactory. If, on the other hand, a computer system is applied in a chaotic situation, it will merely produce the chaos more quickly.

Still another half-truth deals with the threat posed by computers. Many individuals feel threatened by computers, expecting that their jobs will be eliminated. These fears are largely unfounded. Computers are here to stay. Rather than feeling threatened, individuals can attempt to live with computers, by learning something about them. This book can be a step in that direction. For many, this book may be enough; for others it may be only the beginning of a new learning experience. Computers are not to be feared; they are to be used. Trying to resist or ignore the spread of computer systems is both foolish and futile.

Other misconceptions are also still around. Some can be mentioned in passing. It is not true that you have to know "math" to work with or even program a computer. Although some computer systems require skilled technicians to operate and program them, technological improvements are constantly being developed that make it easier for nontechnical individuals to operate and even to program computers.

It is the goal of this book to provide the reader with an operational knowledge of computers and computer systems. Once you have read it, you, as an individual, will have accomplished the following:

1   As a potential computer user, you will be able to discuss computers intelligently with a computer vendor. Any vendor that uses terms and concepts beyond the scope of this book is providing nothing more than a "snow job."

2   You will have established a conceptual foundation upon which a more detailed study may rest, if you wish to pursue the subject further.

3   If you now feel uneasy because computers are suddenly "all over the place" (such as in banks, retail establishments, offices, warehouses, and factories) you will perceive the computer as a new tool to be used, not some mysterious "black box."

4   Finally, if you are a student in a discipline other than computer science, you will also find the book helpful. It can be used as a supplementary text in commercial courses.

part 1

Computer Basics

The material in this section explains the fundamental concepts and facilities of commercial data processing. Examined in this section are the computer itself and auxiliary devices like printers, magnetic tape and magnetic disk storage units, and terminals. This equipment is known as hardware. Also examined are the ways in which data are stored, such as fields, elements or segments, records, files, and data bases. How data are processed and converted into information by computer programs and systems is discussed. And for those wishing more detail on computer fabrication, there is description of electronic computer components.

chapter 1

Processor and Computer Storage

A DATA-PROCESSING ILLUSTRATION

Before describing computer technology, I wish to offer an analogy. Each year, I am obliged to prepare and file four income-tax returns. This ritual includes several tasks. Carrying out the tasks is similar to the processes performed by a computer to complete a job. The analogy, while describing the preparation and filing of income tax forms, introduces some terminology described more fully later in the book. OK, its tax time.

On the day I begin the ritual, I first prepare my data for processing. I go to my file of medical bills, tax receipts, canceled checks, and savings account passbooks. Let's call this stuff *input*. I must also retrieve my booklet of instructions on how to fill out the tax forms. Let's call the set of instructions a *program*. There is, then, a set of precise instructions on how to extract data from my input and do various kinds of arithmetic on those data, transforming them into information that the IRS wants to see on my tax forms.

As I do the arithmetic, I place the results in those places on the tax forms specified in the instructions. Let's call the tax form *output*.

In my case, I must prepare tax forms for the federal government, the State of New York, the State of New Jersey, and the Big Apple. There is a set of instructions for each, four programs. The tax returns must be prepared in sequence, federal first, New York State second, New York City third, and New Jersey last, since certain calculations on one produce results that are used on another. Let's call the entire process of preparing my tax forms, executing all four sets of instructions (four programs), a *system*.

The tools I use in preparing the tax returns are my eyes an *input reader*, my mind and a pocket calculator, a *computer processor*, my memory *computer storage*, a scratch pad *peripheral storage*, and my hand and a pencil an *output writer*.

When preparing my federal income tax form I have to put my canceled checks into batches, a batch for medical payments and a batch for contributions. I also batch my payroll check stubs. I add the amounts from the checks to determine dollar amounts for medical expenses and for contributions. Using the paycheck stub, I add up my medical insurance premiums. We could call this type of work *batch processing*. Let's suppose that in the middle of preparing my Schedule C for total deductions my son Marc asks me to check his mathematics homework. I interrupt my work on the taxes and, using my mind and my calculator, I check his work. This could be called *multitasking* or *multiprogramming*. When I finish Marc's homework, I return with my calculator to the tax work.

A little later on, another son, Jim, asks for the calculator to do a quick multiplication. He uses it for about 30 seconds and returns it. While that is going on, my wife asks how much the last dentist bill was and whether it has been paid. Since I have the bills and checks nearby, I retrieve them and respond to her questions. These two interruptions can be called *interactive processing*. Computer facilities are available so that both interruptions can be responded to in a short interval of time, because everything needed is available. Let's say that the data were *on-line*. There might be several other interruptions of various types that occur before I finish preparing all the tax forms.

When I finish, I take the tax forms that I have prepared in pencil, go to a typewriter, and type up fresh copies. I sign the typed copies, insert them in an envelope, and put them on top of the refrigerator, so they can be mailed at the next available opportunity. There is other mail on top of the refrigerator to be mailed. A collection of output waiting to be distributed could be called a *spool*.

Enough of analogies. Let's now proceed to examine computers in a more disciplined manner. However, as we proceed, recollection of the analogy will facilitate understanding of the concepts and components that are presented.

THE COMPUTER

Think of a *computer* as a box containing two basic parts: storage and the processing unit. This is an oversimplification, as there are actually five basic components: Central Processing Unit (CPU), Storage or Memory, Input, Output, and Control. A picture representation appears in Figure 1.1. Restricting this conceptual discussion to two basic parts for the moment makes for easier comprehension. The idea initially is to emphasize that part of a computer stores or holds information, and

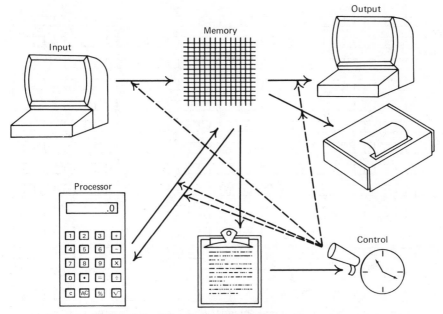

Figure 1.1   The five basic computer components.

another part causes information to be moved around, both into and out of the computer, and from place to place within the computer.

Computer Storage

Functionally speaking, there are two kinds of *computer storage*. One kind, sometimes known as "main memory," "core," or simply "memory," is actually one of the components of a computer. The other kind, frequently referred to as auxiliary storage or peripheral storage, is a separate component connected to a computer by physical wiring. That wiring is called a data path or channel. It is across that path that data are transferred between main memory and auxiliary storage devices. Auxiliary devices receive attention in a subsequent chapter.

The concern here is with main memory or computer storage. In this discussion we call it the storage section of the computer. The storage section contains a number of storage positions, each able to hold one character, that is, a letter, a digit, or a special character like a period or a hyphen. Each storage position has a unique address. The addresses begin at 1 and can run from a couple of hundred positions in small computers to millions of positions in large computers.

Figure 1.2 shows a two-dimensional schematic of a hypothetical

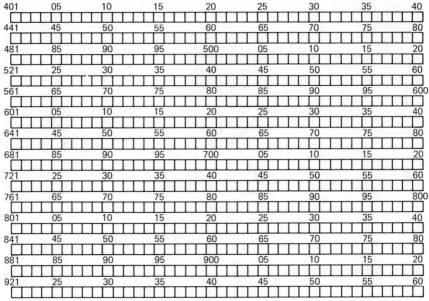

Figure 1.2   Two dimensional schematic of a piece of computer memory.

piece of computer storage. A reasonable analogy would be a crossword puzzle. Each position is uniquely identified and can contain one character of data. Computer storage is actually thought of in a linear sense, the schematic is two dimensional merely for illustrative purposes. In other words, computer storage starts at position one (1), and proceeds continuously to some other position—"n," where "n" represents the last position in computer storage for a particular computer. Figure 1.2 shows schematically a 560-position piece of computer storage composed of storage locations beginning at location 401 and continuing through location 960.

Depending upon the architecture of a particular computer, an addressable computer storage location can contain one or more characters of data. In some computers an addressable storage location can contain several characters of data, in others, only one. For conceptual simplicity, computer storage locations in the following discussions will be of the type that contain only one character of data.

Computer storage holds two basic kinds of data:

1   Data to be operated on, such as payroll information, textual information, inventory information, and so on. The bulk of these data are often stored in files or data bases on peripheral storage devices.

Computers transfer pieces of this information between peripheral storage and computer storage or "memory," in the same way a clerk might transfer several records at a time between a file cabinet and a desk for processing. The file cabinet is like peripheral storage, the desk is like computer storage, and the clerk is the processor. The clerk retrieves some records, makes adjustments to them, returns them to the file cabinet, retrieves some more records, and so on.

2   Data that are a set of instructions that indicate specifically what is to be done to the information when it is in computer storage. To take the clerical analogy a little further, this set of instructions is like the procedure the clerk follows in processing the "records" on his desk. This set of instructions with its specific data, is known as a computer "program."

The terms *program* and *records* receive fuller treatment later on. For the time being, assume that they both exist and appear in the hypothetical piece of the computer storage. Also assume the existence of a means of getting both the program and the record into computer storage. The method for doing so is explained later on. Figure 1.3 shows the same piece of hypothetical computer storage as in figure 1.2. Here it

```
401    05      10      15      20      25      30      35      40
  |J|O|H|N| |A|N|D|E|R|S|O|N| |2|5|0|0|0| |1|1|6|3| |3| |6|0|4| |5|2|5|0|0|0| | |
441    45      50      55      60      65      70      75      80

481    85      90      95     500      05      10      15      20

521    25      30      35      40      45      50      55      60

561    65      70      75      80      85      90      95     600

601    05      10      15      20      25      30      35      40

641    45      50      55      60      65      70      75      80

681    85      90      95     700      05      10      15      20

721    25      30      35      40      45      50      55      60

761    65      70      75      80      85      90      95     800

801    05      10      15      20      25      30      35      40
  |A|4|1|9|4|1|5|T|0|4|3|7|4|3|2|M|4|3|7|4|0|1|T|0|5|5|7|5|2|1| | | | |
841    45      50      55      60      65      70      75      80

881    85      90      95     900      05      10      15      20

921    25      30      35      40      45      50      55      60
```

Figure 1.3 Computer memory containing some data and a small program, before the program has executed.

contains some information: JOHN ANDERSON, who makes $250.00 a week, has a job code of 1163, has three dependents, and works in Department 604. His year-to-date earnings are $5250.00. Also displayed in the second schematic is a simple program which is to add his weekly salary to his year-to-date earnings and move the entire payroll record from one group of storage positions to another. The information on JOHN ANDERSON occupies positions 401 through 437; and the program occupies positions 801 through 830.

The little program contains instructions that, when executed by the processor, will cause John Anderson's salary of $250.00 to be added to his year-to-date earnings of $5,250.00 and will then cause the entire record to be copied from its present location to another location.

The specific location of John's record, the arrangements of the data within the record, the location of the program itself, and the area to which the record is eventually moved—all are determined by the programmer while writing the program. This also will receive greater explanation later. The hypothetical computer instructions are structured as follows:

Position 801: A means add.

Positions 802-807: 419 415 are the ending and beginning storage addresses indicating the location in storage of the $250.00 salary.

Positions 808-809: TO indicates the direction of the addition.

Positions 810-815: 437 432 are the ending and beginning storage addresses indicating the location in storage of the $5,250.00 year-to-date earnings.

Position 816: M means move.

Positions 817-822: 437 401 are the ending and beginning storage addresses indicating the entire payroll record of JOHN ANDERSON.

Positions 823-824: TO indicates the direction of the move.

Positions 825-830: 557 521 are the ending and beginning storage addresses indicating the area to which the payroll record is to be moved.

The schematic in Figure 1.4 shows the same piece of computer storage after two program instructions have been executed. Storage locations 432 through 437 now contain $5500.00 as a result of the addition, and locations 521 through 557 contain the entire record moved but not erased from locations 401 through 437.

In the examples just presented, you may have noticed that there

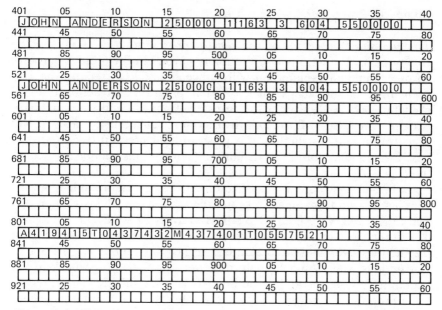

Figure 1.4 Computer memory containing some data and a small program, after the program has executed.

were no dollar signs or decimal points residing in computer storage. It is usually not necessary to store this kind of information, as in most cases there are programming instructions which can add these and other symbols to the data when it is to be displayed in a form that is recognizable to accountants, managers, and other users.

Before discussing the processing unit of the computer, a small digression is necessary. Although the auxiliary storage function was mentioned earlier and will be examined in greater detail later, it should be briefly discussed here, for the sake of clarity. Auxiliary storage is separate and distinct from computer storage or "memory," yet quite often those not familiar with computers are unaware of this fact. Auxiliary storage exists to compensate for the inadequate size of computer storage. Generally, the quantity of data to be kept in storage is far greater than the capacity of computer storage. Picture a clerk in an insurance company. The insurance company has a million policyholders. The clerk can work on five or six of these policies concurrently. Those not being worked on are kept in a file cabinet. Think of the five or six being processed by the clerk as residing in computer storage while the other 999,994 or 999,995 are residing in auxiliary storage.

Computer Processor

The *computer processor* or the *central processing unit* (CPU) of the computer, is, in fact, made up of many parts, but for present purposes an oversimplified explanation will suffice. The CPU executes the program instructions, keeps track of what program instruction is to be executed next, and initiates the transfer of data to and from auxiliary storage. The CPU will execute instructions sequentially, that is, it will execute the first instruction of a program and proceed to execute the next instruction, and the next, until a "branch" instruction is encountered.

A branch instruction is used to direct the processing unit to get its next instruction from an address specified in the branch instruction. It's not unlike "ADVANCE TO ST. CHARLES PLACE" in Monopoly. The branch instruction is often used to force execution of the same set of instructions over and over again. The last instruction of the set of instructions would be a branch, directing the CPU to go back to the beginning of the set of instructions. This is useful if it is desired to execute the same program, repeatedly, each time on a different record from a file. For example, recall John Anderson's record. Suppose that there were a hundred different people and the same action had to be taken on each of them. After John Anderson's record, came Joe Barker's, and after Joe Barker's came Tim Benson's, and so on down to Jeff Zeale's. The instructions of the program would be executed over and over again until Jeff Zeales's record was processed. If Zeale's record was the last record of the file, the processing unit would await further instruction.

Branch instructions can be unconditional or conditional. Unconditional branches disturb the sequential processing whenever they are executed. Conditional branches may or may not disturb sequential processing, depending whether a condition or set of conditions has been satisfied. A longhand example of conditional branch is as follows:

Compare A to B.
Branch to Routine 1 if A is higher.
Branch to Routine 2 if A is lower.
Continue Processing (if A and B are equal).

In an actual set of executable instructions (a program), routine 1 would be a storage address, as would be routine 2. The two branch instructions are conditional. Depending on which condition (high, low, or equal) is met, the processing unit will begin to execute the instructions located at the storage address of either Routine 1, Routine 2, or it will continue processing the next sequential instruction.

The last few pages may make you wonder if that's all there is to a computer. In a conceptual sense, that's all there is. However, in the next several chapters, we will examine other elements which make up a "computer system." *Computer system* is a term that is used to describe either of two entities. First, the term may be used to describe a configuration of equipment including a computer and peripheral devices such as magnetic tape and disk storage units, printers, CRTs, and telecommunications devices. The elements composing this first entity are often referred to as *hardware*. Secondly, the term computer system may also be used to describe a collection of computer programs that run as a group either in sequence or in tandem to accomplish a set of objectives, sometimes called a *job*. An example would be a payroll system. This type of computer system is called *software*.

chapter 2

Auxiliary Storage Devices, Media Control Units, and Channels

PERIPHERALS

The equipment examined in this chapter can be thought of as components of computer systems. As you have seen in chapter 1, the equipment known as a computer is a separate entity. Yet a computer without peripherals is like a brain and a memory without eyes and ears and the ability to speak. Just as a brain and memory cannot function without input and output facilities, neither can a computer.

As stated before, computer storage is usually of insufficient size to hold all the data from all the files needed to complete a job. These data are usually contained in files which are kept on storage media in a form recognizable to a computer. The files are generally read into or out of a computer, a record or a group of records at a time, using devices designed for this purpose. These records can be processed one after another (sequentially) or in no specified order (directly) depending upon the application. Two examples of manual systems illustrate the difference between sequential and direct processing:

Example 1—Sequential processing Suppose you have a collection file of folders for all the people working for Company X. There are 2500 people working for this company. Each employee is uniquely identified by a four-digit employee number, and the file is in order by this employee number. There is a file folder of payroll data for each employee with the tab of the file folder containing the employee number. The complete file is contained in two four-drawer file cabinets. Let's call it the Payroll Master File and call the records Payroll Master Records.

A clerk is given a stack of cards. The stack consists of a couple of hundred cards. There is one card for each employee who has decided to participate in a Savings Bond payroll deduction program. The clerk is given the job of updating the master records of those employees who wish to participate in the bond program. One of the first tasks performed by the clerk might be arranging the deck of cards into sequence by employee number. By doing so, the cards would be in the same sequence as the master file. Applying the bond purchase information to the master records could be carried out sequentially. The first file drawer might be opened and 25 updates could be made; then the second file drawn could be opened and maybe 25 more updates could be applied; and so on. This method would certainly result in the job's being completed more quickly than it would be if the updates were applied randomly because the stack of cards had been left unsorted. In the latter case the clerk might have to open and close a file draw for each update. Processing a group of updates in a particular order, in addition to being known as *sequential processing*, is also known as *batch processing*.

Example 2—Direct Processing   Using the same file, suppose the clerk were asked to find out whether employee number 1436 had a college degree. There would be no need to look at each file folder to find employee number 1436. The clerk would first check the range of employee numbers printed on the front of the file drawers, determine which drawer held the folder for employee number 1436, open that drawer, go to the file folder with the number 1436 on the tab, and find out if that employee had a college degree. The nature of this task is a direct access operation. When using computers, tasks of this type usually require a response within a short period of time. Such transactions are called *on-line* or *real-time* transactions.

MAJOR PERIPHERALS AND MEDIA

Computer programs are written so that they access records in an ordered manner (sequentially) or randomly (directly). There are many variations of both sequential and direct processing, some quite sophisticated, but the basic principle is the same.

There are several types of media that contain the data so that they can be processed by a computer, and also devices that can read the data from the media and get them into computer storage. The devices are often referred to as *peripheral devices*. Although there are many media and devices on the market, this presentation deals with only the most common.*

The most common are as follows:

Media	Device	Function
Paper	Printer	Output
Card	Card Punch	Output
Card	Card Reader	Input
Magnetic Tape	Tape Drive	Input/Output
Magnetic Disk	Disk Drive	Input/Output
Display Screen	Cathode Ray Tube and Keyboard	Input/output

Each of these is given a functional description later. The other storage media not mentioned here—such as magnetic cards, magnetic drum, data cells, magnetic tape, cassettes, mass storage devices, paper tape, microfilm, and microfiche—use the same operational principles that are mentioned, although the mechanics are different.

Paper

Paper is the most-used computer-produced storage medium that is common to both man and machine. Through programming, a computer has the ability to format and print information in various formats, so as to make it understandable to management, to accountants, to personnel administrators, to warehouse foremen, to scientists, or to virtually anyone who wishes to see it. You saw in Chapter 1 that data are generally stored in a computer without formatting. When printed, computer programs format the data so that they become recognizable information.

The printing is done on continuous form paper by a printer. Printers operate at varying speeds. Some can print thousands of lines of 132 characters per line in one minute. This kind of a printer, known as a *line printer*, is designed to print a line of characters across a page, each character at virtually the same instant. Another kind of printer, known as a *character printer*, is similar to a typewriter. Obviously, this type of printer is significantly slower than a line printer and is not regularly

---

*No attempt is made to provide a comprehensive examination of every available device or device type. Rather, the basic device types are reviewed. All other devices are variations or enhanced versions of those reviewed.

used where the volume of data to be printed is great. The typewriter printer is used, however, where printed output of high quality is desired. "Word Processing" computers, used primarily to produce textual output, use a very high quality typewriter printer with a typing mechanism known as a daisy wheel. Sketches of printers are seen in Figures 2.1 and 2.2.

The Card

The 80-column card* until recently was the most commonly used storage medium for getting data into a computer. Many new devices are beginning to reduce dependence on cards as original input media. Eighty-column cards, shown in Figure 2.3, serve as a good introduction because they can be easily explained in some detail and in a manner that facilitiates understanding. The more recent technologies like *key to tape*, *key to disk*, and CRT are explained subsequently.

Once 80-column card technology is understood, little effort is

Figure 2.1   A character printer (relatively low speed).

*There are other types of cards besides the 80 column, including the more recent 96 column; however, the 80 column suffices to illustrate the concept.

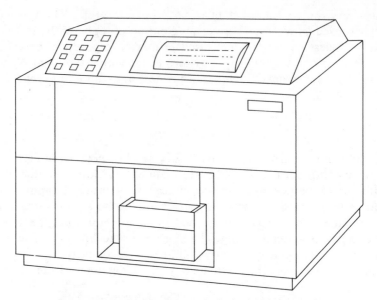

Figure 2.2   A line printer (relatively high speed).

required for the transition in thinking to understanding key to tape, key to disk, and CRT data entry.

Data are entered onto 80-column cards by the use of keypunching machines. A sketch of a keypunching machine appears in Figure 2.4. A keypunch machine has a keyboard similar to that of a typewriter and a mechanism that puts holes in the card. Hole patterns correspond to the characters on the keys. The card is positioned and moved along under the punching station one column at a time. As each column is punched, the card is positioned so that the next column can be punched. Facilities in the machine allow for skipping in the event that some columns are to be left unpunched. Each of the 80 columns of the card can contain one digit, letter, or special character. The second card pictured in Figure 2.3 contains the digits 0 through 9 in columns 1 through 10 of the card, the letters A through Z in columns 12 through 37, and special characters in columns 39 through 64. These data are illustrative only, and have no further use. The printing across the top of the card facilitates reading of the information by humans, as opposed to machines, and was produced by the punching machine at the time the data was punched in.

The 80-column card can contain up to 80 digits, letters, or special characters of information. The card columns are usually segregated into meaningful groups called fields. For example, columns 1 through 4 for a

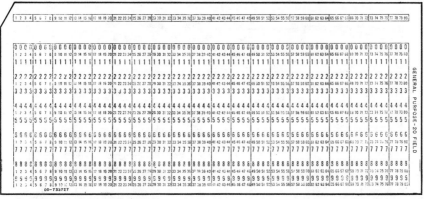

Figure 2.3 An 80-column card (a blank card and a keypunched card).

payroll job could be designated for employee number, columns 5 through 20 for employee name, columns 21 through 26 for weekly pay, and so on. Each employee could be represented by a card. The employee number, name, weekly pay, and so forth are punched into the cards. These cards could be used together with other resources, including a computer, to produce a payroll.

The device that reads the information from cards into a computer is called a *card reader*. The card reader is an electromechanical device that can hold a stack of cards. A sketch of this device appears in Figure 2.5. The cards are read by the reader one at a time. Each card passes through a set of 80 side-by-side brushes that are in contact with a copper roller that has electric current in it. The card acts as an insulator except where there are holes in the cards; the circuitry of the card reader interprets the character by the location of the holes. The impulses generated make their way from the card reader into computer

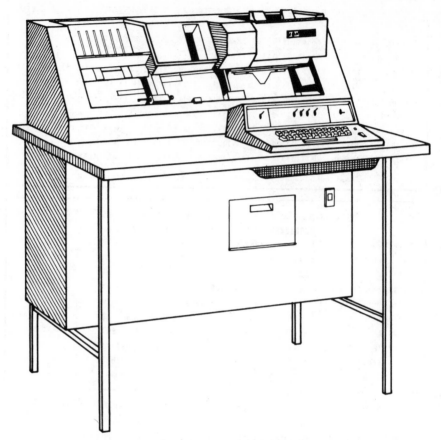

Figure 2.4   A keypunch machine.

storage. Figure 2.6 is a schematic of the preceding explanation.

At this point, it should be apparent how JOHN ANDERSON's record, illustrated earlier, may have gotten into computer storage. The popularity of the 80-column cards is due to its economy of preparation. Most data that are to be put into a computer or onto storage media recognizable to a computer are originally on a paper document, such as an employee time sheet or an invoice. This paper document is often referred to as a source document. The keypunch machine is used to transcribe data from the source document to the 80-column card.

The card can also be used as an output storage medium. Today's output is probably tomorrow's input. A *card punch* is used to punch

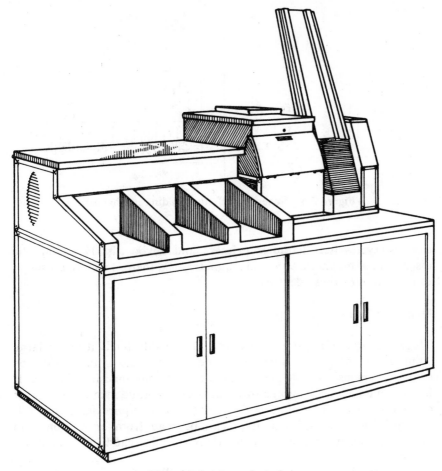

Figure 2.5 A card reader.

data into cards. The card punch alluded to here, however, is connected
to a computer and its activity is directed by a computer. It is quite
different from the keypunch machine that is used apart from the
computer to transcribe data from source documents to cards. Because of
the superior performance of other storage media such as tape and disk,
the use of cards as an output medium is diminishing rapidly.

As stated earlier, a number of devices permit transcription of data
from source documents to magnetic tape or magnetic disk. This equipment may include a combination of several of the following: magnetic
tape devices, magnetic disk devices, cathode ray tube (CRT) display

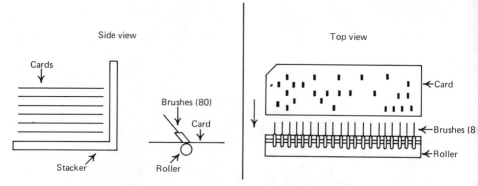

Figure 2.6 Schematic of card reading mechanism.

devices, typewriter-character printers and keyboards. Following the discussion of magnetic tape and magnetic disk, there is a more thorough examination of these devices.

Magnetic Tape

Magnetic tape is a storage medium that readily lends itself to large volume data files and sequential processing.* Reels of magnetic tape come in various sizes. Magnetic tape is also contained in cassettes. It has a tremendous advantage over cards as a storage medium in that it can store on an inch of tape data that would require numerous 80-column cards. In addition, data can be read from or written onto magnetic tape at a much faster rate than it can be read from or punched into cards.

A magnetic-tape device works on essentially the same principles as a reel-to-reel tape recorder or a cassette recorder. The tape passes across a head which reads the data from the tape and passes it into computer storage. After the tape passes across the head, it is taken up by a take-up reel, on a magnetic tape drive or within the cassette. When the processing of the reel is completed, the tape is rewound on the original reel. Figure 2.7 is a schematic of a tape cassette device.

As a reel of magnetic tape is loaded onto a tape drive, five-foot loops of tape fall into vacuum pockets under the reel itself and also under the

---

*Sequential processing—working with one item after another, generally assuming some order in which the items are arranged. The processing of an alphabetically ordered list of names is an example of sequential processing.

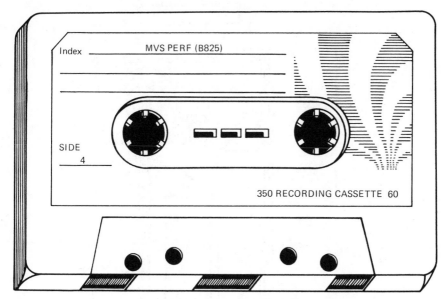

Figure 2.7   A magnetic tape cassette.

take-up reel. These loops provide slack so that the tape will not break under stress, since the drive itself is subject to sudden acceleration and deceleration during start and stop operations. Magnetic tape as a storage medium lends itself to storage of large files of historical data, and most processing of these files is done sequentially. A sketch of a magnetic tape drive appears in Figure 2.8.

An example showing clearly how magnetic tape is used is an over-simplified payroll application. Suppose the existence of a payroll master file containing employee information needed for payroll processing. Such information would include employee number, employee name, hourly pay rate, number of dependents, payroll deductions, year-to-date earnings, and so forth. Also assume that this file is ordered in ascending sequences by employee number; that is, employee 0001 is first and employee number 9999 is last. One final assumption—there is a total of 1416 employees, meaning that although the file is in order by employee number, every number in the range (0001 to 9999) is not assigned to an employee. This is true with most sequential files. The number of employees to be paid this week is 427, and time cards will be submitted for those 427 employees. The time cards contain such information as employee number, hours of straight time, hours of overtime, and so forth. The data from the time cards are keypunched into 80-column

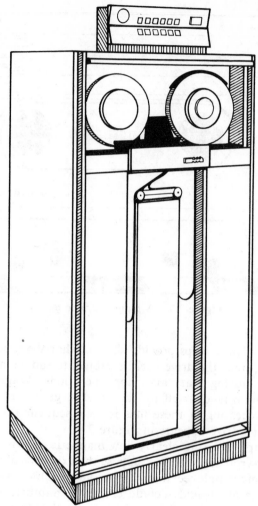

Figure 2.8   A magnetic tape drive.

cards, one 80-column card for each employee. For conceptual simplicity
at this point, assume that a program exists which reads the 80-column
cards containing the employee information and records that information on magnetic tape in ascending sequence by employee number.
There are now two files and two separate reels of magnetic tape. The
data on the employee time card file is then processed against the payroll
master file, using a computer program that could be called a payroll

main process program. It is this program that reads records one at a time from each file and matches the employee number on the employee time card file to the employee number on the payroll master file. When a match is found, the program multiplies hourly rate from the master by hours from the time card file to get weekly gross pay, uses number of dependents to determine taxes, applies payroll deductions, and so forth. Two new files are created on magnetic tape as a result of this process, an updated payroll master file and a payroll check and register file. The payroll check and register file contains the information needed to produce checks and payroll register. The updated payroll master file is a copy of the original payroll master file, except for updated information such as year-to-date earnings for those employees who were paid.

Magnetic Disk

Magnetic disk is a storage medium that lends itself to the storage of large amounts of data for direct processing. Although sequential processing may be, and often is, done on disk, the potential of disk is realized in direct-processing applications. With a *disk drive* any record in a file may be retrieved directly without having to read all the records in front of it.

A sketch of a small scale disk storage device appears in Figure 2.9. Figure 2.10 is a schematic of the mechanics of a disk drive. Sketches of two types of disk storage, the single disk and the disk pack, appear in Figure 2.11. In addition to the disk drive which can hold a single disk, there are devices that can hold many disk packs. The single-disk devices are often used with small computers. The multipack devices are used in great quantity with large-scale computers. A sketch of a multipack device appears in Figure 2.12.

More recently, single-disk devices, in the form of a technological development known as *floppy disk* or *diskette,* represent a significant breakthrough in cost reduction. These disks, no bigger than a 45 rpm phonograph record, are being used in great quantity. Sketchs of a "floppy" being loaded can be seen in Figure 2.13.

Floppy disks or diskettes come in envelopes for protection. Step A in Figure 2.13 shows the floppy being removed from the envelope. Steps B and C show it being positioned for loading into the device that houses it and then inserted into the device, much the same way as bread is put into a toaster. Step D shows it inserted and ready. The term *floppy* probably became associated with these small disks because they are made of material that is flexible and can bend slightly without damag-

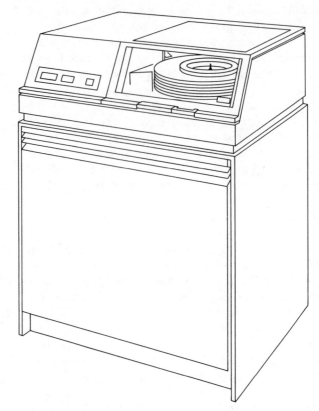

Figure 2.9   A magnetic disk drive (relatively small scale).

ing the data stored on their surface. The disk platters on the larger disks, however, are quite rigid and cannot be bent even slightly without causing irreparable harm to the surface.

A *disk* is a circular platter on which data can be stored. The data can be stored on both the top and bottom surfaces of the platter. A disk pack is a collection of these platters on one shaft which can be placed on a disk drive that is built to accommodate the disk pack. A disk or a disk pack rotates on the shaft of a disk drive at very high speeds. Arms containing the read/write heads move back and forth just above the surface of the disk. On such devices, there is one reading and writing mechanism for each recording surface. These devices are sometimes called *movable-head disk drives*. There are also *fixed-head drives* on

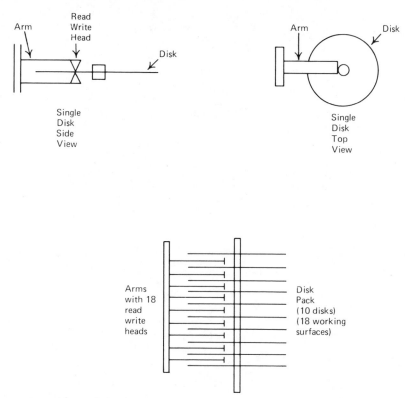

Figure 2.10 Schematic of a magnetic disk read/write mechanism.

which there are multiple reading and writing mechanisms for each recording surface. These devices can retrieve and store data more quickly than can the movable head devices. The fixed-head devices also cost more money to purchase or to rent. The reason for the fixed-head devices' being faster becomes apparent as we examine the way data are stored on disk surfaces and disk packs. Data are stored on the surface of the disk in concentric circles known as *tracks*. On those disk packs containing more than one platter, the flow of the data recording from one track to another is perpendicular rather than parallel. In other words, when a file is being put onto a disk, and a track becomes full, the next track used is the one below it rather than the one next to it. The set of perpendicular tracks on all the platters of a disk pack is called a *cylinder,* and recording is done in this way in order to reduce the amount of arm movement in reading and writing data. Figure 2.14 is a

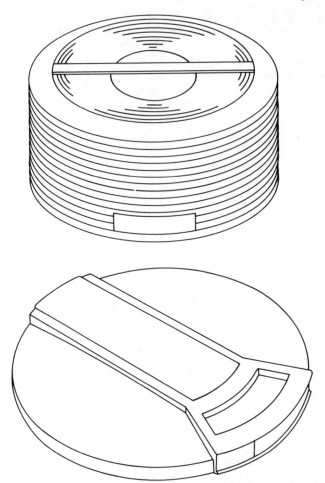

Figure 2.11 Magnetic disk packs.

schematic showing tracks and a cylinder. The track is a physical entity, that is, there is a physical separation of tracks on the disk; the cylinder is a logical entity, that is, a logical collection of tracks. Separation of tracks is a function of hardware; a collection of tracks constituting a cylinder is a function of software.

There is a multitude of methods for structuring files for direct access processing. Disk storage, like computer storage, has *addresses*. For example, cylinder 4, track 6, record 3, is an English language representation of the location of some data. Recall the payroll master file used to illustrate sequential processing in the section on magnetic tape. There

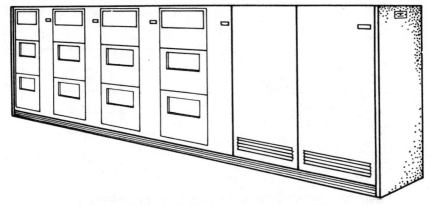

Figure 2.12 A "bank" of magnetic disk drives.

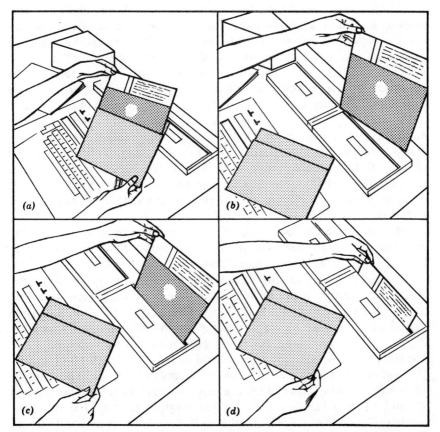

Figure 2.13 Loading a floppy magnetic disk into its read/write mechanism. (Courtesy of International Business Machines Corporation.)

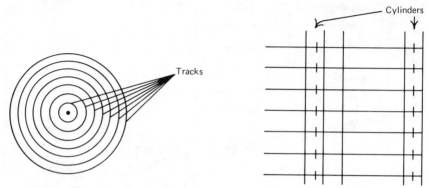

Figure 2.14 Schematic portraying the track and cylinder concepts.

were 1416 employees. Using four digits to represent employee number, there is a total of 9999 numbers that could be used. In the sequential file, employee number was used to order the file in ascending sequence and employee number was also used to search the file; that is, the matching of employee time-card records with the payroll master records. Also the payroll master file was copied onto another tape each time it was used for processing, so that if a new record had to be added to the file (say, for a newly hired employee), it could be written on the new tape in its proper place. On a sequential file, records, in addition to being ordered, are also located next to each other. This is true even though all the possible numbers are not present. Figure 2.15 illustrates this. Employee 142's record is next to the record of employee 6; the numbers 7 through 142 are not assigned to any employees and are not included.

The employee number in the payroll example, in addition to being data about an employee, is also used functionally to order and search. Used in that sense, the employee number is called a *key*.

In a direct access file, just as in a sequential file, the key provides the means of locating the desired record. However, in the direct access file the records are stored on a disk that has addresses. To avoid having to examine each record to see if it is the one for which you are looking, there are ways of using addresses themselves to serve as keys. To illustrate this, suppose the existence of a disk pack with 10 cylinders, 100 tracks, and the capacity to hold 10 records on a track. The cylinder addresses could be 0 through 9, the track addresses could be 00 through 99, and record addresses could be 0 through 9. If the 1,416 employee records should be placed at the cylinder, with track and record addresses corresponding to the employee number, the record desired

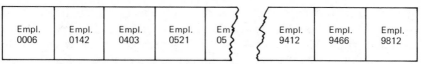

Employee Records on Magnetic Tape

Figure 2.15 Records of data as they appear on magnetic tape.

could be retrieved by examining the employee number and getting the record from the disk address that was equal to that employee number. The following table shows the correlation:

Employee Number	Cylinder	Disk Address Track	Record
0026	0	02	6
0142	0	14	2
0463	0	46	3
0521	0	52	1
0578	0	57	8
.	.	.	.
.	.	.	.
.	.	.	.
9412	9	41	2
9466	9	46	6
9812	9	81	2

An observation should be made, however; using 9999 disk addresses for a 1,416 record file is quite wasteful. It leaves 8583 empty spaces. Even if a growth factor is anticipated, for up to a total of 2000 records, that still leaves 8000 wasted spaces. There are many methods of compacting the disk space required for this file. These methods generally make use of arithmetic algorithms which can operate on the employee number to produce a unique disk address within a specified range, say 0000 to 1999. This process takes any employee number between 0001 and 9999 and by arithmetic manipulation creates a unique number within the range of 0000 to 1999. Caution is to be exercised when planning to do this, for as the number of records within the file approaches 2000, the algorithm begins to break down and creation of duplicate numbers becomes troublesome. Regardless of how well the algorithm is developed, duplicate numbers will occur, and a procedure for handling them must be incorporated in the algorithm.

For a file of 1,416 unique numbers, with a 5% planned annual growth rate and an overflow area of 100 spaces for duplicates, disk space of about 2000 addresses should last for about five years. Those numbers from 0001 to 9999 that will generate duplicates within the range of 0001 to 2000 can be determined ahead of time and consciously avoided, thereby negating the need for overflow space. If the file grows beyond expectations, more space and a new algorithm must be provided. Still, a disk space saving of 80% is accomplished originally by compacting the disk space and developing an algorithm.

When using disk and other direct access storage devices, the acronym DASD (direct access storage device) is often used.

The CRT

Display Screen Cathode Ray Tube (CRT) and *keyboard* are the next medium and peripheral device to be presented here. Figure 2.16 is a sketch of a CRT device and keyboard.

A CRT is used to enter or retrieve data from files or data bases that reside in other storage media. For example, suppose a clerk in the payroll department was asked to find out what John Anderson's year-to-date earnings were. A number of assumptions are necessary to show how the clerk might get the information he wants. The assumptions are as follows:

1 That the CRT is wired to a computer.
2 That the computer has connected to it a disk drive with the disk pack containing John Anderson's payroll record.
3 That programs exist and are in the computer that allow the clerk to (a) request the information, (b) retrieve the information from the file, and (c) display the information on the screen.

Using the keyboard, the clerk keys in a request and, generally within seconds, the information he requested is displayed on the CRT screen. Also, depending upon design criteria in the computer programs, the clerk may be able to change the data that exist on the file by using the keyboard. Although there are many kinds of keyboards, the one used in this example would closely resemble a typewriter keyboard. It would contain all the alphabetic and numeric characters and some special characters like periods or hyphens. Moreover, function keys like "RE-QUEST," "ENTER," "BACKSPACE", and the like would appear on the keyboard.

In addition to CRT and keyboard devices, other types of terminals exist. The most common is a *typewriter terminal*. The typewriter termi-

Figure 2.16 A CRT terminal device.

nal, instead of displaying data on a screen, prints the data on paper. These kinds of terminals are used primarily for direct processing where the data input and data output of a system are of low volume. One would not commonly process an entire payroll on a typewriter terminal, but would use a typewriter terminal or a CRT and keyboard terminal to request specific information from individual records in a file or data base. A typewriter terminal is virtually identical in appearance to the character printer pictured earlier, except that it has a keyboard as well. As terminal devices they may be located at sites remote from the computer.

As mentioned earlier, keypunch machines and 80-column cards are being replaced in great quantity by key-to-tape and key-to-disk devices. Direct entry to a computer through the use of CRT devices is also replacing keypunching and cards.

The basic principles of data entry key-to-tape and key-to-disk devices are similar to those for cards. The medium for carrying the data is different. Errors are less frequent and verification of what has been keyed is simplified. Key to disk devices often have magnetic tape devices in their configurations.

We will examine two more methods of data entry. Though last in this presentation, these methods are quickly becoming the most frequently used. The first is called *remote job entry* (RJE). This method generally makes use of a line printer, CRT with a keyboard and/or a card reader, which are located at a site remote from the computer. The RJE device, often called a terminal, could be located across the street or across the country. In its most common application, data from cards are read into the RJE device card reader or keyed into a CRT device. Those data are then transmitted by telephone lines to the computer. The computer performs operations on the data and transmits return information which is printed out on the line printer. Transmitting data over telephone lines between computers and remotely located devices is sometimes called *teleprocessing*. The subject will receive more attention later on. The sketch in Figure 2.17 pictures a typical RJE device.

The second method is called *interactive processing*. It usually employs a CRT device or a typewriter terminal. In this type of processing the device can be located either remote from the computer or right at the computer site. A terminal that is located at the computer site and not attached through telephone lines is said to be locally attached. Interactive processing is best described by way of analogy. It is like

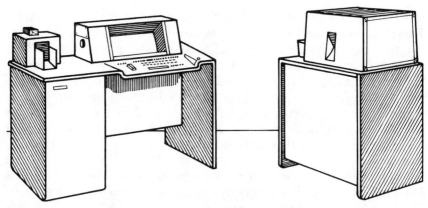

Figure 2.17 An RJE device, a relatively high speed printer.

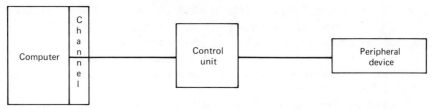

Figure 2.18 A schematic portraying a control unit between a computer and a single device.

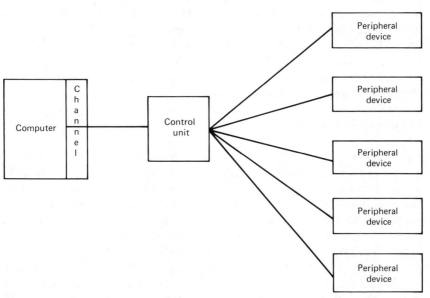

Figure 2.19 A schematic portraying a control unit between a computer and several devices.

having a conversation with a computer. Operational programs exist that can be put into a computer to facilitate this kind of processing. Picture a computer having several CRT devices with keyboards attached to it. These CRT devices are located in several different locations. Included in the software of this computer are programs that can be used to assist programmers in writing more programs, programs that can be used for the processing of textual information, programs that can be used to set up files and process orders, all kinds of programs. In such an environment, computer programmers are able to "code, test, and debug programs."* Secretaries and writers can use the textual processing features. Warehousemen, order entry clerks, and order fulfillment supervisors use the programs for processing orders and preparing invoices.

On-line management information systems and airline reservations systems are other examples of systems that have interactive processing capabilities.

To summarize: Data are obtained from media used by people (source documents), such as invoices, time cards, journal entries, and so forth. These data are entered into computers by keypunching them onto cards or through data entry devices such as CRT, key-to-tape or key-to-disk devices. High speed printers, RJE devices and continuous form paper are used to produce large volume output such as paychecks, invoices, and the like. Magnetic tape and disk are used to store massive volumes of data in files for high speed processing by computers. CRT and typewriter terminals are used to access limited amounts of data from files stored on peripheral devices

Control Units and Channels

Before moving into data structures and computer software, a few other hardware facilities should be examined. The first two facilities are used to interface† computers and the devices just described. These pieces of equipment are often referred to as *channels* and *control units*. Each peripheral device that is connected to a computer is connected through a control unit and a channel. Schematically it is show in Figure 2.18. More than one peripheral device can be connected through the same control unit. This can be seen schematically in Figure 2.19. This does not mean that you can put any number of different types of peripheral devices through one control unit of any kind. Each type of peripheral device has its own control unit. In some cases, the same control unit is designed for use by more than one type of device. For example, a card reader, card punch, and a printer can often use the same control unit. Actually, however, this is merely several control units under one set of covers. In most cases, although a control unit may be able to accommo-

---

*"Code, test, and debug programs" describes a process that a programmer goes through in developing a new computer program. The term *code* denotes the process of writing the instructions which make up the program. *Test* means to run the program on the computer to get results that can be evaluated. *Debug* is a term denoting the error correction processes. Usually a series of test, debug, test again, debug some more, steps are gone through before a program is made operational.

†Interface a word with many uses, can be either hardware or software. An *interface* is basically a component that allows two incompatible entities to interact with one another.

date more than one peripheral device, it can accommodate only one *type* of peripheral device. For example, a tape control unit may be used for up to eight tape devices, but it cannot be used for anything but tape devices. Some peripheral devices have a built-in control unit, and a separate control unit is not required. In more recent equipment, a peripheral device and control unit are one physical unit, and other devices can be connected through it.

A *channel* is a governor of the flow of information between auxiliary storage and computer storage. There is a significant difference in the speeds of computer storage and auxiliary storage. Computer storage moves information at electronic speeds, nano seconds (thousand millionths of seconds), while auxiliary storage moves information at electromechanical speeds, microseconds (millionths of seconds) at best in the fastest devices. The channel compensates for these speed differentials. When speaking of a channel, one can visualize two parts. One part is a small processing unit that shares computer storage with the computer processor. Its functions are specialized, and it executes its instructions concurrently with the processor of the computer in which it resides. The other part is the path across which data are transferred between peripheral storage and computer storage.

A control unit contains the electronics which control the operation of the peripheral devices. Even though a control unit may have many devices attached to it, the devices can operate only one at a time. The control units are attached to the channels of a computer. Since many control units can be connected to a single channel, interleaved data transfer via the channel is possible. In other words, each of the control units is attached to a specific part of the channel sometimes called a *subchannel*. Data are transferred from computer storage to a specific control unit across that control unit's subchannel.

Unfortunately the terminology of channels, subchannels, and control units is not generic to all computer manufacturers. *Computer architecture,* that is the computer equipment design and structure, differs among manufacturers. Equipment like channels, subchannels, and control units are called by other names, such as *bus* or *interface* by some computer equipment manufacturers. The term "interface" has a number of meanings besides that of describing a piece of equipment. Generically it is a common element that is used to reconcile the differences between two or more elements that must communicate with one another. In this context, the term is used to describe an equipment interface resolving the speed differences between computer components and peripheral devices. It is reasonably safe to say that an interface is like a control unit in concept, while a bus is like a channel.

Minis and Micros

"Small computers" are often referred to as *minicomputers* or *microcomputers*. Electronic technology keeps improving toward the point where greater and greater computing power can be concentrated into equipment that requires less and less space. There are currently available pocket calculators that can calculate square roots, compound interest, statistical variances, and the like. These calculators represent some of the most sophisticated hardware that can be mass produced. Minicomputers available now are somewhat larger than pocket calculators, but not much bigger than attache cases. Although the minicomputers cannot yet support the quantity of applications that the large-scale computers support, the processing power of the minicomputers greatly surpasses the processing power of large-scale computers of less than a decade ago. There are some distinct advantages to the use of minicomputers. In addition to much less space, they require far less electrical power and air conditioning than do the large and medium-scale computers now commonly in use. A disadvantage, which is rapidly being overcome, is that software support, such as language compilers and operating systems is not as comprehensive on the minicomputers as it is on the large and medium-scale computers.

Peripheral devices for minicomputers are virtually the same devices that are connected to large and medium-scale computers. Peripheral devices themselves are getting smaller in some cases. For example, tape cassette and cartridge units can be used in lieu of tape drives. Disk drives which store less data can be used with minicomputers. These disk drives require significantly less space than the massive disk storage devices associated with large and medium-scale computers.

A typical miniconfiguration, which includes the processing unit, about a quarter-million positions of memory and control units for about 32 peripheral devices, including teleprocessing control units, can be placed in a rack that takes up an area about 4 feet wide by 4 feet deep and 6 feet high. Often this configuration requires no more than normal room air-conditioning and two or three 115 volt, 20 amp wall outlets for power.

Microcomputers are quite small. They are even smaller than minicomputers. The technology in the field of microcomputers is so dynamic that it is virtually impossible to write something today that will still be true tomorrow. Many microcomputers are currently being used for specialized functions and are generally not programmable in the same sense as other computers. The programming of many microcomputers is done as they are being manufactured. A later chapter examines small computers in greater detail.

There are a few other types of hardware, like telecommunications control units, modems, telephone lines, and virtual storage computers. These are also explained in some more detail within context later in the book.

Bits, Bytes, Fields, Elements (Segments) and Records, Files, Data Bases, and Programs

DATA

In the last two chapters, terms like record, file, and field were occasionally used. The explanations of the terms were superficial and brief. In this chapter, these entities are examined in greater detail.

Bits and Bytes

The smallest pieces of data recognizable to people, programmers excluded, are characters. A, B, C, 1, 2, 3, $ are characters. Programmers are excluded because they, like computers, recognize bits. A *bit* is a binary representation and can have either of two values, zero or one. Bits are dealt with more fully in a later chapter. In order to give you an idea of what bits are like, look back at the picture of the 80-column cards. The holes in the cards are like bits. Suffice to say that it takes a combination of bits to make up a *character*. There is one particular coding structure in which characters are made up of combinations of eight bits. In the trade this type of character is usually referred to as a *byte*. This particular coding structure is known as the Extended Binary Coded Decimal Interchange Code. This tongue twister has given rise to the acronym EBCDIC, pronounced eb sa dick. For those of you who are interested there is a chart in the Appendix containing all characters and their EBCDIC bit combinations. It is in the Appendix for your fun and pleasure, but it is not fundamental to your understanding of anything that follows.

Fields

After characters the next largest piece of data recognizable to people is a collection of one or more characters which define something. A specific quantity of positions to define something is known as a *field*. Social Security numbers would fit in a nine-position field if the hyphens were left out. Another example of a field would be an employee number. Field sizes are determined by analysis of the information to be defined by the field. For example, if a field is to be designed for an employee name field in a payroll record, it has to be defined so that it is large enough to hold the longest name. This is known as a *fixed-size field*. If it is to be of variable size, a couple of additional fixed positions have to be used within the field to define its size. The two drawings in Figure 3.1 illustrate both a fixed-size field and a variable-size field.

Notice the wasted space in the fixed-size field. Eight positions are wasted with the name "CHU" so that a name like "GRABOLOWITZ" can be accommodated. It is only fair to point out that although the variable size saves space, it increases programming complexity. A Social Security number will always use nine positions, but names can vary in size. When a computer program is being written that is going to access fields within records, the programmer must define the limits of the fields within his program. Since a program is written to access fields, the program expects to find the same kind of data in the same place each time it accesses a field. With the fixed-size field, when the name JONES is accessed, six blanks are also accessed. Using the variable-size field, the field length is first analyzed by the program and determined to be 05, so that the name is accessed without the blanks.

Elements or Segments and Records

To be candid, there is a lack of precision in the trade regarding these terms. Definitions vary depending on which equipment manufacturer or software vendor you are dealing with. What IBM defines as a segment

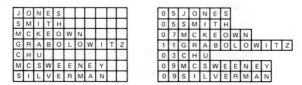

Figure 3.1   Fixed-size field and variable-size field.

may be a data element to some other vendor and to another, a record. This lack of precision contributes significantly to the difficulty in making comparisons among different vendors' software products.

Let's start with the concept of a record. A *record* is a collection of information (fields of information) related to an entity. An entity is generally an item of some kind or, in many cases, a person. For example, a payroll master record for an individual, an item master record for an inventory item, a journal entry for an accounting application, or vote returns from a county are all records. Records, like fields, can be variable length or fixed length. *Fixed-length records* are quite straight-forward, but there are many types of variable-length records. An example of fixed-length records is seen in Figure 3.2. Fixed-length records always have the same kind of data in the same physical location in each record. A program being written to process fixed-length records can define an area in computer storage and, as the records are processed through storage the employee name field and every other field will always be found in the same locations. A longhand section of a computer program to define this area could be as follows:

1   Define an area 36 positions long.
2   Define first 4 positions employee number.
3   Define position 5 as first initial.
4   Define positions 6 through 16 as employee name.
5   Define position 17 through 21 as weekly base pay.
6   Define position 22 through 25 as job code.
7   Define position 26 as number of dependents.
8   Define positions 27 through 29 as home department.
9   Define positions 30 through 36 as year-to-date earnings.

Examples of two kinds of *variable-length records* are shown in Figures 3.3 and 3.4. The set of variable-length records in Figure 3.3 is an example of the kind of records that are delimited by an end-of-record symbol. The last character in each record is the end-of-record symbol. The set of variable-length records in Figure 3.4 is an example of the

Figure 3.2   Fixed-length record.

Figure 3.3 Variable-length record with end of record symbol.

kind of records that contain a *count field* (first two positions, in this case) indicating the length of the record. In the case of the record with the end-of-record symbol, the symbol itself is part of the record. In the case of the record with the count field, which is a count of the number of characters in the record, the count itself is part of the record. The advantages of using variable-length records and variable-length fields is that they occupy less space. However, as is readily apparent, programs written to use these records become somewhat more complex. When one uses variable-length records, merely defining an area as with fixed-length records will not work, since as each variable-length record comes in, the data fields can be in different locations. Therefore, additional programming is required to analyze the count field or the end-of-record symbol and, using some arithmetic, determine where the desired data field is located in each particular record. It is well to note, however, that the count field itself must be in a fixed location (not necessarily first) in each record.

Elements or *segments* are collections of data that generally consist of one or more fields yet contain fewer fields than an entire record. Organizing data into elements or segments makes it possible for computer programs to transfer portions of a record from peripheral storage into computer storage. Segments or elements are used extensively in data base management systems. In such systems, relationships can be established among segments or elements of records in one file and segments or elements in other files. These relationships are given a more detailed treatment in the chapter on data base systems.

Files

A *file* is a collection of many occurrences of the same type of records. Another name for a file that is now in common use, is *data set*. The term

Figure 3.4 Variable length record with record length indicator.

data set is probably more appropriate since it is more encompassing than the word *file*. When one thinks of a file, one thinks of a payroll master file, or an inventory file. However, when one thinks of a catalog or a library (these two items are discussed in more detail later under operating systems), one thinks in terms of a collection of information or a set of data. Since files are also sets of data, the broader term data set is now in common use as a generic name for files, libraries, catalogs, and the like.

Data Base

The term *data base* is quite imprecise. At this point, a few observations can be made. A data base is generally made up of data from a number of data sets. Various elements of these data sets have relationships with one another that cross data set boundaries. For example, a data base for a given corporation might include information from the following data sets: Sales, Inventory, Budgets, Payroll, and Personnel. Some of these data sets contain common information; for example, a payroll data set and a personnel data set would probably contain some redundant data, as would a sales file and an inventory file. There are many theories about combining some or all of a company's data into a single grouping in order to reduce or eliminate redundancies and to make elements of those data available to whoever needs them. This grouping of data is known as a data base. A data base need not be as big as all files within a company or an organization, but can be somewhat smaller. For example, an Election unit for a major television network has a data base of prior election returns. It is composed of a national file, a state file, a county file, a precinct file, a stratification file, and a Congressional district file. Each of these files contains historical election vote data stored according to different schemes. Data bases come in sizes large and small. The larger they get, the more difficult they are to manage and maintain. The sophisticated techniques for structuring these files, such as inverted indexing, chaining, and linking, are quite difficult to implement. Data Base Management Systems (DBMS) software products address themselves to this problem. A subsequent chapter deals in greater detail with data bases and DBMSs.

To summarize, in very broad terms, bits make up characters, characters make up fields, fields make up segments, elements, and records, records make up files (data sets) and relationships among segments and elements transcending file boundaries make up data bases.

PROGRAMS

Computers by themselves, with all their ability to do high-speed calculations and rapid manipulations of large volumes of data, have great potential. However, human effort is required to realize this potential. Systems designers, programmer/analysts and systems programmers and computer operators are the catalysts. *Systems designers* are those individuals who prepare the systems specifications for a business application. Possessing a detailed knowledge of the application and a working knowledge of computers, they prepare report and display layouts, input specifications, input sources, and data flow through the system. *Programmer/analysts*, who generally have a less detailed knowledge of the application but a more detailed knowledge of the computer, prepare the detailed programming specifications for the system. The more senior programmer/analysts review the specifications and develop programming schedules. The actual programming is allocated to some of the more junior programmer analysts. *Systems programmers* are those individuals most familiar with the "nuts and bolts" of computers. They provide support functions and assist in the interfacing of the application programs with the software support facilities of the computer, like operating systems, access methods, data base management systems, and computer networks. All of these software support facilities receive attention in later chapters.

    Computer operators are the individuals who operate the computers. Recently, in installations with large computers, with a large number of software support systems and business applications, operations skills have become specialized, whereas in years past computer operators "did it all." In a complex contemporary environment you find tape handlers, printer operators, console operators, master terminal operators, and technical support specialists. At the same time, in environments with smaller computers and less equipment, the one-man operation can still be found.

Ways to Program

Let's examine *computer programming*. Program instructions are used to tell a computer what steps it must take in order to accomplish a task. The computer "sees" these instructions as a series or a string of numbers. It is necessary that these program instructions ultimately be reduced to the string that is needed.

There are currently five alternative ways of producing these strings.

1   The program can be written in strings, that is in actual machine language.

2   The program can be written in a language which contains instructions similar to an English-language shorthand. These instructions are sometimes known as *mnemonics*. Languages in this category are often called *assembler languages*.

3   The program can be written in a language that is more related to the task to be completed than to the machine on which it is to be run. This kind of language is often referred to as *problem oriented* or *high level* language. COBOL, FORTRAN, and PL/I are examples. COBOL is an acronym signifying COmmon Business Oriented Language, FORTRAN is a shortened form of FORmula TRANslation, while PL/I represents Programming Language One (1).

4   Programs can be written in *interactive languages*. These languages are in the "tool kits" of engineers, statisticians, and financial analysts. With languages expressions can be written in a form closely akin to the user's discipline. APL and BASIC are examples. The initials APL stand for A Programming Language and BASIC stands for Beginners All-purpose Symbolic Instruction Code.

5   Portions of programs can be written in specialized languages. These languages are used to perform particular functions and their instructions can be intermixed among instructions of other languages.

The following pages contain a fairly elaborate explanation of the function of computer programming. If you wish to get some insight into the process that computer programmers have to go through to produce computer programs, I suggest you read the next several pages carefully. If instead, a superficial understanding is all you need, then you can skim it. Let's look at the five alternative ways of computer programming.

Each of these alternatives is considered in turn. There is some overlapping among the alternatives. Furthermore, there has been a general chronological evolution from machine language to high level, to interactive, to specialized languages as far as the methodology of programming is concerned. Exceptions to this general trend occur when phenomena like minicomputers and microprocessors appear on the scene. However, the vast majority of programming done today is in high level languages. As of this writing interactive languages are gaining acceptance among a larger number of people and their use is becoming more widespread.

Machine Language

Machine-language programming presents such formidable problems that this kind of programming is very rare in contemporary computing. The programmer is forced to remember a large number of numeric codes that represent the instructions to be performed. He must also keep track of all storage locations by number, so that specific data and instructions can be uniquely identified at all times. This method exists but it is not used by programmers in the traditional sense. In some contemporary small computers (microcomputers) this kind of programming is still done, but done as part of a manufacturing process. It is known as *microprogramming*. The result of microprogramming is circuitry rather than software.

In some other places, programming in machine language still exists as a curiosity. It is extremely costly in terms of time and money. Moreover, it can be applied only to very small tasks. It would be a virtual impossibility to write today's large, complex programs in machine language.

Assembler Language

The first step in overcoming the impossibility of writing big programs in machine language was the development of *assemblers*. Assemblers introduced two aids which relieved the programmer's burden a great deal—*mnemonic instructions* and *symbolic addressing*. Mnemonic instructions allowed the programmer to write the word "ADD," rather than having to remember that the number "9," (or whatever the actual number for a specific machine) was the machine language instruction for add. The term "ADD" was more meaningful to the programmer. The entire program when listed became easier to read and to follow. A means of translating these mnemonic instructions to machine instructions was a program called an assembler. This program, "the assembler," had as its task the translation of mnemonic instructions into machine-language instructions.

In addition, the assembler also had the task of keeping track of memory locations. In this way, the programmer could use a symbol (a combination of letters, say TAX CALC or EMPL NAME) to express an address in computer memory. This technique, known as *symbolic addressing*, relieved the programmer of having to remember the location of every piece of data and every instruction to his program. In this way, the programmer could reference an employee name by using "EMPL NAME" and during the assembly process, the assembler would determine the address.

In the same way, a programmer would write B TAX CALC (branch to a routine called TAX CALC) and the assembler, while assembling the program, would establish the address of TAX CALC and insert it into the machine language instruction.

The process would work essentially like this. A programmer would establish the address to be associated with each symbol. For example the programmer would write on his coding sheet things like TAX CALC=4420; EMPL NAME=0020; GROSS=0067; TAX=0084. Subsequent instructions might be BRANCH TAX CALC; SUB GROSS, TAX. The assembler would substitute "01" (or whatever the numeric value for a branch instruction) for the branch, and "4420" for TAX CALC. The instruction would appear as "014420" in machine language. "SUB GROSS, TAX" would appear as "9200670084" in machine language, assuming "92" as the numeric value of the subtract instruction.

Later developments had the assembler assign storage locations itself. The programmer indicated where he wanted the program to start and from that point on all addresses were assigned automatically by the assembler. This development had a favorable impact on the function of maintaining and modifying existing programs. Since addresses were assigned by the assembler, each time a change was made to a program and it "reassembled," it was possible that all the addresses would be changed. The programmer would be totally ignorant of the exact location of the data until he examined the printout of his assembled program.

To recap, this process of using mnemonic instructions (also known as *operation codes* or *"op" codes*) and symbolic addressing and having them translated into machine language is called *assembling a program*. The facility for doing this is usually a program called an assembler. The mnemonic op codes and the symbolic addresses written by the programmer are known as the *source program*. The translated program, that is, the machine language version, is known as the *object program*, or *load module*.

The Programming Process

The sequence of the events in getting a program assembled is as follows: The programmer defines his task and writes the mnemonic instructions for that task. He then gets these instructions into a medium that can be read by a computer. This medium could be 80-column cards which are keypunched from the mnemonic instructions on a coding sheet that the programmer has written. Programmers can also code their programs interactively using a CRT device or typewriter terminal connected to a computer. This particular methodology is quickly becoming popular with programmers. More sophisticated assemblers and compilers (to be discussed below) have facilities which not only allow the programmer to code a program interactively but also allow interactive testing and debugging. From the cards or from the CRT, the assembler gets the source program into computer storage. The program to be assembled is "data" as far as the assembler program is concerned. The assembler then translates the source program into an object program or load module. Instruction and data addresses are assigned, areas to hold input and output data are reserved, and the operation codes are put into machine language. At this point the program has been assembled, but not executed or tested.

Usually the first assembly, except for the simplest of programs, contains some syntax errors, misspelling, unresolved symbols, and the like. It is generally possible to eliminate these errors with one or two additional assemblies. Here it is well to caution that merely because a source program assembles without any error, there is no guarantee that the program is correct. All that can be said is that the source program is free from syntactical errors, that the program makes sense and will probably execute. Logical errors that are imbedded in the program go completely undetected and must be removed by the programmer as a result of testing and debugging* the program by actually running it with test data and checking the output for correctness.

The source programs that go into assembly programs are generally coded on a one-for-one basis (one machine instruction is generated for each programmer-written instruction). Traditionally, standardized coding sheets were used for purposes of uniformity and documentation. When coding sheets or a terminal device is used, each line or source code results in a single machine instruction. The programmer may also write comments into the program for documentation purposes. These comments will be printed on the assembly listing or displayed on the screen. When the assembler program prints the output listing on the printer, a print image is created showing the entire source-line entry, and beside it the machine language instructions generated by the assembler. The programmer is thus able to see the entire picture, that is,

*Debugging—finding and fixing logic errors in a program.

his source statements, comments, and the resultant machine language instructions. This is indispensible when debugging a program. When working interactively with a CRT, a programmer can *page* through his program. Each CRT display contains between 20 and 50 lines of the program depending on the device used.

Macros

The one-for-one relationship exists in what are usually called *basic assemblers*. The next significant advancement in programming was the development of the *macro-assembler*. The distinction is that in the operation code field it is possible to write a macro instruction that is not equivalent to a single machine instruction, but is rather a privileged word that the assembler recognizes. The assembler issues a call for a special routine, preassembled and stored in advance, that will analyze the macro and generate more than one line of machine coding. The size and complexity of the macro invoked are limited only by the ingenuity of the programmer who writes the special routine. These special routines are generalized subprograms that, by the specification of parameters, will output the correct machine language instructions back into the calling program just as if the programmer using the macro had instead individually written the instructions himself. Macros can be powerful tools. Macros reduce the amount of instruction writing that a programmer must do to complete a task. In a typical programming department, there are certain parts of tasks that are redundant in every program in the department. Rather than have every programmer write the mnemonics for these common elements, they can be written once and made part of the compiler. Each program that is written can contain statements which can include these common elements within the task.

In the broadest terms, "macro" can be thought of as being of two basic types, input/output macros and arithmetic or logic macros.

Input/output macros are used for reading and writing data files. A programmer usually defines the characteristics of a file and assigns a symbolic name to it. From then on he merely writes a "read" or "write" instruction, specifies some parameters, like record length and file name, and indicates the area or memory that will contain the data. The assembler generates the necessary machine code to execute that data movement. Depending upon the size and architecture of the computer, this can be a fairly complicated string of instructions.

Arithmetic and *logic macros* are employed to cut down on certain repetitive coding wherein arithmetic or logical manipulation is to be made on data. Should a processing unit have no multiply or divide feature, a multiply or divide macro can be written to substitute for the single machine instruction. This would constitute an arithmetic macro. Should it be necessary to examine the contents of a certain data field for characteristics, it would be advantageous to write a macro to manipulate the data logically. This would constitute a *logic macro*. In all cases, the point is that the special macro subroutine is written and debugged only once, although it can be used by many different programmers in many different situations.

Macro assemblers are sophisticated assembly programs that provide an efficient and convenient way to get the job done. The use of macro assemblers makes the programmer's job easier still. However, the use of macros requires some additional education of the programmers using them. The macro-instruction repertoire must be made common knowledge, and the programmer must be familiar with the macro library (the facility for storing macros), its contents, and its use.

Higher Level Languages

Problem oriented or *higher-level languages* were developed in parallel with the development of macro assemblers. Generally defined, these languages are aimed at solving specific classes of problems. Different types of problems are clustered according to similar processing characteristics, and languages were developed to solve these problems. The most common dichotomy that occurs is the natural differentiation that exists between scientific and business data processing. When it is remembered that the problems of scientific computing deal largely with symbol manipulation in mathematical notation as opposed to the problems of data manipulation as they exist in business applications, it is eminently logical that two procedure-oriented languages should develop. Those two languages are household words in computerdom: FORTRAN and COBOL.

No discussion of languages would be complete without a comparison of the relative merits of each. Arguments between assembler language and higher level language advocates still are heard at cocktail parties, in programming departments, and classrooms. No doubt these discussions will continue into the future. Both sides have good reasons for their positions. Appearing here are some observations. The reader is left to make his own judgment on the relative merits of each position.

Several large, disconcerting problems faced the user who wrote his instructions in an assembly language. As new computers were introduced, existing programs had to be totally rewritten. Of course, the rewriting included learning to use a new machine, learning to use a new assembler, rewriting the programs, and then retesting them. Depending upon the number and complexity of the programs involved, this might take many man-years of effort. All of the effort thus expended would merely duplicate what had already been done, and was running on the preceding computer. At the end of the program conversion effort, the user was still in the same place. The resources devoted to the reprogramming could certainly have been better employed in developmental work for new applications. Using assembly languages, there was little or no transferability of programs from one computing system to another.

The assembly languages were sometimes difficult to learn rapidly and always necessitated that the individual know machine architecture in order to use the language. The recruitment and training of new programmers was tedious and difficult because expertise built on one machine was not immediately transferable to another. Those talents that are machine-independent ("a computer is a computer") were always transferable, but a user could not hire an experienced programmer on Model X and have him immediately productive on the new Model Y. In fact, some users theorized (incorrectly) that they preferred to hire trainees because their minds were not cluttered with the knowledge of a previous machine and consequently they could learn the newer computer more rapidly and be productive sooner. Just as there was little or no transferability of programs from one machine to another, there was also limited transferability of programmers from one machine to another.

Documentation

Another factor to be considered when deciding whether to use an assembly language or a higher level language is that of maintaining and modifying programs. Consideration must also be given to the maintaining and modifying of programs which already exist. Functionally, this is known as *program maintenance*. The program maintenance function is one that requires an accurate description of what a program is supposed to do. The text that provides these descriptions is called *documentation*.

Program documentation consists of the following:

a) A general description of what the program does.
b) A detailed description of the workings of the program. This description is known as *program specifications*.
c) A detailed description of the data going into the program (input) and the results (reports and displays) produced by the program (output). A description of a record that is to be used by a computer

program is known as a *record layout*. A description of a report is called a *report layout*. Specially designed forms are often available for this kind of documentation. See Figures 3.5, 3.6, and 3.7 for examples.

Figure 3.5 contains a record layout form for "making a map" of a record. Figure 3.6 is a form used for setting up a dummy report. Figure 3.7 is a record layout form that can be used to describe a record. There are also sheets for *screen layouts* describing displays. Also in the documentation there should be explanations of the data elements that are used by the program, both as input and as output.

This kind of documentation, often neglected, is of inestimable value to a programmer who is called upon to modify a program, written in assembly language, that he has never laid his eyes on before.

Higher-level languages are devised to obviate some of the objections to assembly language coding. Some of the objectives of higher-level programming languages are (1) to provide some sort of self-documentation so that reading the program itself will provide clues to what is happening from a processing standpoint, (2) to enable a program to cross hardware lines so that it is as machine-independent as possible, thereby allowing the transferability of programs, and (3) to facilitate the transfer of people across hardware lines by maximizing the amount of technique and experience that can be applied to the new system. Higher-level languages are more easily learned than assembler languages, and training time is dramatically reduced both for old pros and neophytes.

Programs written in higher-level languages are translated into machine languages by programs that are known as *compilers*. What assemblers do for programs written in mnemonics, compilers do for programs written in higher-level or problem-oriented languages. The introduction of the term compiler also led to the use of another term for the higher-level languages. They are sometimes referred to as *compiler languages*.

The main purpose of higher-level languages is to increase productivity of programmers. However, it is appropriate to observe that speeding up the programming may mean slowing down the execution of the program. As a general rule, the further removed the source language is from machine language, the slower a program will ultimately run. It is true that most compilers generate fairly efficient programs, but they are replete with generalized routines, and in many instances the more general the routine the less efficient the program produced. When programming in an assembly language, the programmer can make use

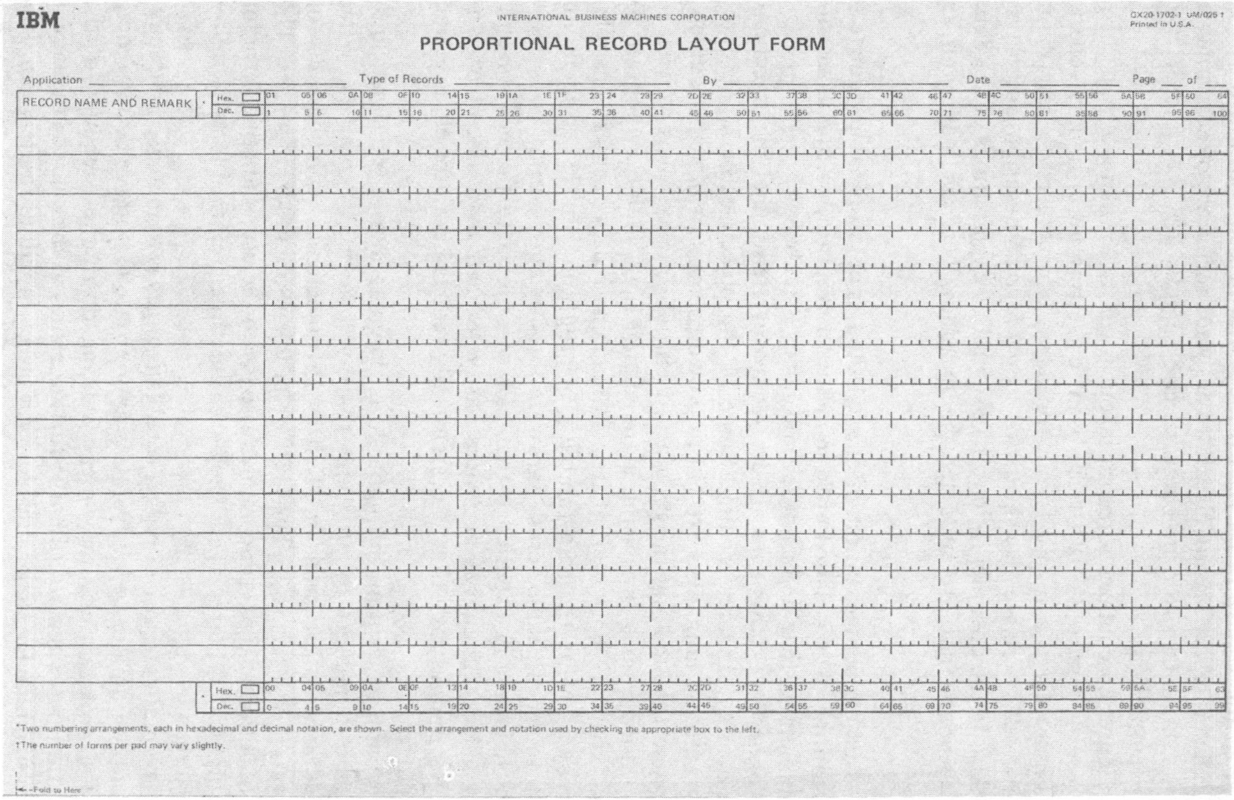

Figure 3.5 Record layout worksheet. (Courtesy of International Business Machines Corporation.)

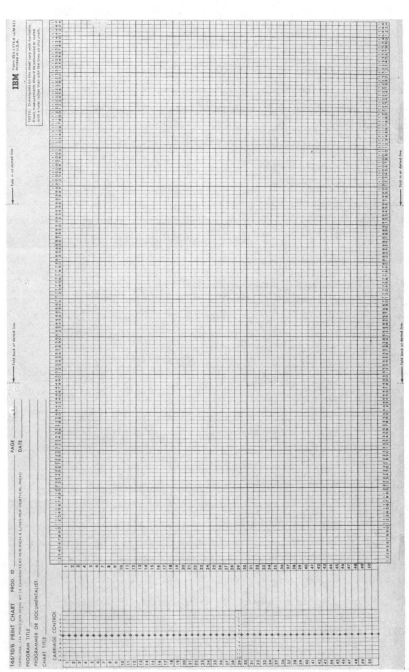

Figure 3.6 Printer spacing chart. (Courtesy of International Business Machines Corporation.)

						PAGE NUMBER OF	
PROCEDURE TITLE RECORD DESCRIPTION –						**PROCEDURE NUMBER**	

LABEL	LENGTH		MODE OF RECORD-ING	COMPUTER STORAGE DEFINITION	REF. NO.	FIELD NAME
	LOG.	PHY.				

A - ADDR, VAL - FULL WORD
B - BINARY
C - CHARACTER, 8 - BIT CODE
D - FLOAT, PT - DOUBLEWORD
E - FLOAT, PT - FULLWORD
F - FIXED PT - FULLWORD
H - FIXED PT - HALFWORD

P - PACKED DECIMAL
R - RELATIVE RECORD NO.
S - ADDR, BASE DISPLACEMENT
V - ADDR, EXTERNAL SYM,
X - HEXADECIMAL, 4 - BIT CD,
Y - ADDR, VAL - HALFWORD
Z - ZONED DECIMAL

SPECIFIC CODE AND FIELD DEFINITIONS
ARE GIVEN FOR THE FIELD REFERENCED
ON 'CODE AND FIELD DEFINITION' SHEET,

Figure 3.7 Record description form (for documentation purposes). (Courtesy of CBS, Inc.)

of "tricks" and take fuller advantage of the computer, because if he knows the machine, he will invariably come up with short cuts to do things. Imagination is required for this. When programming in a compiler language, a programmer usually must stick to the language and is denied access to the personality (poetically speaking) of the computer. He can be as imaginative as he wants to be, and this will stand him in good stead once he knows the language, but he will rarely be able to "play games" with the machine and produce truly efficient programs. In other words, it is possible with mnemonic languages to take advantage of the characteristics peculiar to a particular computer in making a computer program more efficient by speeding up its execution or by reducing the amount of storage that it requires.

While none of this should be construed as opposing compilers, it is intended as a caution that the same program written both ways will often run more slowly when a compiler is used. The program may also require a greater amount of computer storage. Both these conditions may have little to do with the programming talent involved. However, the other benefits accruing to the use of compilers far outweigh this apparent disadvantage. As computer equipment continues to drop in cost, and as compilers become generators of more efficient programs, this disadvantage becomes less objectionable.

Interactive and Specialized

Contemporary developments continue in both assembler and higher-level language compilers. Every minicomputer and microcomputer has its own assembler language. Higher-level languages are too numerous to mention. Among the higher-level languages, FORTRAN and COBOL are the most well known. An interactive facility, the Time Sharing Option (TSO) of the IBM operating system allows the languages to be used interactively. BASIC and APL are two other languages that are often packaged in their own interactive facility. There are other products that facilitate interactive processing, but for entire applications rather than for individuals. These specialized products include: CICS and IMS from IBM. CICS represents Customer Interface Control System and IMS stands for Information Management Systems. Both of these are Data Base/Data Communications systems.

Figure 3.8 pictures some of the more commonly used programmer coding sheets. COBOL and FORTRAN are two of the most common compiler languages, while 360 Assembler is the assembler language for the IBM 360, 370, and 303X lines of computers.

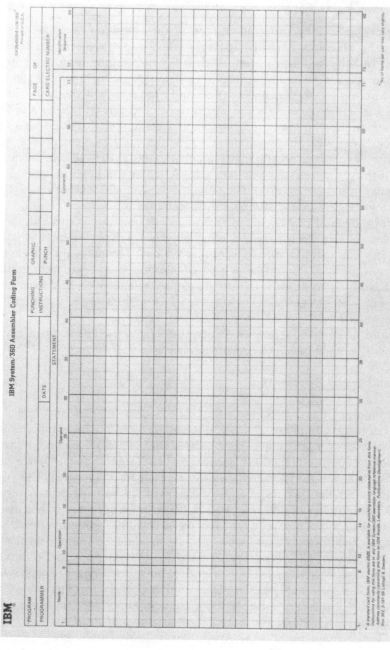

Figure 3.8 Assembler, COBOL, and FORTRAN coding sheets. (Courtesy of International Business Machines Corporation.)

58

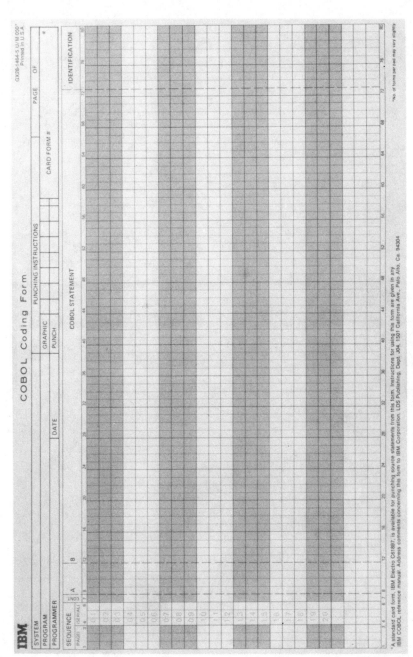

Figure 3.8 (Continued)

59

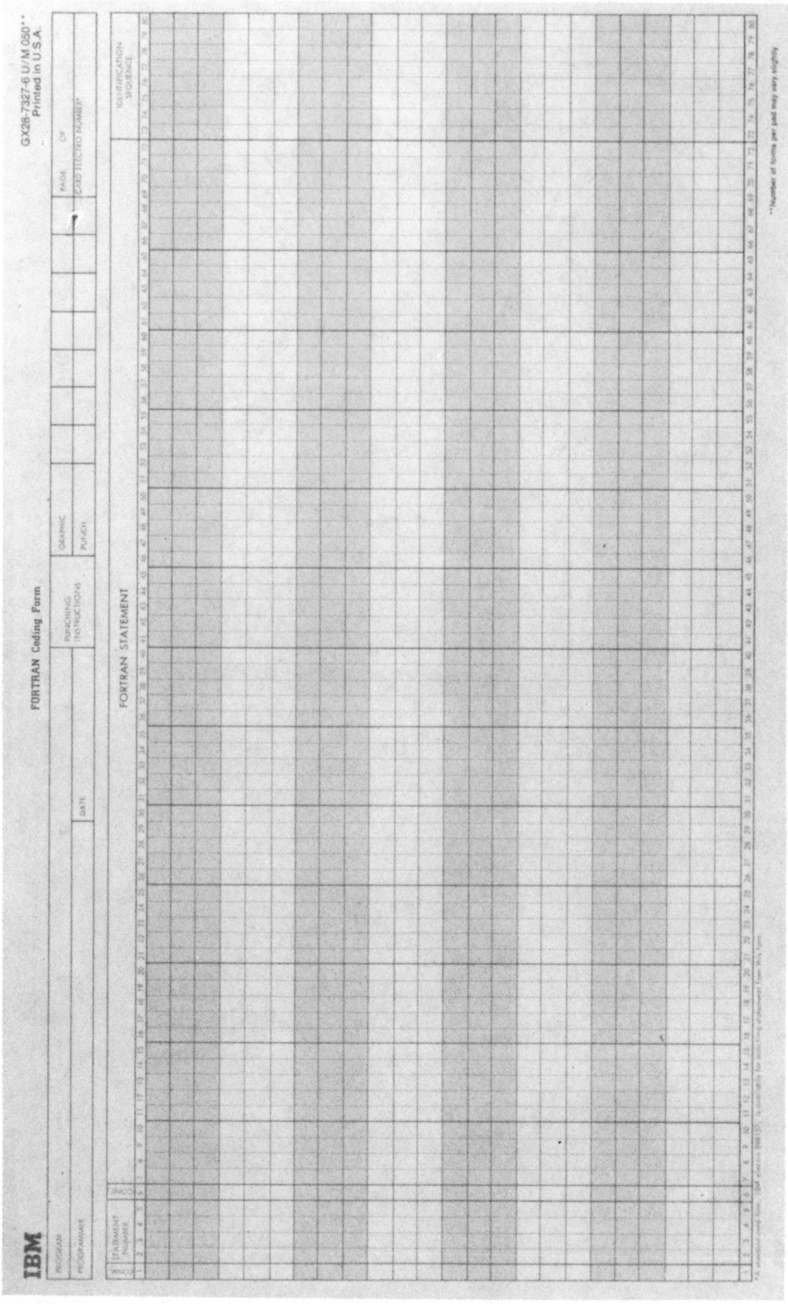

Figure 3.8 (Continued)

60

chapter 4

Systems and Other Facilities

SYSTEMS

This chapter surveys briefly what computer technology can be used for, some related technology, and some of the sophistication required to make a computer a cost effective tool. Subsequent chapters add significant detail to what is surveyed here.

The term "systems" has other meanings in addition to that discussed here. The term is sometimes a synonym for a computer processor or a configuration of equipment, that is, a computer with its peripherals. In this context, a system is defined as a group or collection of computer programs and operating procedures organized to complete a job. For example, a payroll job might consist of many operations, including recording and entering straight time and overtime hours worked in a given week, calculating federal, state, and local income taxes, updating year-to-date earnings, and printing payroll checks and registers. These are just some of the tasks required to do a payroll job. The orderly flow of data through a series of steps required to produce a completed payroll is known as a *system*. A system does not necessarily imply the presence of a computer, but a computer can be used as a tool in carrying out some of the tasks in a system. Typically, a computer system consists of a series of computer programs and operating procedures which are organized to do a job.

Computer systems usually operate in one of two modes, *batch* or *on-line*. A batch system is one in which similar elements of data are batched into groups, and processed one element after another in some kind of sequence. An on-line system is one which single transactions arriving on a random basis are processed as they arrive. The difference between these two modes of operation is time and quantity. An on-line system is more efficient relative to time. The schematic in Figure 4.1 illustrates.

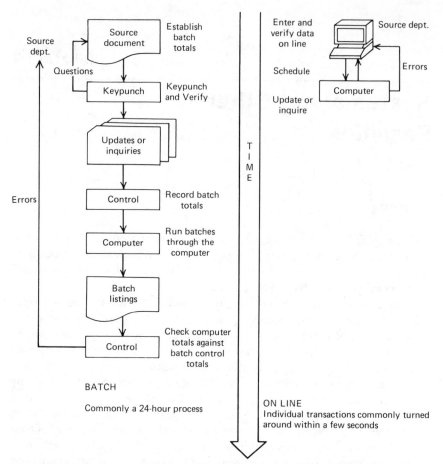

Figure 4.1 A schematic contrasting batch and on-line processing.

OTHER CONCEPTS

There are several other subjects integral to the understanding of electronic data processing (EDP) and computers with which the reader should become acquainted. Each of these subjects is given a broad general treatment. The subjects include: operating systems, teleprocessing, (data communications networks) time sharing, and virtual storage.

Operating Systems

This software developed as a direct result of the inability of mechanical peripheral devices to keep up with electronic computers. Operating systems are themselves programs. They are extremely sophisiticated and complex. One particular operating system—IBM's "O/S"—has a host of technical manuals on its use. Although the facilities provided by an operating system are many, one of the most important is its control of a function called *multiprogramming*. Simply stated, multiprogramming is the ability to have more than one program executed concurrently in a computer. Poetically speaking multiprogramming is an activity where a computer can walk and chew gum at the same time.

The differential in speed between peripherals and computers causes the computer to be idle 90 to 95% of the time when running one job. Operating systems give the computer the facility to make use of this idle time. They do it by allowing one program to execute some of its instructions while another program is waiting for one of its input/output instructions to be completed. While data are passing from a peripheral device through the channel to computer storage, the computer is free to do other work. With an operating system, control of the computer could be turned over to another program that was not waiting for input/output to be completed. It could execute some of its instructions while the first program is waiting for its input or output operation to be completed. If this second program also encounters an input/output operation, it would also have to wait, and the operating system would pass control on to a third program, and so on. A realistic maximum number of concurrently executing programs for multiprogramming is relative, depending on the capacity of the computer and the sophistication of the operating system.

In an operating system environment there must be a priority scheme to tell the operating system which program gets first crack at the computer resources if a conflict arises. Using the example—if the operating system passes control to a second program while a program with a higher priority is completing an input/output operation—the operating system would also see to it that the program with the higher priority gets control back from the second program when the higher priority program completes its input/output operation. The second program's processing would be suspended, so that control could return to the higher priority program.

In addition to the need for operating systems, as evidenced by the idle time in the computer, there are other factors which contributed to the common acceptance of operating systems. The most prominent of these has been the advancement in hardware technology, especially in the area of computer storage. Larger and larger amounts of computer storage are being produced which take up less and less space. Computer storage is also becoming more economical. Although the actual cost of equipment rises, the capability of the equipment rises faster. A common expression for this phenomenon is "More bang for the buck." In the mid 1960s, a computer with 100,000 positions of computer storage was considered large scale. As of this writing, computers containing 2 million positions of computer storage are medium-scale computers. Computer manufacturers now speak of machines with 16 to 32 million positions of computer storage. Even greater memory sizes are forecasted for the not too distant future.

Operating systems themselves take up a large amount of computer storage. As stated before, operating systems themselves are programs. They have other facilities besides the multiprogramming facility. The operating system is also a program, but one with options. It is told which options it should exercise through a language of its own. The language is known as JOB CONTROL LANGUAGE (JCL). JCL instructions given to the operating system are interpreted and acted upon. JCL statements are used to specify numerous *parameters* such as: data set space requirements, the sequence of the job tasks, or steps within a job, or whether a file should be put on tape or disk, to mention just a few.

Other facilities of operating systems include *libraries* and *catalogs*. A library is a facility which is analogous to a public library. Rather than books, an operating system library contains, in addition to other things, data sets or files. They are usually referred to by directories. For example, a programmer can put his source program into a library and free himself of having to handle source program cards. His source program is given a unique name and through JCL, he can refer to that program, and add, delete, or change statements in that program. Computer operators can also refer to data sets or files in similar fashion.

The directories by which items in libraries are located are called *catalogs*. Catalogs are used to hold, in addition to some other things, the names of JCL procedures that are used over and over again. For example, programmers who wish to compile and test programs written in the COBOL language would need, say, 10 or 12 JCL cards to invoke options of the operating system required to do this. Rather than have each programmer make up the cards himself, they could be made up once, named, and put in a library and the name entered in a catalog.

The catalog could be either in computer storage or on a disk. Functionally, this *cataloged procedure*, along with other things already in the catalog, is available to those people who have the authority to use them. When the programmers wish to use it, they make up one JCL card that invokes the procedure, to compile and test their program. Other operating concepts and facilities receive a more detailed description in a subsequent chapter on the subject.

Basic Teleproceessing

The area of *teleprocessing* has become a subject more comprehensive than computers and electronic data processing. Subsequent material in this book deals in greater detail with teleprocessing as it affects computer technology in the form of distributed computer processing and computer networks. The technology of communications is full of "gee whiz bells and whistles." Included are such things as terrestrial microwave radio transmission facilities, satellite communication systems, and optical fiber transmission systems. Plentiful information is available on these subjects and others in telecommunications texts like James Martin's *Telecommunications and the Computer* and *Future Developments in Telecommunications*. Both these texts are in their second editions and are published by Prentice-Hall. For an exhaustive examination of telecommunication technology, these books, by James Martin, are very good.

Within this text, teleprocessing is examined from the day-to-day perspective of the operations manager. Within the trade, teleprocessing is also known as "TP." Teleprocessing facilities permit the use of a computer from a terminal located in a site remote from the computer. The communication channels between remote terminals and a computer are either telephone lines or one of the facilities of TP technology, i.e. satellite, microwave, or fiber. These same facilities permit the interconnection of several different sites. In fact, with the more advanced technologies, the possibilities are virtually limitless.

And yet, while it is now possible to interconnect scores of sites, some fundamental technology underlies it all. There are still obstacles to be overcome before the massive computer networks described by Martin and others are put into place. A great deal needs to be done. The obstacles are not technological, but managerial and educational. Managing these massive networks is going to be a monumental task. Educating managers and training technicians to control, coordinate, maintain, and troubleshoot in a computer network environment is going to require a significant investment of time and hands-on experience.

In order to understand teleprocessing, or any other subject, it is best to begin with fundamentals. Let's do that.

From a hardware point of view, in addition to a computer, basic TP includes four separate kinds of devices:

1   A terminal or terminals.
2   A telephone line or a more advanced telecommunication facility.
3   Modems.
4   A teleprocessing control unit or a front-end computer.

Terminals can be either high speed or low speed. A CRT with a keyboard or a typewriter type terminal is an example of a low-speed terminal. A line printer with a card reader and a CRT is an example of a high-speed terminal, often called an RJE station. The application for which the terminal is to be used determines the kind of terminal device used. In an RJE situation, Job Control Language (JCL) cards, together with the data input for the system, could be read through the card reader and transmitted to the computer. Processing could be done and resulting output transmitted back and printed out on the line printer.

A telephone line usually carries the data back and forth between the computer and the terminal. The service on telephone lines can vary from low volume and speed to extremely high volumes and speeds. Other carriers of data are also employed by teleprocessing applications. As mentioned above, satellite communications, microwaves, and optic fibers are beginning to play a major part in the teleprocessing application development.

A *modem* is a device which is used to interface a telephone line to a computer cable. Think of it functionally as a translator; computer equipment speaks one language and telephone equipment another.

The functional schematic in Figure 4.2 shows the equipment which makes up a teleprocessing facility. Figure 4.2a shows a *dial up* facility and Figure 4.2b shows a *dedicated line* facility. Dial up uses a telephone and connection between terminal and computer is established when needed. It is generally used for low volume applications. The dedicated line facility has a connection that is there whenever needed. It is generally used for high volume applications.

The teleprocessing control unit performs essentially the same functions as the control unit of any other peripheral device. More specifically, it performs the functions of transmission control and character assembly. The control unit for the terminal also performs these func-

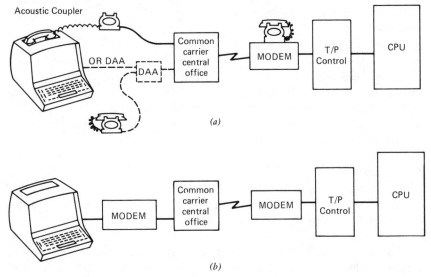

Figure 4.2 Schematics depicting typical telecommunications facilities. (a) A dial up facility. (b) A dedicated line facility.

tions for the terminal. In most teleprocessing environments, the teleprocessing control unit (TCU) and the control unit for the terminal talk to each other, so to speak. This conversation takes place through the modems and over the telephone line and its purpose is to allow the control units to synchronize themselves, before sending or receiving data, and to allow verification of data after they have been sent or received.

Teleprocessing is used together with several types of computer processing. Time-sharing is one of those types. TP is also used to support both batch processing and on-line single transaction processing. In the on-line single transaction method of processing, single transactions arrive randomly from remotely located terminals. Processing takes place, which may include updating of files or data bases. Responses to the transactions are fabricated and returned to the terminal that initiated the transaction. For the single transaction type of processing, the terminal device is generally a relatively low speed device like a character printer, a teletype, or a CRT. In the batch method, a stream of input transactions is sent to a computer, across communications lines or some other telecommunications facility. Processing takes place, updates may be made, and output transactions, generally in the form of reports, are formulated. The reports are transmitted from the computer back to the terminal that initially sent the input.

The batch type of remote processing is often referred to as *remote processing*. In RJE, for example, it is possible to hold report output on a peripheral storage device until processing has been completed and then send it back to the initiating terminal. This process is called *spooling* and the data set in which such report output is held is called a *spool*. It is also possible in more sophisticated TP systems to send output to terminals other than the terminal initiating the transaction.

Time-Sharing

Also known as interactive computing, *time-sharing* is the ability to use a computer and peripheral devices to service many users at what appears to be the same time. The users involved generally have low-speed terminals, with which they converse with the computer. There are compilers in existence that can compile and test a program on a statement-by-statement basis. Two of the more popular languages which use this technique are APL and BASIC. The APL language uses mathematical notation and is generally intended for computer applications that consist of complex computations made on small amounts of input data, that produce small amounts of output data. BASIC on the other hand is a commercially oriented language. Its intended use is with business applications. If large files are needed, they can be stored on peripheral devices at the computer site. Program statements can be written by programmers compiled and tested, one statement at a time, and stored on a peripheral storage at the computer site. The cost of using this service is reasonable, if it is used properly. Care should be taken to see that a minimum amount of time is spent keying in data or having data typed out since low-speed terminals are generally used. Storage of data on peripheral storage at the computer site should also be carefully controlled. These two items, if not watched, can run up a sizable monthly bill.

Basically, time-sharing works by dividing up a period of time—say a second—among many users. Each user gets a fraction of every second devoted to him exclusively. Since input/output operations from peripheral devices, plus the terminals, are very slow compared to the electronic speed of the computer, the fraction of a second is sufficient to handle the user's computer storage and processing unit requirements. None of the many users is even aware of the fact that the other users are getting time. This gives the user the impression that he has the entire machine to himself.

Generally, but not necessarily, the terminals are located at a site remote from the computer. Some companies support their own time-sharing. They either lease or buy a computer from a manufacturer and develop or buy the software to support time-sharing. The time-sharing firms develop their software to support the many types of available terminals. As they market their services, they sometimes enter into an agreement with terminal manufacturers and attempt to make an arrangement or lease or sell both time-sharing service and terminals. In some cases, however, the user may choose to select a terminal of his own preference, such as a communicating word processor, and as long as the time-sharing firm has the software that supports that terminal, an agreement can be made on that basis.

Within large computer centers a time sharing facility called TSO (time sharing option of the operating system) is often present.

Virtual Storage

Although not really new, *virtual storage* is now being offered on a large-scale basis. Essentially, it allows programmers to assume that they have virtually unlimited computer storage at their disposal. Through operating system software, a computer with, say, 2 million positions of computer storage can be made to look as if it had 16 million positions of computer storage. The computer is able, through the use of sophisticated software techniques, and disk devices, to determine which program and data set modules are being used most frequently and keep those modules in computer storage. The modules used less frequently are stored on a direct-access storage device and read into computer storage as they are needed. The whole process is dynamic in that if one of those modules that is initially stored on the direct access storage device begins to be used more frequently, it is then stored in computer storage, and a module initially in computer storage, that now is being used less frequently is relegated to the direct-access storage device.

The concept of rolling in and rolling out modules is known as *paging*. Today's programming is done in what is known as modular programming. Since many of the applications are quite large, programs are written in parts by many different programmers. These parts make up modules. It is these modules, as well as data set modules, that are transferred back and forth from a direct access storage device in the dynamic environment of a virtual storage installation. The shuttling back and forth of modules is accomplished in sets of computer instructions of a certain size. These sets of instructions are referred to as pages. Hence the term paging.

The material presented in this chapter has been brief as it is intended to be merely introductory. Subsequent chapters contain expanded examinations of systems, teleprocessing (from a data processing and computer perspective), and data bases. The more expanded discussions deal with the complexities of getting data from devices to computer storage and from networks to computer storage. The hardware for doing this can be either a control unit or a computer. The software components for doing this are called access methods. Sophisticated file structuring and data bases and data dictionaries will also be discussed in some detail.

First, however, let's look at some of the basic components and subassemblies of computers.

chapter 5

Building Blocks and
Small Computers*

An Analogy

Many owners of automobiles have neither the time nor the inclination to learn anything about how their vehicle works. They just want to get into their car, turn the key, and go. These individuals realize that they must periodically put gasoline in their car, change the oil every once in a while, and get a tune-up once a year. If for some unknown reason, the car breaks down, a mechanic is called and the car towed, pushed, or if possible driven to a service center for repair. In most cases, all the owner cares about is getting the car going again and how much it is going to cost.

And then, there is the other kind of automobile owner who is a frustrated automotive engineer/mechanic who wants to know everything from front bumper to taillight about his car. This type of individual often spends more time tinkering with his automobile and working on it than he does using it for its intended purposes.

There is another kind of car owner; the individual who uses his automobile primarily as a means of transportation but who also wants to know something about automobiles in general and something about his automobile in particular. This individual realizes that to understand the particulars of his car, he first has to understand some concepts about cars in general.

The three attitudes above can also be applied to users of computers. Some computer users just wish to look at the basic operating booklet, plug it in, and start computing. At the other end of the spectrum are the individuals who wish to become familiar with every facet of the equip-

*The chapter was published as an article in the *Journal of Systems Management* in October of 1979. It has been modified somewhat to fit properly into the context of this book.

ment and the systems and programs which make it run. Then, as with automobiles, there is the other kind of computer user. This individual wishes to have at least a basic operational knowledge of the computer system he owns. It helps him communicate with the technicians who support and service the configuration of equipment, systems, and programs in his installation.

Maxi, Mini, and Micro Computers

In the past few years, computers have gone from maxi to mini to micro in size and price. This decrease in size and price does not change one basic fact about computers. Any digitial computer, no matter what its size, is made up of five basic subsystems or components. Figure 5.1 illustrates these components, again.

The *input subsystem* consists of the paths (channels) through which information must pass as it moves from an input device into the computer. The *memory subsystem* stores information which is used for solving problems. As shown in Chapter 1, the information stored is not only the data needed to solve a problem, but also the set of instructions (program) required to solve it. The *processor subsystem* performs the

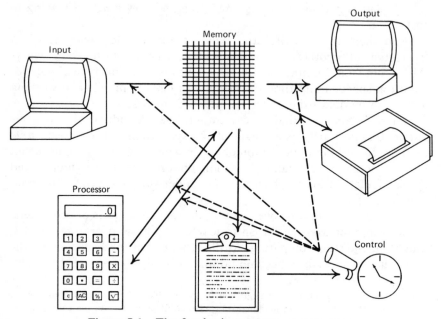

Figure 5.1   The five basic computer components.

arithmetic and logical operations necessary to execute instructions in a computer. The *control subsystem* supervises the activity of the other subsystems. It directs the processing as far as: (a) input of information, (b) storage and retrieval of information, (c) arithmetic and logical processing of information, (d) output of information, and (e) its own activity. The *output subsystem* is made up of the paths (channels) through which information must pass as it moves from the computer to the output devices.

The trend from maxi to mini to microcomputers spans a ten-year period. It began approximately in the mid-1960s and progressed into the mid-1970s. The minis and micros now have processing and storage capabilities equivalent to or greater than most of the commercial computers in use in the mid 1960s. The basic subsystems described above have not changed functionally. The components making up those subsystems, which are examined next, have not changed functionally. All that has changed is that they have become significantly smaller. The sketch in Figure 5.2 indicates the dramatic miniaturization of electronic components in comparison to a pencil.

Even though computers have shrunk from maxi to micro, peripheral devices have not. There are basically two reasons for this. The five basic

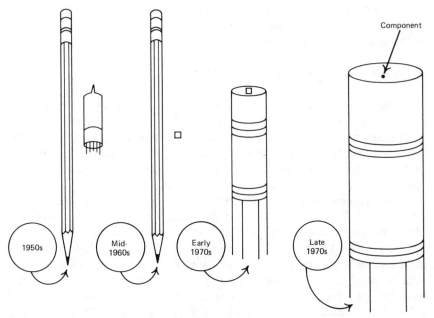

Figure 5.2 The miniaturization of computer components.

subsystems and their components are totally electronic and can be made as small as electronic technology permits. Peripheral devices are electromechanical. Some storage media like magnetic disk and tape are driven on devices which can be reduced in size only as far as mechanical technology permits. The second reason for the limited reduction in size of peripherals is functional. A CRT device is totally electronic, except for parts of the keyboard. However, reducing a CRT screen and keyboard in size as far as electronically possible would result in a screen too small to be seen and a keyboard too small for human fingers to manipulate.

So, peripherals have gone from maxi to mini in some cases, but not to micro. For example, floppy disks or diskettes are conceptually the same as any large-scale disk storage device. Yet they are slower in accessing data, have less storage capacity, and are less expensive. The same can be said for magnetic-tape cassette recorders and cassettes as opposed to magnetic-tape devices and reels of magnetic tape. Although cassettes have less capacity, are slower in retrieving data, and are less expensive than magnetic tapes, in principle they are the same as the larger magnetic tape drives and large reels of tape. Usually, the smaller and less expensive the computer, the smaller and less expensive are the I/O peripherals. This is a generalization, and there are exceptions, but one is more likely to find floppy disks and cassettes on microcomputers than on large-scale computers. CRT input devices are virtually identical to those used on larger computer systems.

Computer Components

The small basic electronic components that are used to make up computers are examined next. The application or grouping of these electronic components is the methodology for fabricating computers. The following presentation of technical material in nontechnical language provides a conceptual understanding of electronics technology and its application in the fabrication of computers.

Within the context of an introductory treatment, as we saw in Chapter 1, it is possible to explain the basic operations and subsystems of a computer without reducing data elements below the level of characters, that is, A, B, 1, 2, 3, and so forth. However, a smaller chunk of information is possible when one deals with a computer at its own level. This piece of data is known as a *bit*. The word bit, a contraction for the term "binary digit," describes in terms of binary numbers a chunk of information which can have either of two values, either "O" or "1." The smallest electronic components have the ability to express two states, and the two states could be called "0" or "1." Combinations of bits make up *characters*. Two of the most commonly used bit combinations schemes are ASCII and EBCDIC. Tables of ASCII* and EBCDIC codes are found in the appendix.

We are getting down to the "bit" level in computing so as to set the groundwork for an examination of basic computer components. A computer works with bits in performing its internal processing functions. When displaying information, a computer combines the bits into alphabetical or numerical characters recognizable by the individuals using the computer.

Let us have a look at some components. They are first examined as stand-alone components; then their functions are explained. Ultimately a collection of these components makes up a computer.

A *diode* is a device that conceptually is like a check valve. It allows current to pass through it one way, but current flowing in the opposite direction is so small as to be negligible.

Semiconductor material is that which benefits from economies of scale. Semiconductors are metallic crystals that are able to share electrons (negatively charged atomic particles) when in a group. These electrons would be the property of individual metal atoms but are shared by all the atoms when in a metallic crystal. A crystal in this case is a metallic union made up of different metals with differing atomic structures. For example, silicon is made semiconducting by being combined with another element like aluminum. A property of the aluminum atom is that it lacks one electron of the number needed to bind it to the silicon. By borrowing, so to speak, from a pool of electrons, to form the bond, it leaves a positive "hole" which can migrate throughout the crystal. In this case, the result is a positive or "p" type semiconductor. In another example, where arsenic and aluminum make up the union, arsenic has an extra electron. This electron enters the pool, and the result is a negative or "n" type semiconductor. When "p" type and "n" type semiconductors are joined and electric potential is applied, current will flow freely or be inhibited, depending on whether the electric potential applied is positive or negative. The junction thus described performs the function of a diode.

A *transistor* is basically an amplifier. Transistors consist of three pieces of semiconductor material, making a sandwich. Transistors are of two basic types, *bipolar junction* (BJT) and *field effect* (FET). The BJT type is a current amplifier, while the FET is a voltage amplifier. Both types of transistor can be fabricated in two ways: "pnp" or "npn."

---

* ASCII—American Standard Code for Information Interchange.

They represent an improvement over vacuum tubes in that they perform the same function, but do so with much less heat. Schematically, transistors can be expressed as illustrated in Figure 5.3.

Where the diode was like a check valve, a transistor is like a gate valve. The base of the transistor is like the gate and control wheel on the valve. With the valve, the amount of liquid flowing through it depends on how far the gate is opened. With the transistor, the flow of current between emitter and collector is determined by the amount of current applied to the base. Since it is an amplifier, a relatively small amount of current applied to the base increases the flow of current by some factor greater than the amount applied to the base. Transistors, like valves, come in various sizes. The designation "pnp" or "npn" signifies the direction in which the current flows either from emitter to collector or from collector to emitter.

The way the basic building blocks are made into components and subsystems is known as the *fabrication process*. Specific advantages and disadvantages exist for each type of fabrication process. Details of most of these processes concern the electronics involved. However, a couple of readily discernible observations can be made.

For the purposes of this survey, three fabrication processes can be reviewed: (1) Bipolar, (2) MOS, and (3) I²L.

1 **Bipolar technology**, also known as *transistor-transistor logic* (TTL or T²L), is the most common of the fabrication technologies. Its components are relatively fast in electronic performance, but are relatively large in size and contain a number of individual components.

2 **MOS**—*Metal Oxide Semiconductor technology* is a fabrication process that results in components that are relatively small in size (miniature is a better word) but whose electronic speed is relatively slow. PMOS or "p" channel MOS and NMOS or "n" channel MOS are two types of this technology. The channel here refers to the slab that produces conduction. The "p" and "n" refer to the basic charge

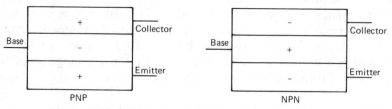

Figure 5.3   Schematics of PNP and NPN translators.

of the channel whether it is plus (positive) or minus (negative). NMOS is five times as fast in electronic performance, but since it is more complex a more expensive fabrication process is required to produce it.

3 *I²L or IIL—Integrated Injection Logic* is the most contemporary microprocessor technology. It combines the packing density of MOS with the speed of bipolar technology.

Computer Subassemblies

Combinations of transistors, together with more commonly known components like resistors, wires, power supplies, and capacitors are the basic building blocks that make up larger components of computers. At this point, the discussion deals with any computer. The specifics of microcomputers and microprocessors will follow later, after the conceptual groundwork has been laid. The next step up is to define some of the larger components made up of the basic building block electronic components just described.

A *flipflop* is a bistate device, that is, one that can be in either one state or the other. A flipflop is a pair of transistors that work reciprocally; that is when one transistor allows current to pass through it, the other transistor does not allow current to pass through *it*. Another property of a flipflop is that once an impulse sets it, it will stay in that state until another impulse clears it. In this way, the flipflop makes pulse input continuously available. Flipflops are relatively costly and are used primarily in registers. A flipflop can store one bit of data.

A *register* is a group of flipflops that can store a fixed number of bits. The size of registers varies from one computer to another, but they are usually the same size in bits as the "word length" of the processor and controller with which they interface in a specific configuration. The *word length* of a computer defines the number of bytes in a single addressable computer storage (memory) location. Recall that bits are the smallest recognizable pieces of data.

A collection of bits makes up a character. For example, eight bits are required to make up a character in the EBCDIC coding structure. The eight bits represented by 11000001 would be the settings of eight flipflops or one register in an eight-bit word machine.

Perhaps the best way to illustrate the concept of a word is to explain it in the context of computer memory. The basic element of memory is also a bit-storing device. Magnetic cores, until recently, were the most commonly used bit-storage devices. Some of the contemporary computer memories are made of metal oxide semiconductor (MOS) materials, and are found in computers of all sizes. The kind of memory with which this discussion is concerned is the memory that is normally considered part of the computer, as opposed to auxiliary memory such as magnetic disk and magnetic tape. Conceptually, computer memory comes in two forms, character and word. In a *character memory*, each storage location of memory contains the number of bits necessary to make up a single character of data, using the coding structure peculiar to that machine. For example, an EBCDIC character memory would have the capacity in each of its storage locations to hold a character made up of eight bits. *Word memory*, on the other hand, has the capacity to hold more than one character in a storage location of memory. For example, a storage location of word memory could contain several positions, each position having the capacity for one character. Each of the characters could be formed using, say, eight bits. The memory would be known as a 64-bit word memory. Each storage location has a unique address, and these locations are sometimes referred to as *addresses*. The picture in Figure 5.4 helps to clarify the concept.

Another basic element in the makeup of computers is the *electronic switch*. Switches are also referred to as *logic gates*. They are found as part of the processor, control, and memory subsystems of all computers.

An electronic switch or logic gate is a device that inhibits or allows an impulse to pass along a single path. There are a few basic types of switches: "AND" switches, where both the signal and the actuation of the switch (which acts as input to the switch) are combined to produce a signal on the output lead, and the "OR" switch, where a signal is produced on the output lead if either a signal or the actuator has input

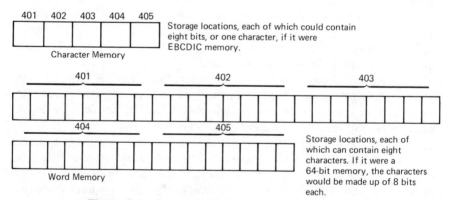

Figure 5.4   Storage locations, character and word.

into the switch. Combinations of AND and OR switches, or as they are sometimes called, *gates*, can be used to construct more complex switches. It is the "AND" and "OR" switches that give a computer basic logical ability. Let's use automobiles again to illustrate, starting with the AND switch. Assuming that I have a car in good working condition; if the battery is ok "AND" I turn the ignition key, the car will start. Both conditions must be present. If the battery is ok "AND" I don't turn the ignition, the car is not going to start. If the battery is dead, I can turn the key till the cows come home, but the car will not start. The "OR" switch reacts to an "either/or" as well as "both" situation. If I wish to stop my car while it is moving, I can apply the foot brake "OR" the hand brake "OR" both. (Although I may have to be something of a contortionist to perform this action). In any event, the car will stop.

Let's summarize a little at this point. Transistors perform a diode or "check valve" function and are made of semiconductor materials. Combinations of these basic elements form basic electronic components such as flipflops and switches. Flipflops and switches are used to make up computer components such as registers and logic circuitry. Combinations of logic circuitry and switches form the major subsystems of all computers. The miniaturization of this technology resulted first in more powerful large-scale computers, as less space was required. Minicomputers followed, and the most recent advances in electronics technology have produced, among other things, microcomputers and microprocessors.

Microprocessors and Microcomputers

Now for a look at microprocessors and microcomputers. A precise definition of micros, just as for minis, is somewhat difficult to arrive at. Yet, the distinction between microprocessors and microcomputers is quite clear. A microcomputer, like any computer, is made up of the five basic subsystems. What makes it a *microcomputer* is the fact that these subsystems are miniaturized.

A microprocessor on the other hand is made up of the computer subsystems exclusive of the memory and the input, and output subsystems. Schematically this is shown in Figure 5.5.

In the world of microprocessors, some of the subsystems are given different nomenclature, but they perform the same functions. For example, the processor subsystem which performs arithmetic and logic function is often called the *arithmetic and logic unit* (ALU). The control subsystem is often referred to as the *controller*, and since both

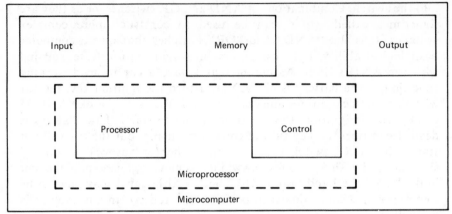

Figure 5.5   Microprocessor within microcomputer.

the processor and control subsystems use *registers*, the registers are sometimes listed as a separate component.

One reasonably accurate definition of a *microprocessor* is: a miniature component, a single integrated-circuit chip on which fit many of the components of processor and control subsystems. A microprocessor is sometimes known as a *computer-on-a-chip*.

The most simple microprocessor is made of the following components:

1   Arithmetic and Logic Unit (ALU).
2   Registers.
3   Controller.

As the chapter's opening analogy attempted to show, one type of car owner likes to know a little something about cars in general so that he can understand his car in particular. The last several pages were devoted to describing some of the components and subassemblies of all computers, and to distinguish microcomputers from nonmicrocomputers. In light of the basic concepts already examined, let's now look at the terminology often used to describe microcomputers in the marketplace.

Any manager or individual or group that is contemplating the use of a microcomputer configuration should be familiar with the following components and terminology:

Central Processing Unit (CPU)
Memory

Random Access (RAM)
Read Only (ROM)
Bus (or data channel)
Input/Output and Peripherals
Front Panels or Face Plates
Software

The CPU of a microcomputer is a *microprocessor*, a very small subassembly which contains an arithmetic and logic unit (ALU) and a control component. The control component is also occasionally called a *clock*. The clock controls the speed at which instructions are executed by the configuration. A degree of caution is advised in ascertaining that the CPU does not house a clock that is too fast for other system modules, such as memory. As any car mechanic knows, too big an engine will damage a transmission or rear axle that has not been engineered to handle it. With a clock that is not in synchronization with other components, there are likely to be some puzzling results as transfers of data are expected to be completed before they actually are completed or as a processor begins to operate on data that it expects to find but which have already been moved elsewhere.

Memory in a microcomputer comes in two "flavors;" RAM and ROM. *Random Access Memory* (RAM) can be read from and written to. It is the kind of memory that can be used to hold application programs, compilers, transient data (data that are being transferred from one peripheral to another and being manipulated in the process), and other software. RAM is measured in bytes (8 bits) or in *k bytes* (k = 1024 bytes). It can generally be purchased in modules of 4k, 8k, or 16k bytes. *Read Only Memory* (ROM) can be read from, but not written to. This type of memory is preprogrammed, that is, it contains a fixed set of instructions. ROM usually contains programs which include simple routines for interacting with a computer system, such as altering or examining computer memory (RAM) locations. The user can obtain ROM modules and put his own programs on them.

In order to interconnect the components of a microcomputer system, a *bus* is required. Standard buses are available. A standard bus is one that contains compatibility among the components of several manufacturers. It is necessary to ascertain that the components the user is planning to interface have a common bus allowing their interconnection.

To attach peripheral devices to a configuration, a special component often called an *interface* (there's that word again), is required for each peripheral device or device type. Peripherals include CRT display devices or typewriter terminals, disk storage devices (both "floppies" and the larger type), and tape cassette devices. Interfaces are of two basic types: *serial* in which data are transferred serially bit by bit along a single path (wire), and *parallel* where data are transferred in parallel across eight paths (wires), eight bits or a character at a time. Functionally, microcomputer peripheral devices are used two ways: as *auxiliary storage* and as *Input/Output* (I/O) facilities. Auxiliary storage is used to hold files or data bases containing information that is to be available to the computer for processing. The most common forms of auxiliary storage media are magnetic disks and magnetic tapes. I/O facilities are used to enter data into a computer and/or to display information that has been processed by a computer. I/O devices include CRT display devices, typewriter terminals, high speed printers, and graphics display devices. By now you may have noticed the functional similarities of all computers; maxis, minis, and micros.

A *front panel* or *face plate* is basically a console with lights and switches by which a user is able to observe and control the internal activity of the computer. Although front panels and face plates look impressive they are really quite superfluous, as most communication with a microcomputer is much more effective using a terminal device. The components just described make up the hardware or "iron" of a microcomputer.

The last subject in microcomputer technology to be examined is software. Without basic software support, a technician would spend unproductive time working with switches and lights on the face plate console just getting the system to perform some basic functions. Software is available which supports basic system monitoring. Assemblers and problem-oriented language compilers are also available. There are varieties of these, and the potential user should question any vendor to find out what the software does.

Uses of Micros

Contemporary microprocessors are being employed in many applications. These have five basic applications, in addition to their stand-alone capability as part of small business-computer systems and as word processors.

1 They are being incorporated into terminal devices, such as CRTs and/or printer card reader configurations. Terminals which have microprocessors included in their design are called *intelligent* or *smart terminals*. Individual terminals can have microprocessors within their circuitry, or in some cases a number of *nonintelligent*

terminals are connected by a cable to a centrally located controller that has a microprocessor in its circuitry. This type of an arrangement is called a cluster. It overlaps two other basic applications, as will be seen below. Microprocessors are often seen in point of sale (POS) terminals.

2 Microprocessors are having an impact on the way computing is done. As shown earlier, microprocessors are often part of a larger computer configuration. Distributed computing is a concept that is emerging because microprocessors are being imbedded in the circuitry of larger computers.

3 Microprocessors are making their presence felt in the field of data communications. Microprocessors are included in the circuitry of Teleprocessing Control Units (TCUs). Tasks that historically have been performed by the main computer can be off-loaded into a TCU that contains microprocessors.

4 Microprocessors are being used in programmable controllers. These devices, historically known as process controllers, have been used to control manufacturing processes. The small size of microprocessors has led to applications formerly impossible because of size constraints. For example, in automotive engineering, microprocessors are used for emission control and nonskid braking.

5 In the area of consumer products, the arrival on the scene of the small pocket calculator represents the beginning of microprocessor products that can serve the individual consumer. Electronic games represent a more frivolous application.

Programming of microcomputers can be done in three basic ways:

1 **Direct machine coding**—that is, by the use of external toggle type switches, "zeros" and "ones" (bits) are directly loaded into the machine using the face plate console. This is tedious and should be confined to small programs.

2 **English-language-like nmemonics**—these are symbols that are used by programmers to make their task less tedious, but nmemonics must be assembled into machine language before the program can be executed.

3 **High-level languages**—that are problem oriented rather than machine oriented. Programs written in these languages must be compiled and assembled before they are executable by the machine.

What is on the market in microprocessors:

1 *Monolithic*—These are complete configurations of components on one piece of semiconductor with limited programming and limited speed. They usually have read-only memory (ROM) and limited random access memory (RAM). An example is the small programmable calculator.

2 *Chips sets*—These contain microprocessor and other components including ROM, RAM, and I/O device interfaces. Faster than monolithic, they also take up more space.

3 *Bit slice*—These are parallel processors that are coupled together. They can be used as building blocks in an expandable application. Programming (software) and interfacing are complex.

4 *Complete Microsystem*—This describes a complete system and support from the manufacturer.

Recently micros have found their way into the general purpose computer marketplace, where they promise to make their presence felt. The recently announced microNOVA by Data General Corporation is an example. Although much of its promotional literature is still directed at the electronics engineer, the microNOVA can use some of the software used by the larger minicomputer NOVA from the same company. The microNOVA has a FORTRAN IV and BASIC compiler and can support a number of peripheral devices.

As technology continues to effect a reduction in both size and price of computer and peripheral components at an ever-accelerating pace, selection becomes more complex. A potential user has a difficult time deciding to spend x dollars now for a computer system that may be obsolescent in a year, or as a product that can outperform it appears on the market at $x/2$ dollars. In some ways, micros appear to be now where minis were in the early '70s. When minis were first marketed, their early promotional literature was directed at the electronics engineer. Yet now one would be hard put to distinguish between a mini and a nonmini either by reading promotional literature or by actually using the equipment. A few years from now, it will also be difficult to discern micro from mini from midi from maxi from whatever. It is not overly difficult to identify extremes. There is obviously a difference in capability between an IBM 3033 and a micro NOVA. And yet these machines both have the same five basic components. They are fabricated using the same basic components and subassemblies. A computer is a computer, no matter what kind of prefix you give it. The prefix "micro" and "mini" are imprecise. The distinction between "mini" and nonmini has become quite blurred, and within the next few years the distinction between "micro" and nonmicro will also blur.

part 2

Computer Software

This section deals with major system-software components. These components are to be distinguished from application software. Application software or programming is the occupation of a significant number of individuals in the computer profession and it is a highly visible entity. System software is not highly visible, but its activity consumes a significant amount of resources, both human and machine. The complexity of the system-software function depends upon the complexity and size of the computer installation. Although computer complexity ranges from the single computer installation to the "wall to wall" installations of MCAUTO and other large corporations, elements of system software are found in all of them.

The elements of system software described in this section are those of the IBM Corporation. Other computer manufacturers and software vendors have similar products. Yet the IBM system software products are comprehensive enough to serve as a vehicle to describe system software products generically. Chapters 8 and 10 use many IBM buzzwords and deal with some highly specialized technology. They contain the most difficult material in the book for the uninitiated.

The chapters in this section deal with the most complex and often overlooked aspect of using computers. Systems software supplies a user of a computer configuration with the potential to do "all kinds of things." The proper care and feeding by skilled technicians of that systems software go a long way toward the realization of its potential.

chapter 6

Control Programs
or Operating Systems

A Little History

As we have already established, contemporary computer technology is made up of basically two elements. Known in the trade as hardware and software, these two elements include equipment (the hardware), as well as data and programs (the software). Equipment includes computers, peripheral devices, communications lines, modems, and storage media, all of which is nothing more than a pile of junk without software. The equipment has tremendous potential and when given specific instructions on how to act on specific data and to produce information from those data, it can do so with phenomenal speed and accuracy. To restate what has already been established, data are that which is operated upon by computer equipment, and programs are the instructions by which computers operate upon the data.

Since 1960 computer technology has increased in conjunction with electronics in capability and sophistication. The computers in use during the early 1960s had speed and accuracy capabilities that allowed them to perform tasks with significantly increased efficiency. These early machines, such as the IBM 1400 and 7000 series, using magnetic tape and magnetic disk storage devices, made possible great improvements in the storage and processing of data. However, the hardware and software technology at that time permitted the processing of one task at a time. An entire configuration of computer equipment, that is, processor, storage, auxiliary storage input/output (I/O) devices, programs, and data were combined to accomplish a single task. Figure 6.1 illustrates this concept.

Even though the processing of data with such a configuration resulted in significant improvements in speed and accuracy, it soon became obvious that even greater speed and accuracy were possible. Technological improvements in the speed of computer processors,

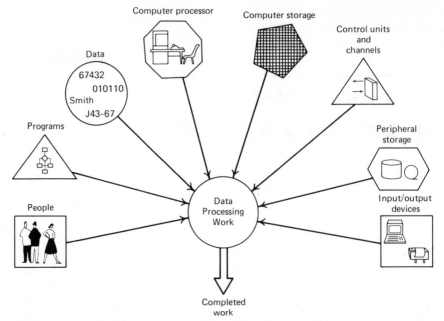

Figure 6.1 The elements that are combined to perform data processing work.

together with improvements in both speed and capacity of computer storage, resulted in those components' being idle 90–95% of the time when processing the one task. Auxiliary storage and I/O devices were just not able to keep up with the computer. Improvements in I/O devices were also being made, but the limitations imposed by mechanics prevented them from keeping pace with computers, which were electronic and not restrained by mechanical limitations. To address this situation of idle time and unused capacity, computer manufacturers and software designers began to think about developing a *superprogram* which would allow the attachment of many I/O and peripheral storage devices and additionally would permit the computer to process several tasks concurrently.

The Concept

The way it would work would be something like this. The superprogram would be developed to function in the main or central processor of a computer. It would control all devices and also suspend processing of one task and commence processing of another when directed to do so. In addition to the superprogram in the central processor, several smaller processors, sometimes known as *channels*, would be incorporated into the same computer. While the channels were performing one type of task, the central processors could be doing something else. Under the superprogram as devised, the channels generally perform the function of transferring data between auxiliary storage or peripheral devices and computer storage. This process is an order of magnitude slower than the central processor speed, so that while data are being transferred, the central processor is free to do other work. It is the function of the superprogram to direct the processor to do this other work. The super-program is known as a *control program* or an *operating system*. Although the tasks performed by an operating system are varied and complex, the operating system itself is nothing more than a computer program. It differs from a typical computer program only in its functions and complexity. In concept, an operating system enables a computer to "walk and chew gum at the same time."

OPERATING SYSTEM

Most computer manufacturers and vendors of small business systems that use computers provide some kind of control program or operating system which runs on their equipment. There are few, if any, commercial data-processing computers marketed today that do not have some kind of operating system included. Perhaps the largest of these operating systems is IBM's operating system, which has become affectionately known as "OS" (pronounced "oh es") or as "Big Ozz." An examination of the function of OS, since it is probably the most comprehensive, can serve to explain operating systems in general.

Let us first define an operating system more formally. An *operating system* is an integrated set of computer programs used to make efficient use of the facilities of a configuration of computer equipment. It, the operating system, is a manager of functions. Specifically, OS has three major management functions, the management of jobs, the management of tasks, and the management of data.

The management of jobs is an external interface, that is, the function of managing the transfer of jobs into and out of the processing streams. A *job* is defined as a specifically defined set of work to be done. Processing a payroll is an example of a job. So also is the "start up" and the "close down" of a computer configuration.

The management of tasks is an internal function, the management of carrying out the internal tasks necessary to complete jobs. A *task* is defined as an element of work, an operating system program module, that is part of the process in getting a job done. The *fetching* (loading into computer storage) of a program is an example of a task. To help distinguish between job and task, consider the following manual system illustration. In processing a payroll manually, the calculation of taxes and deductions is part of the job. Turning on the adding machine is a task.

Retrieval of employee records from the file cabinet and the procuring of time cards are part of the data management function of producing a payroll. *Data management* in an operating system manages the transfer of data elements and information between peripheral storage devices and computer storage. Data can be thought of as physical or logical records of information or segments of data bases.*

JCL

How does the operating system know what to do? Communication with the operating system is achieved by *Job Control Language* or JCL. The concept of JCL is simple, yet its application can be complex. Learning how to use JCL effectively requires a learning curve of classroom training and experience. The length of the curve varies depending upon the technical sophistication of the installation and the technicians using it. Job control language is used by nearly all types of technicians from application programmers to systems software specialists and operations technical support technicians. JCL statements are entered into the computer by means of 80-column cards or through a terminal device. Most statements are of three major types, JOB statements, EXEC (execute) statements and DD (data definition) statements. There are a few other statements such as delimiter statements and comments statements, but the JOB, EXEC, and DD statements make up the bulk of JCL in use. A basic JCL statement is in the following format:

// name   verb   parameters

---

*Using the payroll example, the record for one employee or the time card for one employee would constitute a logical record. A group of records for several employees or a handful of time cards might constitute a physical record containing several logical records. Within a computer configuration, it is possible to block several logical records in one physical record for the sake of more efficient processing. Within data bases, pieces of records in one file can be related to pieces of records in other files. The pieces are known in some data-base systems as segments. Data-base management systems, which are large complex computer programs in their own right, use operating systems data management programs to transfer segments of data between data bases that reside on peripheral storage devices and computer storage.

By convention, OS JCL statements use the first two positions for slashes, the next eight positions for names and the next four for the verb. The remainder is free form with commas as delimiters. The two slashes (//) are used to identify JCL statements uniquely from other types of data. Names are used to differentiate one JCL statement from another. The verb indicates the type of JCL statement and also provides specific instruction to the operating system that results in some action taken by the operating system. JOB, EXEC, and DD are verbs. The parameters and their use introduce the complexity into JCL. There are many parameters and each of them has several options. One of the options is a *default option*. The default option allows the JCL user to omit the specification of an entry for a parameter. The action taken by the operating system in such a case is the action that the developers of the operating system believe would be the most common option selected. Since there are many parameters and several options for each, including a default, it is not difficult to understand how complex an operating system and JCL can become and why it may take some time to acquire the training and experience to use it effectively.

JOB Statement

The JOB statement contains information telling the category or class of the job. This information is used by the operating system to eliminate contention between jobs requiring the same resources by preventing these jobs from running concurrently. This so-called *job class information* also helps provide a *job mix* for more efficient use of system resources. It also aids an installation to process high priority work more quickly. Assigning jobs to specific classes depends on determining the processing characteristics of jobs in an installation. When the characteristics are known, a balance can be established by the concurrent processing of jobs with offsetting characteristics. For instance, jobs with high input/output activity can be run concurrently with jobs having high processing requirements by assigning them to two different classes, the classes themselves having configuration resources available concurrently. All this work comes under the heading of job management. The facilities of the job management function of the operating system are invoked to perform the work specified in the parameters.

EXEC Statement

Many jobs consist of several steps. The job control language EXEC statement notifies the operating system to execute a step that is named in the parameter portion of the statement. The step is usually a program of some kind that resides in an operating system library (another operating system facility to be discussed later). Other parameters in the EXEC statement help the operating system to locate the program. Operating systems libraries, including a program library, are often stored on magnetic disk storage devices. Once the desired program is located, it is copied into computer storage, at locations partially determined by the job class of which the step is part. Once in computer storage, it is ready for execution. Whereas the JOB statement invokes facilities of the job management function, the EXEC statement invokes facilities of task management. When the job step (program) is in storage, that is, loaded and ready to execute, there are additional resources needed. These additional resources are the data that resided in files or data bases, or both.

DD Statement

The DD statement defines the files and/or data bases from which and to which data and information are transferred during the execution of the job step. The DD parameters include the names of files and/or data bases used, their location, device type on which they reside, whether they are input (already existing) or output (to be created or existing to be updated), and other file and/or data base characteristics. Because of the number of DD statements and the number of options for each parameter, it is this part of JCL that can be most complicated. File and data base technology itself is often quite sophisticated and this adds to the complexity. DD statements invoke the facilities of the data management function. Figure 6.2 contains a list of the JCL statements, also called *job stream*, that might be used to get some automobile maintenance done. Also shown in the illustration are some of the tasks that might be performed during the job of automobile maintenance. The tasks would not appear in actual JCL; they are included merely for illustrative purposes.

A Contemporary Operating System (MVS)

As stated earlier, operating systems can be of varying sizes and complexity. OS in one of its most current versions, called OS/VS2, (MVS), short for Operating System Virtual Storage, Release 2, Multiple Virtual Storage, may be the most comprehensive of all. To examine all the facilities of such a system would fill a book. As a matter of fact, there are nearly 20 technical manuals of significant size devoted to it. Rather

```
// Job      Six-month check, change oil, and lubricate

// Step 1        remove old oil, check for problems
                 (Tasks)    raise car on lift
                            remove plug from oil pan
                            drain old oil
                            replace plug in oil pan
                            remove old oil filter

//DD             (Data Mgmt)        get new oil filter
                                     get grease gun
                 (Tasks)    lubricate fittings
                            visually check exhaust system
                            visually check springs and shocks

// Step 2        add new oil
                 (Tasks)    put oil in car
                            clean breather cap
                            replace breather cap

// Job      Tune up engine and carburetor

// Step 1        tune engine
                 (Tasks)    remove old spark plugs
                            open distributor
                            remove old parts, points, condenser etc.

//DD             (Data Mgmt)        get new spark plugs
                                     get new distributor parts, points,
                                     condenser etc.

                 (Tasks)    put new spark plugs in engine
                            replace distributor parts
                            colse distributor
                            start engine
                            check timing, adjust if necessary
                            turn off engine

// Step 2        tune carburetor
                 (Tasks)    remove old air filter

//DD             (Data Mgmt)        get screw driver
                                     get new air filter
                 (Tasks)    put in new air filter
                            turn on engine
                            adjust idle and mixture screws
                            check transmission fluid
                            turn off engine
                            check master cylinder

/*   end of job stream
```

Figure 6.2   A JCL or job stream illustration.

than attempting to cover all aspects, the next several pages examine the main features of OS/MVS, features which are found in varying degrees of sophistication in many operating systems. Those features examined include:

Virtual Storage (paging and swapping)
Data Management (access methods)
Job Entry Subsystems (input queues)
Spooling (output queues)
Utilities & Language Compilers
Libraries
System generation utilities—SYSGEN (installing an operating system)
Catalogs

Virtual Storage

Many contemporary operating systems include a virtual storage feature. Basically, *virtual storage* is peripheral storage. However, some special circuitry, an increment of improved high speed computer storage, and a software algorithm are combined to produce fast and efficient transfer of selected data between peripheral storage and computer storage. The data being transferred in this particular case are program modules. The program modules are from both application and control program libraries. A virtual storage system allows the user to act as if the computer were two, three, or even four times as large in terms of memory as it actually is. For example, when generating, that is, setting up the operating system for a 4 million byte* computer, it is possible in a virtual environment to specify that the machine actually has a 16 million byte storage capacity. Users of that machine configuration can treat it as a 16 million byte machine. Those technicians serving in a support role, systems software programmers and operations technical support personnel, perform something of a juggling act to keep the system performing effectively. Operating environments have a tendency to change periodically. Because a virtual storage environment is generally specified in anticipation of a certain situation, when that situation changes, adjustments are necessary. Making these adjustments is one of the tasks performed by systems software programmers and operations technical support personnel.

*Byte—position of computer storage.

Paging and Swapping

A virtual storage operating system in action makes use of two techniques called *paging* and *swapping*. Both these techniques move data between peripheral storage and main storage. The difference between the two is in the amount of data they transfer. Paging transfers data in small increments. In OS/MVS paging is done in increments of 4K*. Swapping involves transferring larger increments, usually an entire program. Swapping is used essentially to make efficient use of configuration resources. However, the distinction between the objectives does on occasion become blurred. When all is said and done, virtual storage operating systems have virtually produced what was once known in the U.S. Army as blivit†.

Access Methods

The data management facilities of an operating system transfer file and data base records and data elements between peripheral storage and computer storage. The IBM operating systems, from the earlier versions of OS up to the most current OS/MVS version, include data management facilities that are called access methods. There are, within the operating system, several access methods. Each access method can handle a specific type of file organization. There are sequential access methods for handling sequential files and direct access storage access methods for retrieving data elements directly from files. There are also access methods for telecommunications and for the more sophisticated file structures. All of these access methods have acronyms made up of the initials of the words which attempt to describe their function. A partial list includes:

BSAM	Basic Sequential Access Method
QSAM	Queued Sequential Access Method
BDAM	Basic Direct Access Method
ISAM	Indexed Sequential Access Method
TCAM	Telecommunication Access Method
BTAM	Basic Telecommunications Access Method
VSAM	Virtual Storage Access Method
VTAM	Virtual Telecommunications Access Method

*K—1024 positions (bytes) of memory.
†Blivit—10 pounds of (expletive deleted) in a 5-pound bag.

Every operating system that is able to perform many concurrent tasks and can deal with data entered from many terminal devices concurrently has within itself access method programs of some sort. The programs may not be called access methods, but they do perform the data management function, that is, they transfer data from peripheral storage devices to computer storage. Those access methods with the term "telecommunications" as part of their name effect the transfer of data from telecommunications control units to computer storage. The telecommunications control units themselves interface with a communications network consisting of terminal devices that can be located either local to the computer configuration or remote from it. In other words, a telecommunications control unit can be connected by cable to a terminal device in the next room or connected by a telephone line or a satellite link to a terminal device on the other side of the country. In many contemporary computer configurations, the telecommunications controller is a computer itself. In such configurations, access method programs are both in the main computer and in the telecommunications controller. In cases where the telecommunications controller is a computer, it is occasionally referred to as a *front-end computer*.

Job Entry Subsystem (JES)

A Job Entry Subsystem, called JES in OS/MVS, is that feature that reads jobs into the system, schedules jobs for execution, and processes output from the jobs. JES is interfaced to the operating system through another component called the *subsystem interface*, which is also used to interface other subsystems, including user written subsystems. Job entry subsystem processing consists of five stages. In the input stage, an input stream is read in from a peripheral device such as a card reader, magnetic tape, direct access device, or a terminal. The input stream, which may include both JCL and data, is stored on a direct access device in a data set called a spool.

The next stage of processing is done by the converter. Taking the JCL from the spool data set, the converter merges it with any other JCL that may reside in a procedure library (JCL already stored "in the computer") and converts it into a form recognizable by the computer processor. If any JCL syntax errors are detected by the converter, the job is placed on the output queue, and diagnostic messages are included. If there are no errors, the job is placed on a priority queue to await processing.

Execution is the next stage of JES processing. When resouces become available for processing, a job is selected by priority within job class. Then the necessary resources are reserved (allocated) for the job. While executing is going on, there is an access method within JES that transfers data among input spool data sets, computer storage, and output spool data sets. When the job completes its processing, it is placed on an output queue to await further processing.

The fourth stage includes analysis of certain output characteristics and matches them to device characteristics, determining routing of output. The external writer processes the output to the appropriate device. The last stage involves releasing spool space when the job is completed. This stage is called the *purge*.

There are other functions of job entry subsystems that make them quite sophisticated. For example, a job entry subsystem can reside in one computer and act as kind of traffic cop, directing input to several other computers to which it is physically connected. There are still more, but those covered here should serve to illustrate the functions.

Utilities

No operating system would be complete without a set of *utility programs*. The utility programs are those used to perform functions common to operating system environments. If such programs do not come with the operating system, the user must either purchase them from another vendor or write them. With OS/MVS there are a number of utilities. There are system utilities which are used to manipulate collections of data and operating system control information. Data set utilities are used to manipulate data elements including fields, records, or entire data sets. There are also independent utilities that operate in support of the operating system but do not require the operating system in place in order to execute. The names of the utilities are somewhat amusing to the uninitiated. In its inimitable style, IBM has bestowed some magnificently meaningful acronyms to these utility programs. The following lists serve both to inform regarding utility program functions and to amuse with utility programs' names. The lists contain some of the utilities. They are not exhaustive.

System utilities—:

IEHATLAS assigns alternate tracks for use when defective tracks are indicated on a direct access storage device.

IEHDASDR *initializes* (makes ready to be used by labelling) direct access storage device packs (called volumes). It is also used to dump (copy) a volume from disk to tape and to restore (copy) a volume from tape to disk.

IEHMOVE moves or copies collections of data.

IEHPROGM builds and maintains system control data.

Data set utilities—:

IEBCOMPR compares records in sequential or partitioned data sets.*

IEBCOPY copies, compresses, or merges partitioned data sets; can select or exclude specified members during a copy operation, can rename or replace selected members of partitioned data sets.

IEBGENER has the ability to copy sequential data sets or to convert sequential data sets to a partitioned organization.

IUBUPDTE can incorporate changes into sequential or partitioned data sets.

Independent or stand-alone utilities include:

IBCDASDI, which initializes direct access volumes and assigns alternate tracks.

IBCDMPRS, which can dump and restore the contents of a direct access volume.

These utilities and others are part of the OS/MVS operating system. Since this particular operating system is extremely large and comprehensive, it contains a multitude of utilities. Smaller operating systems may not contain as many. In cases where utilities are not part of an operating system package, they can either be purchased or written by an internal programming staff.

Compilers

Language compilers are programs. Their function is to translate statements written by computer programmers into instructions that are executable by a computer. A complete discussion of programming languages and compilers was presented in Chapter 3. The discussion here deals with the mechanics of computer program preparation.

Partitioned data sets—those data sets that reside on a direct access storage device and whose members are individual sequential data sets. Also, partitioned data sets include a directory that points to each member. Partitioned data sets are generally used to store programs and procedures; in those cases they are called *libraries*.

The compiling of a program in an operating system is a three-step process. Once a program is coded, the first step of the process is completed. Through JCL statements, the compiler is invoked and the programmer-written statements are translated into machine-executable instructions. Once a computer program is compiled, certain addresses are assigned to the instructions and to storage areas designated to hold data elements from files on which the program is to act. This completes the second step and the program is then in what is known as *object form*. The third step of the compilation process is called a *link*. An operating system function called a *linkage editor* combines the program with whatever other modules are required for the program to execute its desired function. These other modules might include certain access method modules and even other application programs. Once the linkage editing step is completed, the program is stored in its appropriate library, is ready, and can be called for execution by the operating system. Figure 6.3 illustrates.

Libraries

As mentioned briefly in the footnote on partitioned data sets, libraries are used to store programs and procedures. Within a comprehensive

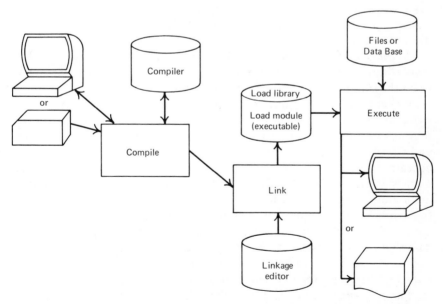

Figure 6.3   The process of preparing a computer program for execution.

operating system like OS/MVS there are several libraries, but basically they all hold programs or procedures (called *procs*). Some of the OS/MVS libraries include the nucleus library, a macro library, a procedure library, and various application program libraries. There are more, but a review of these is sufficient to explain how libraries are used. The *nucleus library* contains the programs which form the nucleus or heart of the operating system and are, for the most part, always resident in computer storage. The nucleus library programs are basic and essential to the functioning of the operating system. In addition to residing in main computer storage, the nucleus is also stored in libraries. It is stored on one library in the same form as it is in the nucleus. In this form it is in what is known as *load form*, which means in the form in which it is executed by the computer. In this form it can refresh the nucleus in the computer storage whenever necessary, such as those times when the computer must be started up after a shutdown period. The nucleus is also stored in another library in what is known as *source form*. Source form is not executable by the computer, but is rather in a form recognizable to a computer programmer. Although it is possible to make emergency modifications to the nucleus in load form, most commonly modifications are made to the source form. Getting the nucleus from source form to load form is accomplished by compiling. The compiling of the nucleus is a special type of compilation called a *system generation*. Known as a SYSGEN, or simply a GEN, this process is examined in somewhat more detail below following the discussion of catalogs.

A *macro library* contains program modules commonly used by several different programs. Rather than have individual programmers write the statement for routines that are common to several programs, it is more efficient to write the routine once, store it in a library, and make it available to all who need it. These modules, called macros, are stored in a macro library, often called MACLIB. Examples would be OPEN and CLOSE statements for files. Both opening and closing of files in an operating system environment are fairly elaborate routines containing numerous instructions. In OS/MVS, the macros are part of the operating system; they need not be written. Application programmers, when requiring open and close routines for their files, merely write OPEN and CLOSE statements consisting of a few parameters, such as file name and record sizes. When the program is compiled, the compiler interprets the macro instructions and generates the necessary instructions for the computer to execute in opening and closing the files.

The *procedure library*, called PROCLIB contains job control language statements. As shown earlier, a series of JCL statements is required to specify information so that the operating system can acquire the resources to get the job done. Most of the JCL procedures are used over and over again, as jobs are run on a daily, weekly, or some other cyclical basis. A computer operator is able to invoke the appropriate procedure by issuing a single command.

Application program libraries are used to hold application programs. Like the nucleus, application programs can also be stored in source and load form. In load form they are retrieved by the operating system when needed to execute the functions for which they were written. Typical applications are payroll, accounting, inventory, order entry, and various inquiries and updates involving an organization's on-line files and data bases.

Catalogs

How does an operating system keep track of what's in all these libraries? An operating system keeps track of all library information as well as file and data base information by means of a catalog. In OS/MVS, the system catalog acts as a central information point for *volumes* (magnetic tapes and disks primarily) for space available within the configuration, for data sets, and also for other catalogs. Additionally, within OS/MVS, there is an elaborate access method called Virtual Storage Access Method (VSAM). A subsequent chapter examines VSAM in considerable detail. Actually, something of a misnomer, VSAM has nothing to do with the concept of virtual storage and it is a lot more than an access method. In the OS/MVS operating system, the VSAM catalog is the system's main catalog. It is called the *master catalog*. In addition to its function as an access method, VSAM is additionally the data manager for the operating system. Other operating systems also contain catalog functions that are not as elaborate as those found in OS/MVS.

Generating an Operating System

Installing and servicing an operating system can be an elaborate process involving the attention of several skilled technicians in an OS/MVS environment. With smaller computers having smaller and simpler operating systems, the technical support supplied by the vendor of the system may be sufficient. The management of an organization will support as complex a computer environment as it perceives needed. In a small organization where the application needs include a small-order entry, billing, and receivables system, a small computer with a small operating system is all that is required. In a large organization, where large data base storage and rapid retrieval of elements from that data base are required, a large computer having a comprehensive operating system may be needed. In such an environment, technical skill is required in both quality and quantity.

An operating system like OS/MVS contains literally hundreds of programs. In addition, it is quite often necessary to acquire other software products to support a large computer environment. Communications networks and data base managements systems are examples. In addition, there are sometimes several large scale computers in a single installation. All of the software products found in such installations are constantly being enhanced and improved. New equipment is almost continually being introduced that must be supported by the software, precipitating further modifications. Periodic system generations, some partial, some complete, must be performed to keep an installation functioning.

As stated earlier, a SYSGEN is a compile process or a series of compile processes. Although they are somewhat time consuming and tedious, the compilers do not represent the most difficult aspect of installing and servicing an operating system. Troubleshooting and interfacing operating systems with other software present greater difficulties.

The first step in performing a SYSGEN involves identifying all the variables that the generated system must support. This includes specifics on the computer configuration, the devices, the modules required, the *nodes* (devices) in the communications network, and other information describing the configuration to be supported. The specifics are entered on statements in the form of parameters. The actual GEN is a two-stage process. The first stage describes the equipment configuration, the system control program, access methods, and installation routines that are to be included in the system together with the selected options of the operating system to be used in the installation. The output from the first stage is input into the second stage of the GEN. The output of the second stage is the new system and listings describing it.

chapter 7

Data Base Management
and Data Dictionaries

Isn't a data base just a collection of files? Haven't we been dealing with data bases all along? Isn't all this hullabaloo about data bases just some more MIS/EDP smoke sent up to cloud issues and mystify the uninitiated? What is a data dictionary? What is a data directory? What is a logical data base as opposed to a physical data base? There is a virtually endless list of questions about data bases, data base systems, and the technology related to them. In this chapter data base and related technology are examined. The concepts and functions of these technologies are not too difficult to understand, yet the technical skills required to implement them are detailed and specialized. At the technical level, there isn't an individual alive who could master it all. There is too much material, it is very involved, and it changes significantly on a regular basis. Merely staying abreast of a half dozen data base-related software products constititutes a full-time job. Yet, on a conceptual level, it is possible to maintain an operational knowledge of what these software products are capable of doing.

DATA BASE

A data base is more than a collection of files. It is a collection of data elements* that have various relationships to one another. Although

---

*Data element—in data base management systems there are a number of different terms used to describe logical groupings of data. In some systems, IMS/VS for example, an accessible logical unit of data is called a *segment*. In others, like IDMS an accessible logical unit of data is called a *record*. Still others, TOTAL, for instance, deal with *elements of data*. This proliferation of terminology adds to the difficulty of analyzing the differences among data-base software products. This is doubly true where the term *record* is used, since it has an entirely different meaning outside of the technology of data base systems. I have arbitrarily chosen to use the term *data element*. As it appears in this chapter, data element refers to an accessible logical unit of data consisting of one or more fields of data, that could be, but is usually not a complete logical record.

there is a high probability that some of these relationships take the form of what is commonly understood to be files and records within files, there are additional relationships that transcend file and record boundaries.

Everyday examples that illustrate data bases include the Bible and a library. In the case of the Bible, let us first use the King James Version. In it there are 66 books. Each of these books could be considered a file, and basically each file is sequential and can be processed by reading from the first verse to the last verse. Each book is subdivided into chapters and each chapter into verses. Each chapter is numbered and so are the verses. So, in addition to sequential processing, it is also possible to carry out direct processing with the King James Bible; an individual can turn to some specific information within the Bible if he knows the book, chapter, and verse. We can see how the Bible is like a collection of files, but how can it be used to illustrate a data base?

Over the years, Bible scholars have developed many techniques and tools for correlating data within the Bible. One of the individuals was a fellow by the name of Scofield. He developed a scheme of using margin notes to relate data elements in one section of the Bible to related data elements in other parts of the Bible. The margin notes were like "pointers" which contained the addresses (book, chapter, and verse) of related data elements. Figure 7.1 contains a page from a King James Bible which is devoid of the margin notes and Figure 7.2 shows a page from a Scofield Reference Bible which contains the margin notes. The difference between the collection of files in the King James Bible and the data base in the Scofield Bible is the margin notes or pointers that establish relationships that transcend book (file) boundaries. Both illustrations use pages from the Gospel According to John. Both pages include some verses from the third chapter of this book. In verse 14, there is a reference to something that is recorded in another book. The book is the Book of Numbers, which is a completely separate book (file). There is a relationship between a data element (verse) in the file (book) John and a data element (verse) in another file (book) Numbers. It is relationships like this that make a data base more than just a collection of files.

A library could also serve to illustrate the principle. In a library are many books (files). Some books have footnotes. These footnotes serve to establish relationships between data elements in one book (file) and data elements in other books (files).

25 And needed not that any should testify of man: for he knew what was in man.

CHAPTER 3

THERE was a man of the Pharisees, named Nĭc-ŏ-dē-'mŭs, a ruler of the Jews:

2 The same came to Jesus by night, and said unto him, Rabbi, we know that thou art a teacher come from God: for no man can do these miracles that thou doest, except God be with him.

3 Jesus answered and said unto him, Verily, verily, I say unto thee, Except a man be born again, he cannot see the kingdom of God.

4 Nĭc-ŏ-dē-'mŭs saith unto him, How can a man be born when he is old? can he enter the second time into his mother's womb, and be born?

5 Jesus answered, Verily, verily, I say unto thee, Except a man be born of water and *of* the Spirit, he cannot enter into the kingdom of God.

6 That which is born of the flesh is flesh; and that which is born of the Spirit is spirit.

7 Marvel not that I said unto thee, Ye must be born again.

8 The wind bloweth where it listeth, and thou hearest the sound thereof, but canst not tell whence it cometh, and whither it goeth: so is every one that is born of the Spirit.

9 Nĭc-ŏ-dē-'mŭs answered and said unto him, How can these things be?

10 Jesus answered and said unto him, Art thou a master of Israel, and knowest not these things?

11 Verily, verily, I say unto thee, We speak that we do know, and testify that we have seen; and ye receive not our witness.

12 If I have told you earthly things, and ye believe not, how shall ye believe, if I tell you *of* heavenly things?

13 And no man hath ascended up to heaven, but he that came down from heaven, *even* the Son of man which is in heaven.

14 ¶ And as Moses lifted up the serpent in the wilderness, even so must the Son of man be lifted up:

15 That whosoever believeth in him should not perish, but have eternal life.

16 ¶ For God so loved the world, that he gave his only begotten Son,

that whosoever believeth in him should not perish, but have everlasting life.

17 For God sent not his Son into the world to condemn the world; but that the world through him might be saved.

18 ¶ He that believeth on him is not condemned: but he that believeth not is condemned already, because he hath not believed in the name of the only begotten Son of God.

19 And this is the condemnation, that light is come into the world, and men loved darkness rather than light, because their deeds were evil.

20 For every one that doeth evil hateth the light, neither cometh to the light, lest his deeds should be reproved.

21 But he that doeth truth cometh to the light, that his deeds may be made manifest, that they are wrought in God.

22 ¶ After these things came Jesus and his disciples into the land of Judæa; and there he tarried with them, and baptized.

23 ¶ And John also was baptizing in Æ-'nŏn near to Sā-'lĭm, because there was much water there: and they came, and were baptized.

24 For John was not yet cast into prison.

25 ¶ Then there arose a question between *some* of John's disciples and the Jews about purifying.

26 And they came unto John, and said unto him, Rabbi, he that was with thee beyond Jordan, to whom thou barest witness, behold, the same baptizeth, and all *men* come to him.

27 John answered and said, A man can receive nothing, except it be given him from heaven.

28 Ye yourselves bear me witness, that I said, I am not the Christ, but that I am sent before him.

29 He that hath the bride is the bridegroom: but the friend of the bridegroom, which standeth and heareth him, rejoiceth greatly because of the bridegroom's voice: this my joy therefore is fulfilled.

30 He must increase, but I *must* decrease.

31 He that cometh from above is above all: he that is of the earth is earthly, and speaketh of the earth:

99

Figure 7.1 A page from the Bible to illustrate a file.

Left margin notes:

a See v. 3, note

b Cp. Ezek. 36:25–27; Jn.4:14; Eph.5:26; Ti.3:5–6

c Holy Spirit (N.T.): vv. 5,6,8; Jn.3:34. (Mt.1: 18; Acts 2:4, note)

d See Mt. 6:33, note

e 1 Cor. 15:50; see Jude 23, note

f KJV listeth

g KJV master

h v. 32; Jn.8:14

i Cp. Phil. 3:19

j Cp. 1 Cor.2:14

k Cp.Prov. 30:4

l Christ (first advent): v. 13; Jn. 3:31. (Gen.3: 15; Acts 1:11)

m See Mt. 8:20, note

n Inspiration: v. 14; Jn.4: 37. (Ex. 4:15; 2 Tim.3: 16); Num.21: 9)

o Sacrifice (of Christ): vv. 14, 16; Jn.6: 33. (Gen. 3:15; Heb.10: 18, note)

Main text:

How can a man be born when he is old? Can he enter the second time into his mother's womb, and be born?

5 Jesus answered, Verily, verily, I say unto thee, Except a man be *a*born of *b*water and *of* the *c*Spirit, he cannot enter into the *d*kingdom of God.

6 That which is born of the flesh is *e*flesh; and that which is *a*born of the *c*Spirit is spirit.

7 Marvel not that I said unto thee, Ye must be *a*born again.

8 The wind bloweth where it *f*|willeth|, and thou hearest the sound of it, but canst not tell from where it cometh, and where it goeth; so is every one that is *a*born of the *c*Spirit.

9 Nicodemus answered, and said unto him, How can these things be?

10 Jesus answered, and said unto him, Art thou a *g*|teacher| of Israel, and knowest not these things?

11 Verily, verily, I say unto thee, *h*We speak that *which* we do know, and testify *to* that *which* we have seen; and ye receive not our witness.

12 If I have told you *i*earthly things, and ye believe not, how shall ye believe, if I tell you *j*heavenly things?

13 And no man hath *k*ascended up to heaven, but he that *l*came down from heaven, *even* the *m*Son of man who is in heaven.

14 ¶ And, *n*as Moses *o*lifted up the serpent in the wilderness, even so must the *m*Son of man be lifted up,

15 That whosoever *p*believeth in him should not perish, but have eternal *q*life.

16 ¶ *r*For God so *s*loved the

*t*world, that he *o*gave his only begotten *u*Son, that whosoever 1*p*believeth in him should not 2perish, but *v*have everlasting *q*life.

17 For God sent not his Son into the *t*world to *w*condemn the *t*world, but that the *t*world through him might be *x*saved.

18 ¶ *y*He that *p*believeth on him is not *z*condemned; but he that believeth not is *z*condemned already, because he hath not believed in the name of the only begotten Son of God.

19 And this is the *aa*condemnation, that light is come into the *t*world, and men loved darkness rather than light, because their deeds were evil.

20 For everyone that doeth evil hateth the light, neither cometh to the light, lest his deeds should be *bb*reproved.

21 But he that doeth truth cometh to the *cc*light, that his deeds may be made manifest, that they are *dd*wrought in God.

Last testimony of John the Baptist

22 ¶ After these things came Jesus and his disciples into the land of Judæa; and there he tarried with them, and *ee*baptized.

23 ¶ And John also was baptizing in Ænon, near to Salim, because there was much water there; and they *ff*came, and were *ee*baptized.

24 For John was not yet cast into *gg*prison.

25 ¶ Then there arose a question between *some* of John's disciples and the Jews about purifying.

26 And they came unto John, and said unto him, Rabbi, he that was with thee beyond *the* Jordan, to whom thou barest *hh*witness,

Right margin notes:

p Jn.6:47

q Life (eternal): vv. 15, 16; Jn.3: 36. (Mt. 7:14; Rev.22: 19)

r Gospel: vv. 16– 17; Acts 5:42. (Gen.12: 3; Rev. 14:6)

s Rom.5: 8; 1 Jn. 4:9

t Gk. kosmos. See Mt.4:8, note

u Isa.9:6

v Assurance-security: v. 16; Jn.5: 24. (Ps. 23:1; Jude 1)

w Or judge

x Lk.9:56; see Rom. 1:16, note

y Jn.6:40, 47; Rom. 8:1

z Or judged

aa Or judgment

bb Eph.5: 13

cc See 1 Jn.1:7, note

dd Jn.15: 4–5; 1 Cor.15: 10

ee Cp.Jn. 4:2; see Acts 8: 12, note

ff Mt.3: 5–6

gg Mt.4: 12; cp. Mt.14:3

hh Jn.1:7

---

of God (Gal.3:26; 1 Pet.1:23) and a partaker of the divine nature, the life of Christ Himself (Gal. 2:20; Eph.2:10; 4:24; Col.1:27; 2 Pet.1:4; 1 Jn.5:10–12). And (5) in view of Ezek.36:24–26, Nicodemus should have known about the new birth. Observe the correspondence between the "clean water," the "new spirit," and the "new heart" of the Ezekiel passage and the "water," "Spirit," and new birth ("born again") of Jn.3:3,7.

1(3:16) Belief in the N.T. denotes more than intellectual assent to a fact. The word (Gk. *pistis*, noun; *pisteuō*, verb) means *adherence to, committal to, faith in, reliance upon, trust in* a person or an object, and this involves not only the consent of the mind, but an act of the heart and will of the subject. "Whosoever believeth in him" is equivalent to "whosoever trusts in or commits himself to him [Christ]." Belief, then, is synonymous with faith, which in the N.T. consists of believing and receiving what God has revealed. See Faith, Heb.11:39, *note*.

2(3:16) Greek *apollumi*, translated "marred," Mk.2:22; "lost," Mt.10:6; 15:24; 18:11; Lk.15:4, 6,32. In no N.T. instance does it signify cessation of conscious existence or of consciousness. Instead, it indicates here that state of conscious suffering which continues eternally and is the inevitable result of sin. See 1 Cor.5:5, *note*.

Figure 7.2 A page from the Bible to illustrate a data base. (From *The New Scofield Reference Bible.* Copyright © 1967 by Oxford University Press, Inc. Reprinted by permission.)

DATA BASE MANAGEMENT SYSTEMS (DBMS)

A data base is a passive entity. It contains data and when those data are related to other data and presented in graphic, tabular, or display form, they become information. But the data base itself is passive; it is acted upon. The mechanism for storing and retrieving and to some degree manipulating data is a *data base management system.* The initials DBMS are often used to express data base management systems. Such a system is a set of tools that provide a user with access to the data in a data base. In a library, some of the elements of the DBMS would be a card catalog and a librarian. A Bible scholar might use a concordance, which is an inverted file containing all the words in the Bible in their immediate context and pointers to their book, chapter, and verse locations, and a Bible dictionary as tools in retrieving information from the Bible.

Most data base management systems are designed with a facility to load data into data bases and also the additional facility of allowing a user to make ad hoc requests for information in the data bases. The potential is there, yet it is the responsibility of the data base designer and the user to structure the data base in such a way that accurate information can be retrieved in a *timely* and *efficient* fashion.

Another analogy may help. It is possible for an architect to design a kitchen with all kinds of potential. However, it is still the responsibility of the individuals who are going to use that kitchen to put the pots, pans, utensils, canned goods, and so forth, into place, so that when some of the equipment are to be used to produce something, they can be reached with a minimum of steps. It is possible, despite the potential designed by the architect, for the users of that kitchen to store things so that when retrieval is necessary there would be substantial extra activity and confusion.

There are numerous DBMSs on the market today. Some are quite well known like TOTAL, IDMS, IMS, SYSTEM 2000, DATACOM, ADABAS, IMAGE, IDSII, DMS 1100, and DMS-11. Many of these systems come from manufacturers of computer equipment; others come from software vendors. Some of the DBMSs are flexible in their capabilities and possess a high degree of tunability in their performance in a particular environment, but require highly skilled technicians in support. IMS is probably the best example of this. Others have somewhat less capability, and a low level of tunability, but do not require highly skilled technical support.

DATA BASE STRUCTURES AND TECHNIQUES

Several terms are used to describe the way data elements are related in data base management systems. A survey of promotional literature and user manuals of DBMS products reveals a lack of agreement on precisely what these terms are intended to convey. Yet to ignore the terms completely would be totally unsatisfactory in a survey such as this. And so the paragraphs and illustrations that follow identify and describe with a reasonable degree of accuracy the terms hierarchy, network, relational, pointers, inversion, indexing, and logical relationship.

Hierarchy

A *hierarchical structure* is a logical structure in which elements of the hierarchy can be subordinate to only one other element. A single element, the *root*, is at the top of the hierarchical structure. A hierarchy, like all the other structures, is a logical construct, that is, the way data are structured logically, not physically. The physical storage of data in a hierarchical structure is linearly, with the logical structure preserved by sequence or by means of *pointers* that are carried as separate fields within the data elements in the hierarchy. Figure 7.3 illustrates the hierarchy both logically and physically.

Network

A *network structure* is one where virtually any data element can be related to any other data element. As opposed to a hierarchical structure, it has more flexibility, but control is less. Actually a hierarchical structure is a kind of a network with some rules governing it. On the other hand a network can often be subdivided into several hierarchical structures resulting in redundant elements in the hierarchies. Figure 7.4 shows a network logically and physically.

Relational

A relational structure is a logical construct of related fields, organized into fixed length data elements. A relational data base is realized through a process called *normalization* that can be applied to get the structure into what is known as *third normal form*, its most efficient form. Much work remains to be done to make relational data bases a practical reality for large data bases. To some, relational data bases are

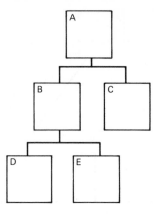

Assuming that the established way to
read the hierarchy is top to bottom,
left to right, i.e. A, B, D, E, C the following
represent physical storage of the
hierarchy:

Physical sequential

Physical with pointers

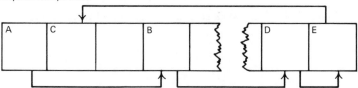

Figure 7.3 A hierarchical structure, logical and physical views.

the epitome of data base development. To the commercial user of data
base systems they are still logical, with physical capabilities more of a
promise than a reality. When they become a reality, they will either use
a lot of computer storage, or will require an extremely sophisticated
retrieval language. The greatest problem with relational structure is
that the term means different things to different people.

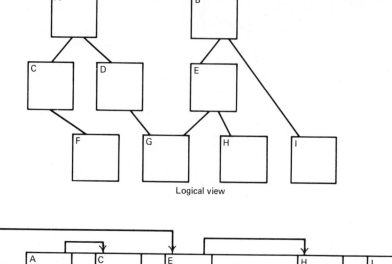

Logical view

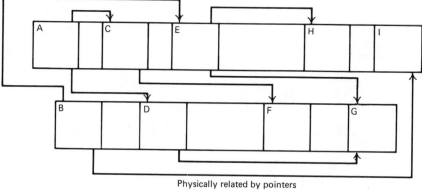

Physically related by pointers

Figure 7.4   A network structure, logical and physical views.

Pointers

The techniques for supporting data base technology, that is, getting it
from logical to physical, basically revolve around the use of *pointers.*
Pointers are actually the addresses of storage locations. In Figure 7.3,
7.4, and 7.5, the arrows depict the storage addresses. For instance the
arrow pointing from E to C, in Figure 7.3 represents the storage address
of C. Included in the data within data element E is the provision for the
storage address of the next data element in the hierarchical structure. It
is usually carried in a special section of the data element called *prefix.*
In more elaborate structures, the prefix can become large, as many

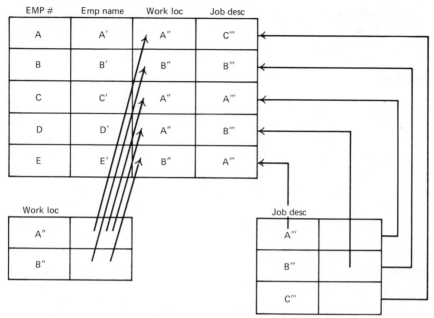

Figure 7.5 Inversion.

relationships are established through the storage of addresses. Techniques such as inverted lists, indexes, and logical relationships are established by means of pointers.

Inversion

Inversion makes use of the actual data values carried in data elements. The values for a particular field are grouped into a table or list along with pointers that point back to their occurrences within the data elements. Figure 7.5 conveys the idea of inversion. Inversion methodology is useful in facilitating rapid response when retrieving information. When values are kept in tables or lists, the answers to many questions are already fabricated. In Figure 7.5, the question "How many employees work at the A location?" is answered by counting the pointers associated with the A "value." In a conventional file, each record in the file would have to be examined to get the answer to that question. However there is a price to be paid for inversion—additional storage space is required for the tables. Furthermore, additional and more complex processing is required for updates, as the tables and pointers must be adjusted to reflect additions and deletions. The greater the number of inverted fields, the greater the amount of time that must be spent to maintain files.

Indexing

Indexes also use pointers. They are used in much the same way as the index in a book, identifying page numbers of which the indexed value appears. There are several kinds of indexing. Examples are *primary indexing* and *secondary indexing.* The primary index in all probability reflects the primary retrieval mechanism or maybe the primary sequence of the file it is indexing. Secondary indexes are alternate retrieval mechanisms into the same file. For instance, the primary index of a payroll file might be the employee number. Most retrieval and processing is probably done using that number. Yet it is possible to establish a secondary index on Social Security number. Retrieval of records is also possible using the secondary index, even though the records of the file are in a sequence other than that of the secondary index. A telephone directory also illustrates the idea of secondary index with the yellow pages providing the alternate retrieval mechanism. Figure 7.6 shows indexing.

Logical Relationships

Logical relationships are relationships that are set up among data elements in different files. The relationships are established by means of pointers. The Scofield Bible and the footnotes cited earlier are illustrations of this concept. Figure 7.7 illustrates the concept of logical relationships. A data element in a record in file A can "point to" a data element in a record* in file B. A relationship is established through the software of the data base management system. More complex relationships are also possible. In Figure 7.7a, a data element in the record of file A points to a data element in the record of file B. This is a unidirectional logical relationship. In Figure 7.7b a data element in a record of file C "points to" a data element in a record of file A, while at the same time a data element in a record in file D "points to" a different data element in file A. Also note that it is possible for relationships to be two directional or bidirectional. The data element in the record in file A that is "pointed to" by the data element in the record in file D also "points" back to that data element in the record in file D.

*Record—used in this context as a conventional record, like a master record in a payroll file.

EMP #	Loc
A	100
B	110
C	120
D	130
E	140
F	150

Primary
Index

Soc Sec #	Loc
N	120
O	140
P	130
Q	150
W	100
Z	110

Secondary
Index

Loc	Emp #	Emp Name	Soc Sec #	Work Loc
100	A	XXX	,W	AFL
110	B	YYY	Z	CIO
120	C	ZZZ	N	CCC
130	D	TTT	P	ABC
140	E	LLL	O	CBS
150	F	RRR	Q	NBC

Figure 7.6 Indexing.

This brief survey barely scratches the surface of what is involved in data base management systems technology. However, the survey serves to show how complex it can be. For example, in a given situation, it is quite possible that a prefix portion of data element is larger than that portion containing application data. If a data element were part of a hierarchical structure, part of a fully invented list and included in a logical relationship, it would contain several pointer fields in its prefix. It can become very complex. It is probably this complexity that has given rise to the feeling among many that all DBMS activity is "done with mirrors."

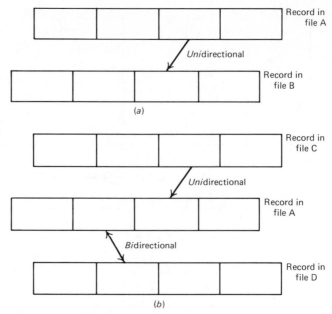

Figure 7.7   Logical relationships.

OTHER ASPECTS OF DATA BASE MANAGEMENT

One of the truly amazing things about data base management systems software is that it works according to specifications. When contemplating whether to use DBMS software, the reliability of the systems should not be of great concern. For the most part they are very reliable. However, getting involved with DBMS does confront a user with several concerns. With all these involved relationships among data elements, what happens if a data base has to be recovered? How often should a data base be copied for backup purposes? How long does it take to copy? What about documentation? Do data bases have to be reorganized? How often? How long does that take?

Most data base management systems have a set of utility programs that perform functions such as copying data bases, recovering data bases, and building data base structures. If a utility is not available to perform a required task, there is usually an additional software facility or aid that can be purchsed separately. Typically data base reorganization, backup, recovery, restore, back out, copy, and restart programs are part of the DBMS package. At the present time, data dictionaries are not. Data dictionaries, indispensable documentation tools in a DBMS environment, are examined more fully below. Although some of the other facilities like copy and reorganization are included in the package, they can involve elaborate and complex procedures and be time consuming in execution on a computer. Copying a large data base with multiple logical relationships and several indexes is going to take a substantial amount of computer time. Frequent reorganizations should not be necessary if the data base design and structure are carefully planned and implemented. They too are time consuming.

Other utilities include programs that monitor activity that take place in the DBMS as it executes. Reports can be produced that contain statistics about the DBMS's performance. These can be used by technicians as an aid in "tuning" the system to perform better. Other statistics can be helpful to the end user in determining bottlenecks in the system.

Since data base management systems seem to be so complex, why are they used at all? Some authors could supply 30 reasons for using DBMS. This book will give four. Each of the four has a corresponding trade-off related to it. The reasons for using a DBMS are cited below, and the trade-offs appears at the end of the chapter. The advantages to using a DBMS are:

1　A DBMS has the potential to reduce the amount of redundant data carried in an organization's files.

2　It has the potential to increase application programmer productivity by removing from the application programmer the concern for file design and file handling.

3　It has the potential to make data somewhat independent of programs.

4　Because of the relationships among data elements established and supported by a DBMS, it is possible to transfer greater amounts of data for each logical input/output instruction. THE DBMS itself has the facilities to handle all the physical transferring of data.

Further mention is made of these advantages in the following discussion of data dictionaries and data base administration.

DATA BASE ADMINISTRATION AND DATA DICTIONARIES

Currently a great deal of attention is being given to data base management systems software. This software has the potential to enhance any information system, by relating data elements in one file with those in other files. Yet there is also potential for a great deal of confusion if some kind of control is not maintained in the use of DBMSs. Control can be exercised by the efforts of individuals who perform the function of data base administration. A tool that can be used in the performance of that function is a data dictionary. In order to understand this function and this tool a little better, a closer look at DBMS mechanics is necessary. Also in this discussion, the advantages of using DBMS cited above are clarified further.

In a DBMS environment, files or data bases are designed and described independently of the application programs that are to use them. In more conventional or traditional file-oriented systems each programmer had to describe and in some cases even design the files that his program was going to use. In the DBMS environment that is not the case. It has become the function of data base administrators to design and describe files or data bases. Functionally, the job is more complex and requires greater technical skill because of the relationships transcending file boundaries that make up data bases. DBMSs come with facilities for performing the data base description function. The facility is commonly called a Data Description Language (DDL). The DDL capability of DBMSs is the foundation for DBMS advantages 2 and 3 above. The relationships among data elements are such that the conventional structures that currently exist for data storage, namely records and files, are becoming more nebulous and are being replaced by structures like data elements and data bases. The actual establishing of these relationships begins to bring about a reduction in the number of times a data element must physically be present in a data base. If a data element can be physically present once in one file and pointed to from two other files, then it is logically present in three places, but need be physically present only in one. This capability is also a function of the DDL and underlies advantage 1.

A second facility of DBMSs is the Data Manipulation Language (DML). It is this facility that underlies advantage number 4. Basically DMLs are input/output (I/O) languages. DML instructions are able to bring about the storage, retrieval, and updating of data elements within data bases. The I/O instructions of DMLs are used with conventional programming languages like COBOL, to interact with data bases. The I/O facilities of conventional programming languages cannot store and retrieve data where data bases are used. The additional complexity of data transfer among several files concurrently is beyond the capability of conventional programming language I/O instructions. To restate advantage 4, a DBMS has within itself input/output capabilities that can allow a programmer to write a single I/O instruction that can retrieve data from several files when that program executes. In conventional or traditional systems the programmer would have to write a separate I/O instruction for each file referenced.

The skill of the Data Base Administrator (DBA) determines the degree to which the potential of a data base management system is realized. Data base administrators are responsible for the design and description of the data bases in both logical and physical form. The physical form involves the actual laying out of the structure to hold the data elements in the computer system. The logical form involves two functions. The first is the establishing and subsequent description of the relationships that are to exist among data elements. The second is the design and descriptive subsetting of logical and physical structures for individual application programs. When a data base is put together, there is always at least one application that is to use it. Often, there are several. The number of separate programs that have access to the data base can number from several to several hundred. One idea behind a data base is to have a degree of data independence, where individual programs would access only those portions of data base records needed for a particular application program. There is terminology to describe the results of this data base definition work.

The DDL term to describe these subsets used is *subschema*. A *schema* is a global definition, that which describes the entire data base structure. A subschema describes a subset. Figure 7.8 illustrates, using a hierarchical model.

Data base administration requires a combination of skills that are both political and technical. The technical skill is required to perform the design and description tasks. The political skill is required to keep track of, document, and explain in nontechnical terms what is being done. A tool that can help DBAs keep track of and document their work is a data dictionary system. A *data dictionary* is two entities: data bases and a system.

1 *Data dictionary* data bases or files are used to hold data describing data. The files of a typical data dictionary contain data base descriptions, both schema and subschema. Schema definitions contain data base characteristics and attributes such as size of the data base, the data base name, data base record length, number of data elements in a data base record, the storage structure used to define the data base, and so on. Subschema definitions include field level descriptions, key descriptions, key lengths, data element names, programs that can use it, relationships to other data elements, and so on.

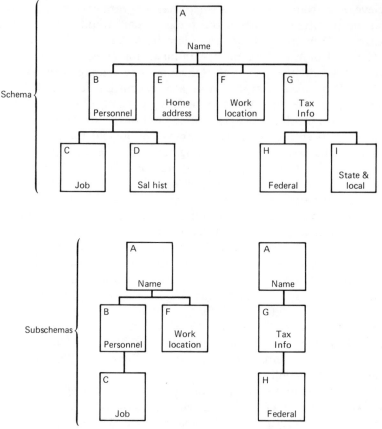

Figure 7.8   Schema and subschema.

2 A *data dictionary* is also a system, that is, a collection of programs that performs services. In addition to the obvious functions such as updating their own files and reporting on their own contents, some data dictionaries have other capabilities. Some have facilities for producing DDL statements describing schemas and subschemas. These statements, in turn can be used as input to the data base management system. This type of facility relieves the DBAs of the need to describe the data twice, once for the data dictionary and once for the DBMS. Some data dictionary systems also can produce data base structures that can be stored in computer libraries and subsequently used by programmers when compiling their programs. The consensus is that in conventional systems environments, data dictionaries were nice to have; in DBMS environments, they are virtually indispensable.

In conclusion, it is advisable to evalute the trade-offs to the advantages offered by data base technology. This is offered not to discourage the use of data base, but rather to provide an awareness that there is a price to be paid. Advantage number 1 cited the potential to reduce data redundancy. The trade-off is an increase in processing complexity. Processing takes longer and problems are more difficult to isolate when something goes wrong. It is the old space/processing time trade-off. Advantage number 2, the increase in productivity of application programming is offset by the increase in complexity of file or data design and description. A brand new technical support function, the DBA function, is created. As with all people costs, it is expensive. Advantage number 3, that of data independence is a fairly clear-cut advantage, once the system is functioning. Start-up time to establish it in the first place is complex and time consuming. Advantage number 4, the ability to reduce the amount of logic that an application programmer must develop to access data from multiple files is also a clear cut advantage. The one off-setting factor, which can be major from time to time, is isolating the responsible software element when something malfunctions. Data base management systems are not installed in a vacuum. They are installed in computer environments and integrated with other software products, whose facilities are often used by the DBMSs. The facilities in the DBMS that permit data transfers from multiple files just add another layer of software to an already complicated environment. Isolating problems in this type of environment occasionally means bringing together several software specialists from different areas and getting them to cooperate in finding and fixing the error. Because of other commitments, time schedules, and other pressures, this can sometimes be quite difficult to do.

However, in spite of the difficulties, hundreds of data base management systems are in operation. There is no doubt that the DBMS technology can function. It is not easy and it is costly, but it can be done.

chapter 8

Access Methods for Files and Data Bases

What the heck is VSAM? Perhaps a better question is: What the heck is an access method? or "When is an access method an access method and when is an access method not an access method?" BSAM and BDAM are access methods, but HSAM and HDAM are not, or at least not in the same sense. Just because an acronym ends in AM, that does not make it an access method. The past several years have seen a rather sizable increase in the use of acronyms. Their use to describe the input/output routines of operating systems software is but one example. Terms like BSAM, QSAM, BDAM, ISAM, BTAM, and others have been part of the MIS/EDP vocabulary for years. Other terms like VTAM, VSAM, HSAM, HDAM, and TCAM are more recent arrivals on the scene. This chapter will tell what an access method is, describe the various types, and give a short narrative on their evolution. Following that will be a fairly comprehensive overview of a contemporary access method called VSAM and some observations about its facilities.

ACCESS METHOD

An *access method* is a set of computer programs containing instructions that effect a transfer of data between computer storage and either input/output devices or auxiliary storage devices. As we have seen in an earlier chapter, data are generally transferred between an auxiliary storage device and computer storage using an electronic data path known as a channel or a bus. Data can be structured in four basic organizations and stored and retrieved by means of access methods that have been developed to handle data in these organizations.

Other data handling methods are variations of or enhancements to these four basic kinds of handlers. The four are:

1 Serial—access of one data element* after another as the elements are physically stored.

2 Sequential—access of one data element after another as the elements are arranged according to a key, that is part of the element.

3 Direct—access of selected data elements one data element at a time by means of a key, regardless of physical or sequential arrangements.

4 Indexed—access of data elements, by means of an index, either one at a time, or one after another according to a key which is part of the index as well as being part of data element itself.

Many computer equipment manufacturers include access methods as part of the software that accompanies a computer equipment configuration. The most universally known access methods are probably those found in computer installations housing IBM equipment. Some of them have been around for several years. Sequential Access Method (SAM or more correctly BSAM basic and QSAM queued), Basic Direct Access Method (BDAM), Indexed Sequential Access Method (ISAM), and Basic Telecommunications Access Method (BTAM) are probably the most commonly known. Other computer equipment manufacturers have access method software for their computer configurations which performs essentially the same functions as the IBM products. The names of the access methods specify the kind of data organizations that they handle. SAM handles sequential data, ISAM handles indexed data, and BDAM handles directly accessed data. BTAM and other teleprocessing access methods like Virtual Telecommunications Access Method (VTAM) and Tele-Communications Access Method (TCAM) handle data that enter the computer system from a telecommunications network. Data base management systems access methods like HSAM, HDAM, HISAM, and HIDAM handle data in a data base environment. These are examined more closely below.

Access method software is usually one of many features of a larger software package known as an *operating system*. As we have seen, operating systems are themselves sets of computer programs that are usually quite sophisticated and elaborate. It is operating system software that enables computers to carry on *multiprogramming*, that is, the concurrent processing of more than one task, one of which may be the execution of some access method instructions.

*Data element—the term *data element* is used generically here in all four definitions, describing some logical entity, a record, or a segment of data.

Evolution

In the early 1960s there were no operating systems. Currently in some of the smaller computer configurations there are no operating systems, and the computer configuration processes one task at a time and transfers data from or to one device at a time. Where there are no operating systems, there are no access methods either. In situations like this the computer processes one task at a time and executes the necessary transfers of data as the data elements are needed. When the task needs a data element, the computer executes a *read* or *get* to retrieve it. When the task is ready to put out a data element, the computer executes a *write* or a *put* to put it out. These gets and puts or reads and writes are sometimes referred to as INPUT/OUTPUT systems (IOS) or INPUT/OUTPUT control systems (IOCS). These IOS or IOCS operations make up one of the functions of an access method. When one task is running at a time, the process of getting data in and out of the computer is a relatively simple one.

Yet there are more elaborate configurations, consisting of multiple channels, with each channel containing numerous auxiliary storage or peripheral devices, like magnetic disks, drums, and tapes as well as input and output devices like CRT terminals, printers, and card readers. In these more elaborate configurations, the computers through the facilities of operating systems have the capability of concurrently processing several tasks, increasing the complexity. There may be hundreds of data input/output devices, and tens or even hundreds of disk and tape devices. Simple IOS and IOCS are insufficient to coordinate and handle all the input/output (I/O) activity. To address this situation of data handling and coordination, more sophisticated techniques are required. *Data buffering* or *buffer pooling* techniques that allow different data files dynamically to share a common area of computer storage have been developed. Access and transfer of data intermixed from several devices on a single channel, (one of many variations of a technique called *multiplexing*), is another sophisticated methodology that is employed. These and other techniques make up an *access method*.

As indicated above, data base management system access methods like HSAM, HISAM, HDAM, and HIDAM add a further level of complexity. These access methods, so called because they end in AM, signify the following:

Hierarchical Sequential Access Method (HSAM)
Hierarchical Indexed Sequential Access Method (HISAM)

Hierarchical Direct Access Method (HDAM)
Hierarchical Indexed Direct Access Method (HIDAM)

These are not actually access methods, that is, they do not themselves bring about a transfer of data between computer storage and auxiliary storage devices. Rather, these so called access methods act as an interface between application programs using hierarchical structures in IMS/VS data base management system environment and the actual access methods such as VSAM. Basically the difference is quite simple. Application programs accessing conventional files access the data they need by using access methods. Application programs using IMS/VS hierarchical files access the data they need through the hierarchical interfaces, which in turn access the data using the access methods. Figure 8.1 illustrates.

Let us now turn to a particular access method, called VSAM, in order to get a more detailed look at what an access method is all about.

VSAM

A number of access methods are used in various installations. Some are user developed; some are computer vendor supplied. One such vendor supplied product is the Virtual Storage Access Method (VSAM) from IBM. A treatment of this access method illustrates the kind of functions performed by a contemporary access method. Theoretically, it is conceivable that VSAM in time could replace all of the IBM supported data storage and retrieval access methods currently in use. This would include SAM, ISAM, and BDAM, the sequential, the indexed sequential, and direct access methods. It does not include BTAM and TCAM,

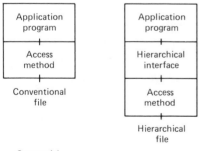

Convential
data access

IMS/VS data access

Figure 8.1 Conventional data access and data base data access.

which handle the transfer of data between communications devices and computers. There is, however, another access method from IBM called VTAM, Virtual Telecommunications Access Method, discussed in a later chapter, which is replacing the currently used BTAM.

The VSAM access method uses a catalog. The catalog contains a substantial quantity of information about VSAM data sets and direct access storage device (DASD) volumes or packs on which those data sets reside. Because of variations in operating systems and in machine configurations, there are several ways in which catalogs can be set up. Yet the kind of information contained within VSAM catalogs is consistent, although its physical organization may be slightly different in one installation as opposed to another.

VSAM can also be thought of as a subsystem of the operating system in which it is contained. As such, it consists of logic modules that perform numerous functions associated with the allocation of space for data sets, catalog housekeeping functions, and the recovery from some types of error situations. It performs these tasks in addition to the IOCS functions. As Figure 8.2 shows, VSAM can also be conceptualized as an interface between an application program and peripheral storage devices. VSAM handles physical records when transferring data between its own input/output buffers and application program work areas.

The VSAM Catalog

Within the VSAM catalog, one may find both VSAM and non-VSAM data set names listed. Associated with these names is information about

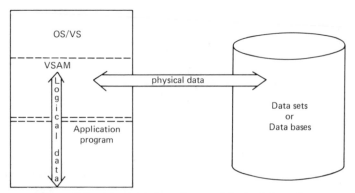

Figure 8.2   Physical data flow and logical data flow.

the data sets, such as the type of DASD device (3350 or 3330 for example) and volume serial number of the DASD device on which the data sets reside. In addition, the VSAM catalog keeps a pointer to each section (called *extent* in VSAM) of a data set that is fragmented. The VSAM catalog also keeps statistics on the maintenance done on the data set, such as additions and deletions and the amount of space still available for the data set. Data set attributes are also kept in the VSAM catalog. These attributes include physical record size, storage area sizes (called *control intervals* in VSAM), and the location of the key field in those records containing a key field. Two new terms, *extent* and *control interval*, have been introduced in this section. A closer look at the fundamentals of VSAM should clarify the meaning of these and other terms as they are used in the context of VSAM.

As an access method, VSAM is more sophisticated than most. It does more for the user, but it also costs more in terms of processing input/output operations (system overhead). VSAM catalog usage and maintenance add overhead to that environment. What the user gets by incurring that overhead is more secure data and data sets that are less likely to be damaged through error or mischief.

VSAM Data Sets

Within VSAM, there are three types of data sets:

Key Sequenced Data Sets (KSDS)
Entry Sequenced Data Sets (ESDS)
Relative Record Data Sets (RRDS)

A Key Sequenced Data Set (KSDS) is one in which records are stored in sequence according to a key. The original KSDS when loaded is in both logical and physical sequence. As inserts are made over time, logical sequence is maintained by means of an index that is part of a KSDS data set. Physical sequence is only partially maintained. Records in a KSDS can be accessed either by key through the index or by their position relative the beginning of the data set.

In an Entry Sequenced Data Set (ESDS) records are stored in the manner in which they enter the data set. Additions to an ESDS data set are stored at the end of the data set. Retrieval of records in an ESDS is by their position relative to the beginning of the data set.

A Relative Record Data Set (RRDS) is a string of fixed length blocks, each identified by a relative record identifier. Searches and inserts are made using this relative record identifier or number.

Logical And Physical Storage Using VSAM

As do all access methods, VSAM contains a set of program instructions that transfer data elements (again used generically) between defined areas in computer storage and defined continuous areas of peripheral storage. These areas have various names in various access methods; in VSAM they are known as *control intervals* (CIs). The size of these CIs is a variable, that is, it is determined by the user. CIs are application and device dependent, in the sense that if they are defined incorrectly for a specific environment (device and application), computer performance can be affected in an unfavorable way. A CI usually contains a number of logical records, although it is also possible for one logical record to span several control intervals. Aptly enough, these are known as *spanned records*. A control interval can thus be defined as a continuous area of auxiliary storage used by VSAM for storing data records and control information describing those records. It is also the basic unit of information transferred by VSAM between auxiliary storage and computer memory. CI size can vary from one data set to another, but within one data set its size is constant. Its size is determined by the user or in default by VSAM itself. In the default option, VSAM determines CI size using two pieces of information, the type of peripheral storage devices being used to store the data set records and the amount of space provided for VSAM input/output buffers in the application program. A pictorial view of control intervals is shown in Figure 8.3.

A group of control intervals make up what is known as a *control area* (CA). A VSAM data set, depending upon its size, is contained within one or more control areas. A control area can also be defined as that portion of a data set at which the VSAM modules perform checks for data integrity as records are added to a data set. Additionally, control areas are used to distribute, throughout a key sequenced data set, free space as a percentage of control intervals per control area and CIs are also used to store portions of the index adjacent to the data set. Control areas and control intervals are logical storage considerations. Physical storage considerations must also receive attention.

On a particular unit of a peripheral storage device, known as a

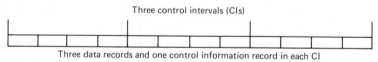

Three control intervals (CIs)

Three data records and one control information record in each CI

Figure 8.3   Record blocking, or VSAM control intervals.

volume, exclusive space can be set aside for use by VSAM. Other space on the same volume can be set aside for non-VSAM use. Completely separate from and independent of VSAM, volumes (individual disk packs and individual tapes), have tables of contents. Within an individual volume's table of contents (VTOC) a segment of the storage space defined specifically for VSAM usage is known as a *data space* in VSAM terminology. The space requirement can be extended beyond its originally defined size to include up to 16 additional areas that need not be adjacent to one another on the volume. These additional areas as we have already seen are called *extents*.

VSAM Data Set Organization

Now that a basic understanding of the meanings of VSAM terminology has been put forth, a more detailed examination of VSAM data sets, using that terminology, can be conducted. A Key Sequenced Data Set (KSDS) is one in which there is an index that relates key values to the relative locations of data records in a data set. The key in the index is the same as the keyfield(s) in the data record itself. The key is the same size and is in the same positions in every record in the data set. The values that reside in the key fields of the data set's records cannot be changed. For the retrieval and insertion processes, VSAM uses the index to locate records.

A KSDS index has several levels, the exact number depending upon the size of the data set. The highest levels are called collectively the *index set* and the lowest level is called the *sequence set*. As with all types of indexing and logical structuring techniques, the relationships in key sequenced data sets are maintained by using pointers. The pointers are actually cylinder and track addresses of locations on direct address storage device volumes. The sequence set points to the control intervals containing the data records of the data set. In direct access processing, using a key, VSAM follows what are called *vertical pointers* from the highest level index down to the sequence set and ultimately to the data. When processing sequentially, VSAM uses only the sequence set and follows what are called horizontal pointers, going from one sequence set record to the next. It uses the vertical pointers only from the sequence set in retrieving the actual data from the control intervals.

When a KSDS is initially loaded, it is in both logical and physical sequence. Free space is distributed throughout the data set either by leaving control intervals partially full or by leaving intermittent control intervals totally empty. When insertions are attempted there is a possibility that an insert becomes impossible because of lack of sufficient space between two existing records. The insert is then made in one of the areas of free space. Logical sequence is maintained in the index, but physical sequence is lost. In the physical makeup of the index, there is a *data compression technique* that increases the number of entries that can be made in an index record. The technique eliminates from the front and back of the key those characters that are not necessary to distinguish it from an adjacent key entry.

Entry Sequenced Data Sets (ESDS) are those which have no index. VSAM keeps track of ESDS records, when they are initially loaded or subsequently added, by their *relative block address* (RBA). Access to these records can be achieved in several ways. The user can create his own index using RBAs. It is also possible to construct a cross reference table using RBAs. Direct access is also possible, employing a user developed algorithm which can convert keys into relative block addresses.

Relative Record Data Sets (RRDS) also have no indexes. An RRDS is a string of fixed-length blocks, each of which has a number. The numbers begin with "1" and continue as high as the number of records in the data set. Each record in the data set occupies one of the blocks. All of the blocks need not be filled. The blocks of a RRDS are contained in control intervals just as in KSDS and ESDS data sets. CI size is determined by the user, as is the RRDS block size. Processing of RRDSs can be by key or by control interval. The relative record number, that is, the number of the record within the data set, is used as a key, when processing by key.

With KSDS and ESDS, it is possible to establish *alternate indexes*. Alternate indexing is provided to help reduce the amount of redundant information that must be kept stored even though organized differently for separate but related applications. A classic example is the payroll master file, whose primary index has employee number as a key. Data elements from this same file could also be accessed by a personnel system by means of an alternate index with Social Security number as the key.

Access Method Services (IDCAMS)

Access Method Services is a program with multipurpose functions that is used in working with VSAM. It is employed in the definition of VSAM data sets, the loading of VSAM data sets, building of alternate indexes, developing catalogs, converting non-VSAM to VSAM data sets, copying data sets, backing up data sets, and several other functions.

By entering commands and providing parameters, a user is able to direct Access Method Services activities. This can be done through an input job stream on cards or by interaction through a TSO (Time Shared Option) terminal. In addition to commands like DEFINE, ALTER, and REPRO, there are a set of conditional statements like IF, ELSE, DO, and END that allow the user to alter the sequence in which a series of commands is executed. This is done by examining and resetting indicators that the access method services facility has set to specify status information when those command executions have been completed.

Included in the facilities of VSAM are the *IMPORT* and *EXPORT functions*. The EXPORT function instructs the access method services facility to copy a VSAM data set in the form of a sequential data set onto a storage volume so that it can be moved to another system. The volume can be tape or disk. Exporting can be permanent, where the catalog record is deleted and the storage space freed, or it can be temporary. In the latter case, two copies are maintained, the original VSAM data set and the copied sequential data set. EXPORT can be used to make a backup copy of a VSAM data set and should the original become unusable, the IMPORT function could be used to bring the exported copy back into the system. The EXPORT and IMPORT functions can both be used to disconnect and to establish relationships between user catalogs and the VSAM master catalogs. Both functions are invoked by commands of the same names, that is EXPORT and IMPORT.

There is little doubt that VSAM and VSAM-like access methods have arrived and their use is a foregone conclusion. Yet there are a few things about VSAM that can affect an operation that the salesman doesn't talk about. VSAM "just kind of sneaks up on you" and the next thing you know, you've got it.

Using VSAM

There are several areas that are affected by the arrival of VSAM. Those areas are systems software, teleprocessing software, data base systems software, operations technical support, DASD coordination, technical services, and application programming.* Each of these areas is affected differently.

---

* These functions are specific to CBS, an organization with a centralized corporate MIS function which includes a corporate data center and an MIS technical support of divisions that have their own systems and programming departments. However, other organizations having similar functions can benefit from the comments here.

The system software group is the most heavily affected group because the support of operating system software, which includes access methods, falls within its jurisdiction. VSAM is part of MVS, which is a current version of IBM's operating system. Because, as you have seen earlier, VSAM is rather elaborate, with catalogs and data management facilities not present in earlier access methods, the systems software group has to acquire quickly some training and experience in order to gain command of VSAM. A minimum of three IBM courses must be taken by systems programmers to begin to get this expertise. They are:

VSAM—Using Access Method Services
VSAM Coding for Assembler Programmers
OS/VS VSAM for System Programmers

Concurrent with the training of the systems programmers in the systems software group comes the experience of setting up the catalog, defining VSAM data sets, and encountering some of the surprises that this new access method offers. The surprises do not constitute insurmountable obstacles; they are merely troublesome. Yet ways must be devised to deal with them.

In addition to dealing with these difficulties, the systems software group is saddled with the tasks of developing standards for VSAM usage, putting together a billing algorithm, and establishing security procedures for VSAM data sets. Again, these are not insurmountable obstacles, but they are tasks that require time, technical expertise, and coordination among several groups.

The teleprocessing software group and the data base systems software group are more users than supporters of VSAM facilities. Yet the systems programmers in these two groups are responsible for the interfacing of their own software systems like CICS/VS and IMS/VS with VSAM. These individuals must also participate in the same education curriculum as the programmers in the systems software group. The teleprocessing systems and data base systems programmers receive their experience by working side by side with the programmers of the systems software group as the initial attempts at VSAM usage are made.

The three software support groups that perform the functions just described are the type often found in a corporate data center. So too are two operational groups that are impacted by VSAM. These two are the Operations Technical Support (OTS) group and the DASD coordination group. The OTS group is responsible for monitoring and to some extent controlling the processing that goes on in the data center. Among other things, the individuals in the OTS group can change job control language (JCL) statements in order to improve an application's performance. The introduction of VSAM, with the catalogs that were not part of the earlier access methods, require that OTS technicians be more aware of the packs' contents than ever before. The DASD coordinator, whose function it is to "move data sets around" on DASD devices for the sake of efficiency, has to be knowledgeable in the workings of VSAM catalogs, organizations, and structures.

A technical services group or a group with a slightly different name, may be part of a corporate MIS function but is not necessarily directly connected with the data center. At CBS, some of the individuals in this group serve as the corporate Data Base Administrators (DBAs). They are a highly skilled group, thoroughly trained and experienced in the disciplines of file structures and data base organization. The introduction of VSAM adds another level of complexity to their function, as VSAM is another access method with which the DBAs must become familiar. This knowledge of and experience with VSAM must be added to the experience required to deal with the HISAM, HDAM, and HIDAM or similar structures found in data base management systems. A knowledge of both these areas contributes to an effective and efficient installation of data base management system applications.

Within divisional systems and programming departments, individuals must also become acquainted with VSAM, so as to be able to use its facilities in developing applications, either data base or conventional.

In order to prepare for the use of VSAM at CBS, a committee was formed consisting of individuals representing the various groups. A list of topics was developed and subcommittees were set up to make recommendations on each area to be considered. The topics developed were:

Education
Standards for MVS, CICS, and IMS
Utility support
Billing
Security
DASD coordination
Standards for usage

Several meetings were held during which the subcommittees' reports were discussed. The reports from the subcommittee were used as the foundations for the VSAM usage that followed. For example, much of the material in this chapter was originally a report from the education subcommittee that was used to begin VSAM education. It was distributed to interested individuals and preceded formal education courses.

In spite of the difficulties and surprises connected with VSAM, there seems to be little doubt that IBM is committed to this methodology, not only in large mainframes, but also in smaller systems. The IBM System 38, for instance, has concepts and language that are quite similar in its microcoded operating system and data base management system. For example, instead of Entry Sequence Data Set (ESDS), the System 38 uses the term *arrival sequence file* but the idea is the same.*

* Throughout this book and perhaps most obviously in this chapter and in Chapter 10, I acknowledge what may appear to you to be an IBM bias. However I am convinced that using IBM products to explain concepts is valid. IBM uses the term *access method* to define the software used by IBM equipment in transferring data between peripheral devices and computer memory (VSAM) and between a telecommunications network and computer memory (VTAM). Other manufacturers may call such software something else and may have other names for their particular products. The term access method is an IBM term. And yet all manufacturers' software contains some program modules to bring about data transfer between computer memory and peripherals or networks. The explanation of VSAM and the subsequent (Chapter 10) explanation of VTAM suffice to give a working or operational knowledge of what such program modules do.

chapter 9

Teleprocessing and Distributed Processing

Vocabulary

The title of this chapter might have taken several forms because there are several terms that are often used interchangeably with those in the title. Teleprocessing, for example, is also known as *telecommunications* or as *communication systems*. Quite often the initials TP are used to connote teleprocessing. Distributed processing also is used interchangeably with other terms such as *distributed systems, distributed computing*, and *networking*. In actuality, each of these terms describes a different segment of a technology made up of several related components. At best, definitions of TP, networks, distributed systems, and the rest are as many and varied as the books and articles that contain the terms. In this chapter, as each term is introduced, a short definition is given. The concepts behind the term are really quite simple. However, the "nitty gritty" technical skills required to implement TP systems and networks are substantial.

Some basic definitions:

1 *Telecommunications* describes the technology, basically hardware, used to establish a communications link between two or more locations.

2 *Teleprocessing* (TP) describes the hardware and software components in communications based systems using both computer and telecommunications technology.

3 *Networks* (in this chapter) describe both the hardware and software components in a total system consisting of one or more computers and terminal devices linked together by TP.

4 *Distributed systems* describes a type of network, where computers, files, and/or data bases are "distributed" in an orderly fashion in several locations.

5 *Distributed processing* (computing) describes a situation in a net-

work, where computer processing takes place in several locations that are linked together electronically and/or by TP.

6 *Distributed data base* describes a situation in a network in which a data base is "distributed" according to application requirements among several locations.

In the pages that follow, there is a more detailed examination of these separate but related technologies. As you can see from these definitions, the concepts are quite simple. Yet, the questions that must be answered before distributing a data base, for instance, are both numerous and involved. For example: Does the data base get distributed by file, by record, or by data element? Is the updating of the main data base done on-line or in batch? How often does synchronization take place between the distributed portion and the main data base? How much redundant data have to be kept in the main data base and in the distributed portion? What is the recovery procedure if the distributed portion is ruined (for whatever the reason)? These questions and many more must be addressed before distributing a data base. But I am getting ahead of myself, let's get back to basics. First, let's look at TP.

TELEPROCESSING HARDWARE

As stated above, TP is made up of hardware and software components of both computer and telecommunications technology. The purpose of this combined technology is the transfer of data among computer systems* by means of common carrier communication facilities, such as telephone lines or one of the more sophisticated facilities like microwave or satellite. These same hardware and software facilities, used in sophisticated configurations of computers and peripherals located in sites remote from one another, are part of what are known as *distributed systems* or *networks*.

Let's first take a look at TP hardware, that is, the equipment used to form a communications link. Figure 9.1 shows it in its simplest form.

The computer has already been thoroughly examined. The Teleprocessing Control Unit (TCU) is a device that has evolved in its complexity. In its original form it performed some very basic functions such as serial to paralled conversion from bits to characters of data coming out

---

* *Computer systems*—the term is used in its broadest sense here, that is, encompassing both hardware and software elements of a computer equipment configuration and computer software.

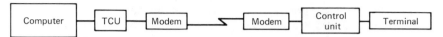

Figure 9.1 Simple teleprocessing equipment schematic.

of the modem. In its present form, the TCU is actually a computer itself. In addition to the functions it originally performed, it now does work that had been done by the host* computer. Since it is a computer, the TCU is programmable and through software it is able to carry out such tasks as assembling and switching messages.

A *modem* is a device which translates between computer equipment and telephone equipment. Since the data appearing in computer equipment cannot be handled by telephone equipment and vice versa, the modem acts as an interface between these two types of equipment. The term modem is actually a contraction for the two terms *modulate* and *demodulate*, these two words being the technical terms describing the process of converting analog or wave telephone signals to digital or pulse computer signals.

The line between the modems is actually a telephone circuit somewhat like the one used to connect the two instruments used during a telephone conversation. Several grades of lines can be used; the larger the quantity of data to be transmitted, the higher the quality of the line required. There are also several ways in which data can be coded to be sent across communications lines. Two of these, the ASCII and EBCDIC, have the coding structures shown in the appendix of this book. Until recently, the five-level Baudot code used in teletype transmission was the most often used. Even in today's sophisticated systems, it is still supported because demand for it is high, it is relatively inexpensive, and the teletype equipment using it is still quite reliable. However it is also rather slow and the need to move larger amounts of data has led to the development of new methods. The teletype equipment operates in what is known as *start/stop* or *asynchronous mode*. One bit at a time is sent over the line and start and stop control elements precede and follow each character sent. This type of transmission was developed to accommodate the keying ability of teletype operators and it was in use long before computers were a factor to be reckoned with. When computers first began to use TP, teletype technology was there, so it was used. Generally stop/start technology is used with devices that can process between 30 and 60 words a minute.

Host—term used to distinguish a particular computer in a network. The term receives more attention later in the chapter.

In order to accommodate faster transmission of data, synchronous transmission modes were developed. The most commonly known is probably IBM's Binary Synchronous mode, known as BISYNC. In synchronous mode, data is transmitted with the transmitter and receiver synchronized so that the start/stop elements are not needed. Originally this type of transmission permitted between 240 and 480 words a minute to be transmitted. Current communications capabilities, such as microwave and satellite, permit thousands of words to be transmitted in a minute.

The control unit at the other end of the communication line in Figure 9.1 is similar in function and in evolution to the TCU. Originally it served to handle basic control functions for the terminal. In its current form, it is also often a computer. Frequently, there are several terminals attached to it, in some cases even different types of terminals. The terminals themselves are a variety of devices. For interactive use, that is where the terminal user has kind of a dialog with the computer system, there can be typewriter or CRT terminals. For batch jobs, where relatively long streams of input are entered and relatively long reports of output are returned, there are card readers, tape drives, and line printers. Frequently, the device for handling these types of jobs are peripheral systems made up of a control unit or a small computer, and several of these devices as well as some CRTs, and perhaps a typewriter type device. In more simple configurations, made up of a control unit, printer, and card reader, the system is known as a Remote Job Entry (RJE) terminal. In more sophisticated configurations, where computers are involved, a distributed processing system may exist.

TELEPROCESSING SOFTWARE

Even in its most primitive form, teleprocessing software is complex. In a primitive system, there is only one computer involved. That computer, known as the host computer, or more simply the *host*, controls all of the activity in a teleprocessing arrangement. The term host has greater significance in distributed systems where several computers are involved, as we shall see later. Some functions are performed by the hardware, but the TP software oversees all other activity and exercises initiative, so to speak, on what goes on in the system. Figure 9.2 shows schematically the TP software as it fits within a computer system.

There are varying degrees of sophistication in TP systems. In primitive systems, all the software is in the host computer. In TP systems where the local control unit itself is a computer, much of the software

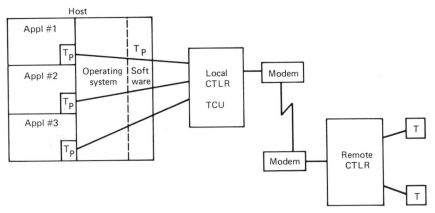

Figure 9.2 Teleprocessing software schematic.

for TP functions is in that computer. Such computers containing TP software control functions are sometimes called *front end computers* or *front end processors*. A futher degree of sophistication is added when the remote control unit is also a computer, also containing TP control software. This computer handles tasks related to the terminal devices connected to it. The schematics in Figures 9.3 and 9.4 contrast a primitive TP software configuration with a more complex configuration.

In the primitive configuration, messages are transmitted back and

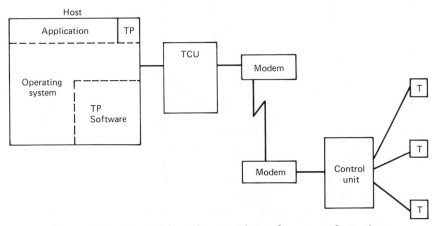

Figure 9.3 A primitive teleprocessing software configuration.

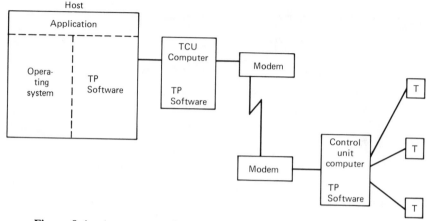

Figure 9.4 A more complex teleprocessing software configuration.

forth between terminal devices and the host computer. For example, a user sitting at a terminal device in Chicago may wish to ask how many copies of the Herman Wouk novel *War and Remembrance* were sold in February. Making the basic assumptions that the host application library has a program module that can handle this type of request and that a book sales file is available to that host, this request could be entered by keying it into, say, a CRT terminal. Once keyed in, the message, or the transaction as it can also be called, travels through the remote control unit, remote modem, telephone line, local modem, TCU, and arrives at the host. A response is fabricated and returned to the requesting terminal along the same route as it came. This kind of transaction is probably the simplest that can be imagined, and yet the TP software to handle it is relatively complex.

Let's look at some of the TP software functions required to process such a fundamental type of transaction.

In order for a terminal to be recognized as wanting to submit a transaction to a computer, the terminal has to get the computer's attention. The terminal can call up the computer by telephone, interrupt what is going on in the computer and get in that way. This is what is known as a *dial up* facility. Dial up is not reflected in these illustrations, but the contrast can be seen in chapter 4, Figure 4.2. The illustrations reflect a *dedicated TP line connection* between the computer and the terminal. In such an environemnt, the host computer periodically inquires if the terminal has anything to send. This inquiry process is known as *polling*. Typically in a TP configuration, terminals are polled several times within a ten-second period of time. Polling is one feature of a TP software task called *line control*.

In a typical TP environment, there are many terminals either making inquiries or entering data concurrently. Software modules or programs are required to receive these messages, locate the proper application program to handle them, load that program into computer storage, and pass the message to that program for processing. Upon completion of processing, TP software is also required to get the response back to the requester. In addition, TP software programs are required to handle any errors that might be encountered in the transactions coming in. Sophisticated TP systems have substantial error recovery capabilities. Simple systems merely reject the transaction and notify the terminal that sent it. TP software also must have the capability of keeping a log of transactions, and a data base or file of records that have been updated by the transactions. This log is used for both recovery and restart in the event of a computer malfunction. Additionally TP software must manage *buffer pools* in a TP environment. Buffers are the area of computer storage set aside as staging areas to hold transactions and messages as they wait to be processed or sent to terminals. As is readily discernible, even in a simple TP environment, the software must be quite sophisticated.

In the more elaborate TP environments the software becomes more complicated because more hardware elements are involved. In Figure 9.4, the amount of TP software in the host is greater. Some TP functions are contained in the TCU computer and in the remote controller. The functions are needed for coordination of activity among three computers, host, TCU and remote controller.

DISTRIBUTED PROCESSING OR COMPUTER NETWORKING

The conceptual line separating teleprocessing and distributed processing or networking can be difficult to discern. Let's just say that several computers linked together over common carrier communications facilities make up a network. There are several ways in which computer networks can be established. One of these kinds of configurations could be called a *distributed system*. Figure 9.1 pictures what could be called a *point-to-point network*. A point-to-point network involves a computer having a TP line or lines with only one terminal device on each line. It constitutes the simplest network configuration. Increasing complexity just a bit would result in a *multipoint* or a *multidrop network*. In this type of configuration the computer can have one or more TP lines connected to it, with more than one terminal device connected to each line. The number of lines and the number of terminals on each line are functions of the complexity of the TP software that must handle the configuration. In networks where several devices are connected to a computer in a site remote from the host that computer is sometimes referred to as a *concentrator*. Other kinds of networks are the *hierarchical*, the *distributed* and the *star structured*. Figure 9.5 pictures the concept a hierarchical network. Modems, control units, and TCUs are omitted for the sake of schematic simplicity.

In a hierarchical network, each computer in the hierarchy performs a different level of task. This kind of structure is often used in real-time process control. The small computers provide the actual process control and pass the events taking place in the process up to the supervisory computers at the next level. The supervisory computers coordinate the activity of the smaller computers. They also report status, part, and subassembly counts to the host. The host computer supervises the activities of the medium-scale computers and prepares management information in the form of planning, inventory control, and exception reports and displays.

Figure 9.6 shows a *star structured network*. Control units, TCUs, and modems are eliminated from the schematic for the sake of simplicity.

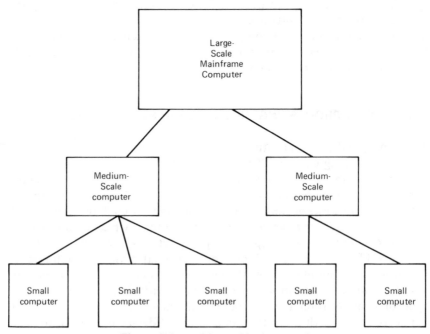

Figure 9.5   A hierarchical network.

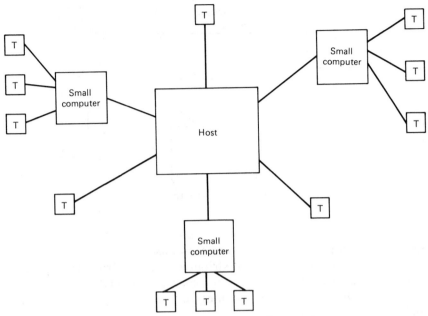

Figure 9.6 A star structured network.

In a star network configuration, all users communicate with a centrally located host that has total control over the entire system. It is a simple type of network to control because all activity (transactions and messages) move toward or away from the host. If any of the remotely located small computers wish to communicate with one another their activity must pass through the host. The host acts as a controller and a message switcher passing messages among the small computers.

The distributed system is pictured in Figure 9.7. Modems etc. are eliminated again for simplicity's sake.

A *distributed network* can be described as one in which one computer is connected to another by means of a common carrier communications facility. A network can be fully or partially distributed. A partially distributed network has several computers, each with its own set of users, having a means of communication among them. In Figure 9.7 this type of network could be reflected in the relationship between the A, B, and C nodes. In a fully distributed network, each computer is connected to several others in the network. Figure 9.7 in its entirety conveys the idea of a fully distributed network. In this type of network, easily the most complicated, many questions should be addressed before imple-

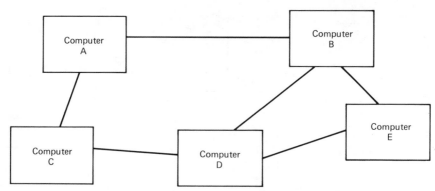

Figure 9.7 A distributed system.

mentation is attempted. The performance and reliability of such a system, once implemented, hold great promise.

Before discussing the fully distributed network from an organizational perspective, let's examine some concepts associated with distributed processing. The concepts are message switching, packet switching, and switched circuits.

In a *message switching* situation, a complete message is transmitted to an intermediate point, at which it is stored for an interval of time, and then transmitted to its intended destination. Message switching systems have been around for years. Teletype networks have been used for this function. In more recent years, the device in which the message was stored was called a message switching computer. There are several computers designed specifically to perform such a function. The messages themselves are routed to their proper destinations based on information that is carried within the message itself.

Packet switching is a somewhat more sophisticated way of transferring data in a network. In a packet switching setup, messages are fragmented in an orderly way, and formed into separate *packets*. The packets are transferred to their destination, where they are reconstituted into their original message format. The purpose of the fragmentation is to take advantage of available network facilities. In an actual network situation, it is often possible that separate communications channels are available to transmit small pieces of data, whereas a channel for a large message might not be that readily available. It is quite possible that a message, in packet form, could be sent across several different paths to its destination. Careful analysis of the application and the network can reveal whether the processing overhead of fragmenting and rebuilding of messages is a viable trade-off against the buffer space and time needed to send long messages.

Switched circuits or *switched lines* simply refer to the electrical connection that is made between devices where there is to be communication between them. This electrical connection is subsequently disconnected when the communications made between the devices is completed. The circuits used are thereby freed up to be used in other communications. An everyday example is a telephone call. When an individual answers the telephone, a connection is made. When the two individuals have finished their communications, they hang up the phones, and the connection is broken. The circuit is free to be used in other communications.

AN ORGANIZATIONAL PERSPECTIVE

Distributed processing could be considered as the deployment of computers to points in a network where they are most cost effective. The basic idea is off-loading from the host those functions that can be performed more effectively using another facility, most likely a small computer. Distributed processing seems to contain the advantages of a centralized processing environment without sacrificing the advantages of decentralized facilities.

The main organizational idea behind the use of a distributed system is very political in nature. In a word, compromise. Large corporate data processing facilities have become burdened with overhead. Corporate computers contain massive superstructures in the form of operating systems, data base management systems, and teleprocessing monitors. A considerable amount of the processing power of the large main frames, is spent in coordinating and housekeeping functions. As a result less and less resources are available to process applications. In the best large data centers, service is generally reasonable but costs are high. In the worst, the computers are often consuming themselves in their own overhead.

On the other side of the coin, a number of stand-alone computers in various departments results in duplication of effort. Each group having its own computer has to develop or purchase its own operating system, data base management systems, and teleprocessing monitor. Yet many of the potential users of computers in a decentralized environment feel that the price is worth paying, just so they can have more control over the service they get.

It comes down to this: distributed systems or distributed processing seems to offer a compromise solution to the decentralization/centralization dilemma. At the same time, technical considerations cannot be minimized. In spite of grandiose "umbrella schemes" like IBM's Systems Network Architecture (SNA) and AT&T's Advanced Communication Services (ACS), the technology needed to make it all work is still being developed. Application analysis is also more complicated than in traditional systems, because of the additional factors involved. Error routines to compensate for situations involving system failures are more complicated because several technologies are in use concurrently in distributed systems. Yet distributed systems and other types of networking appear to be the direction of the future. Although there are complexities and potential difficulties, there are also some encouraging aspects. For example, many tasks that were once software are now being done by hardware. This increases reliability. Computers and peripherals continue to drop in price. Finally, it seems that in the technology area the only thing that is constant is change, rapid change. Distributed processing and networking appear to be adaptable. Both SNA and ACS, mentioned earlier, have been designed with adaptability in mind. If a new device is developed, it can fit right in. At the level closest to the equipment, technical expertise is still required, but within the overall design of these systems, the kind of changes that in the past caused severe discomfort should be easier to take.

chapter 10

Access Methods for
Computer Networks

ACCESS METHODS

As explained in Chapter 8, an access method is a set of computer programs that is used to transfer data between computer memory and peripheral storage devices. Data can be stored on these devices in several ways. Data can be stored in records, within files in much the same way as the cards are stored in the card index file in a library. This method of storage is called *sequential*. Data can also be stored in records in specific locations assigned to hold certain records, like the pigeonholes in a large organization's mail room. This method of storage is called *direct access*. Data stored in library books that are located by using the card index is stored according to a method known as *indexed sequential*. The receiving of data as it arrives and routing it, as with a telephone switchboard, is known as *teleprocessing*. There are access methods for teleprocessing also.

Each of these access methods consists of several programmed routines, that is program modules that have already been coded, compiled, and thoroughly tested. The specific modules required in a given set of circumstances are made part of an application program as that specific application program is compiled and linked, that is, being prepared for execution by a computer. It all goes something like this. As an application programmer codes an application program, there are instances where that program needs to get information from a file, needs to put information into a file, or needs to handle data coming from or going out to terminal devices in a communications network. The programming statements that effect the required data transfer are generally *access method macro instructions*. These macro instructions are statements containing an operation code like GET or PUT, together with several other parameters. These parameters include such information as file or data base name, physical and logical record length, device type, or terminal type. This information is used, during the compile and link phase of program preparation, to tailor the input and output instructions. Specific modules from the access method used are included in the program based on the parameters specified. If, for instance, the physcial record length was 1000 and the logical record length was 100, modules would be included to break out the single logical records from the physical record or block of ten. Perhaps, in a teleprocessing environment, a specific type of CRT terminal is in use. That type of terminal would be specified by the programmer in the access method macro statement. During the compile and link, the appropriate modules for that terminal would be included in the executable program.

Networking

In the contemporary electronic data processing environment consisting of data bases and computer networks, there is a noticeable trend toward simplifying the application programming function. One of the ways this is being brought about is in the shift of the job of specifying access method parameters to the specialized technical functions of the Data Base Administrator (DBA). In a data base environment parameter selection is one of the functions of a DBA. In a computer network environment, selection of these parameters is a function of a Data Communication Administrator (DCA).

Both DBA and DCA signify organizational functions, not individuals. Individuals are required to staff the functions, but depending on the size and complexity of the environment in which they must perform, the number of individuals can vary from one individual performing both functions up to a staff of 30 or 40 including managers and a director or even a vice-president. The "dust" surrounding the DBA function has finally begun to settle. The confusion surrounding the DCA function is just beginning to be stirred up.

Computer networking is about to explode, if it hasn't done so already. The technology is in place, but the skills to use and above all to support and maintain this technology are still being developed. The prerequisites for these skills are possessed by the technicians and programmers who have been working for the past several years in conventional programming and systems environments. However, the newer technologies of data base and computer networking, which are closely related, require that a significant amount of training be given to those individuals having the prerequisites. This training cannot be rushed. The transition is not unlike taking an individual who has been working on internal combustion engines on small airplanes and moving him into a shop that maintains Boeing 747 jet engines.

Networking Strategies

Access methods represent only a part of the technology needed to support computer networks. Within a computer network, there are likely to be several computers, several communication controllers, numerous communication lines, hundred of terminal devices, terminal control units, data bases, application programs, operating systems, access methods, and communications protocols. Several major corporations, such as IBM, AT&T, and Digital Equipment Corporation in the computer and communications industries, have announced strategies or architectures that contain the technological components mentioned above in order to make implementation of computer networks a reality. One of these strategies is Systems Network Architecture. Called SNA, it constitutes IBM's approach to computer networking. Within SNA are all the components of a computer network: computers, communications lines, access methods, and so forth. The schematic in Figure 10.1 illustrates the computer and peripheral device components (hardware) in an SNA computer network. Included may be one or more large-scale computers, peripheral storage devices like magnetic tape, magnetic disk, printers and CRTs, controllers, and communication lines. Within such a computer network the various components must be able "to talk to one another" electronically. This function of talking back and forth is sometimes known as an *interface*, that is, such and such a printer can be interfaced with such and such a computer. Interfacing the components of a network is a function of both electronic circuitry and computer programs (software). Figure 10.2 contains a schematic similar to that in Figure 10.1, illustrating software elements. Both Figure 10.1 and Figure 10.2 portray the elements found in a computer network. The network portrayed is illustrative only and is very simplistic. In reality, computer networks are significantly more complex and contain many more components than shown in the illustrations.

As seen in Figure 10.2 access methods can be categorized into two types, those which transfer data between computer storage and peripheral storage devices or batch input/output devices (discussed in Chapter 8), and those which transfer data between computer storage and communications network via its controller. The access methods for effecting data transfer between computer storage and peripheral storage, although present in a computer network, are not peculiar to a computer network. In Figure 10.2 they are listed as SAM, ISAM, BDAM, and

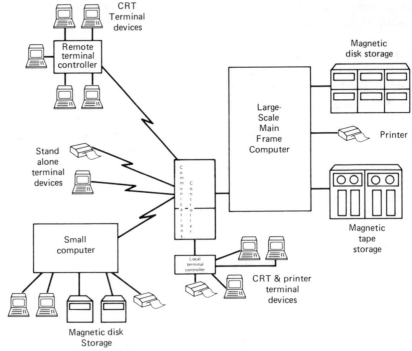

Figure 10.1 The computer and peripheral devices (hardware) in an SNA network.

VSAM. Not listed is another access method called **BPAM**. Their full names as well as the differences among them were explained in detail in Chapter 8. A brief review follows.

NON-TP ACCESS METHODS—A REVIEW

BSAM and QSAM

SAM signifies Sequential Access Methods of which there are two, *basic* (BSAM) and *blocked* or *queued* (QSAM). Data elements or data records that are processed sequentially are stored in order according to a key on storage media such as a magnetic disk or tape. One of the most usual orders in which such data are stored is *ascending numeric*, that is, records with higher numbered keys follow those with lower numbered keys. Basic (BSAM) stores one data element or record in an area of

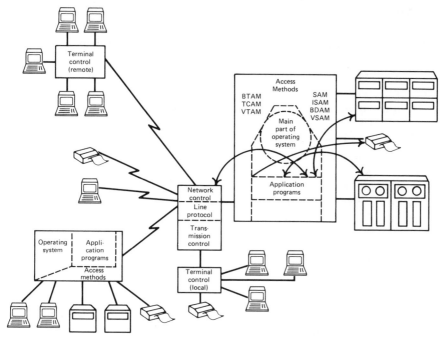

Figure 10.2 The software components found in an SNA network.

storage that is the same size as the data element or record itself. Queued (QSAM) stores several data elements or records in an area of storage that is of sufficient size to contain several data elements or records. The use of the Queued Sequential Access Method permits the transfer of several records between computer storage and a peripheral device with the execution of a single input/output (I/O) operation. Of course, a greater amount of computer storage is required to hold queued or blocked data. The trade-off is space for processing. Basic (BSAM) requires more processing but less space. Analysis of a particular application and the job mix of a particular environment determine which of the sequential access methods is suitable. For example, imagine a payroll clerk who has to prepare a couple of hundred pay envelopes and must update each payee's year-to-date earnings at the same time. If the clerk's desk is large enough, it would be possible to transfer several employees' file folders from the file cabinet (queued) to the desk. Those files could be processed and returned to the files and several more could be retrieved. If the desk was not large enough, only one file could be transferred at a time (basic), and one access to the file cabinet would be required for every transaction processed.

BDAM

BDAM is the Basic Direct Access Method. This method is used to transfer data elements or records that are addressable by their location on storage media. Although the data elements or records could be stored sequentially, most often they are not. They are frequently stored in locations whose storage addresses are determined by applying an arithmetic algorithm to their key. The result of the algorithm is a storage address. The most commonly used storage medium for this access method is magnetic disk. Data records or elements stored in direct access files or data bases are generally used in applications where transactions requiring data from one or perhaps a few records or elements arrive more or less randomly. For example, an automobile parts supplier has his stock of parts stored in bins and on shelves so that he can quickly respond to requests for those parts that are made in a random fashion.

BISAM and QISAM

ISAM is the Indexed Sequential Access Method. This access method was developed as an attempt to combine the characteristics of sequential and direct access methods. Basically the idea was to store data elements or records in files or data bases so that both sequential and direct processing could be applied to them. An index or series of indexes stored the keys of the records or data elements in sequence. Retrieval of records or elements is accomplished by way of the index. There is both a basic (BISAM) version and a queued (QISAM) version of the indexed sequential access method. As with most hybrids, ISAM has advantages and disadvantages. For instance, it has an advantage over sequential access methods because file maintenance is possible without recopying of the entire file. One of the disadvantages lies in the fact that ISAM files require reorganization more often than BDAM files.

BPAM

Basic Partitioned Access Method (BPAM) is used to store data elements and records used primarily by technical support personnel. It is something of a "souped up" BSAM. It is used to store operating system Job Control Language (JCL) procedures, source programs, and load modules,* data elements that are generally stored in operating system

---

* Programs in executable form.

libraries, and similar data. To state it simply, BPAM is used to store groups of sequential data sets.

VSAM

VSAM, Virtual Storage Access Method is something of a misnomer. It has nothing to do with virtual storage and it is significantly more complex and encompassing than the access methods just discussed. VSAM supports three separate methods for storing data elements or records. VSAM has its own catalog, a feature not part of the other access methods. Because of the catalog and the complexity involved with its use, more technical expertise is required to support VSAM. Instead of access method, a more apt categorization of VSAM might be a data management system.

The access methods just described have given rise to some terminology that, once understood, facilitates further explanations. The terminology includes the terms *logical record, physical record, GET, PUT, READ*, and *WRITE*. The distinction between a logical record and physical record is simply a function of blocking or using a queued access method. A physical record is the record or data element transferred in an input/output operation. If there are several records or data elements within a physical record, each of them is a logical record. For example, if the payroll clerk retrieved 10 employee file folders from the file cabinet, he would have retrieved one physical record and 10 logical records. The GET, PUT, READ and WRITE instructions are used to bring about the transfer of data elements or records between computer storage and peripheral devices. The GET and PUT operations are used with queued access methods, while READ and WRITE are used with the basic access methods. Just as there is more work for the clerk when he retrieves 10 folders, he must isolate them one at a time to work with; there is also more work for the computer using queued access methods, as one logical record at a time must be isolated from the block retrieved. However, this additional work is done at computer speed and results in significant time saving relative to doing ten input/output operations involving a peripheral storage device.

TP Access Methods

The access methods are those used to transfer data in the form of transactions between terminal devices in a communications network and computer storage. Virtual Telecommunications Access Method (VTAM) is a good example of one of the most current, most elaborate, and best known access methods of this type. There are others, including Basic Telecommunications Access Method (BTAM), which has been around for a number of years. It is now something of an anachronism. Yet it is a relatively simple, straightforward, and reliable product. Another Telecommunications Access Method (TCAM) is more elaborate than BTAM in that it does more.

BTAM

Compared to VTAM and TCAM, BTAM is somewhat limited. If an installation were to support BTAM only, each application program that requires interaction with a terminal device would have to contain a number of the necessary modules to communicate with that device. An application programmer when writing a program would include BTAM macro instructions for the I/O operations. These I/O instructions would include read and write operation codes and other parameters specifying the device type with which communications were to be made. During the compilation and link editing of the application program, the necessary BTAM modules would be included in the application program's load module. The program could use only that terminal, and the terminal would be the exclusive property, so to speak, of that program. Without additional software, no other application program would be able to access that device. Consider for a moment, two application programs trying to establish communications or trying to transfer information between the device and the computer at the same time, with no other software to act as a "traffic cop." If you try to call someone on the phone and the person you are calling is using the phone, you get a busy signal. If you were simultaneously to feed two different radio stations into a speaker, you'd get garbled, unintelligible noise. So too, BTAM unaided by some other monitoring or "traffic cop" software is limited, leaving the BTAM user with several responsibilities. It is the user's option either to secure other software or to develop it in order to address these other responsibilities. TCAM, as we shall see, contains additional software that gives it additional traffic cop capabilities that can be used in a communications environment. It is a queued access method, that is, it uses data sets to queue messages that are received from or to be sent to terminal devices in a communications network. The schematics in Figure 10.3 and Figure 10.4 illustrate the architectural difference between BTAM and TCAM. BTAM is shown in Figure 10.3 integrated into another software product called a communications monitor.

BTAM is intended for use with a communications network with a small number of lines or with a communications monitor. The facilities

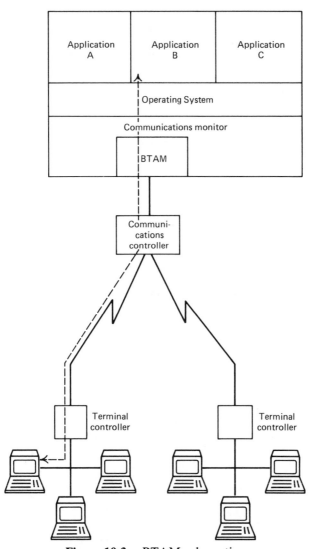

Figure 10.3 BTAM schematic.

of BTAM become available as part of a user's operating system when that system is generated. With BTAM, an installation possesses an access method that can generate input/output control system (IOCS) routines for several different types of terminal devices. However, it is not a complete communications system. The additional responsibilities must be addressed. Included are: the development of application pro-

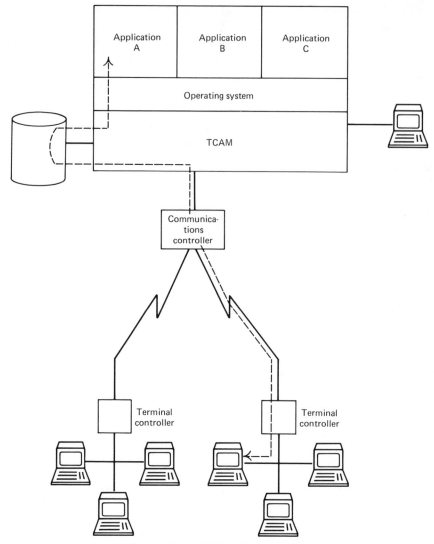

Figure 10.4   TCAM schematic.

grams, testing for exception conditions, and determining the control, flow, and disposition of data, routing and/or queueing of messages, and the development of routines for network scheduling and allocation functions. Quite often an installation either develops or purchases software to perform these additional functions. In such cases, BTAM is used as a component of such software. For example, the Customer

Information Control System (CICS), an IBM software package that interfaces a telecommunications network with transaction-oriented files or data bases and multiple application programs, and Information Management System/Virtual Storage (IMS/VS), a data base data communication information system, are the kind of software systems that can use BTAM.

TCAM

TCAM, on the other hand, has within itself some capabilities of a network manager or a traffic cop. For example, it has a message queuing facility and a message switching facility. As such, it is more than an access method; it is actually something of a communications network manager. Figure 10.4 shows this. Unlike BTAM, it does not require additional software to perform communications system management functions. TCAM has its own routines for interacting with the terminal devices; TCAM does not use BTAM routines. However, in concept, BTAM could be thought of as a subset of TCAM, since TCAM includes "BTAM-like" functions. TCAM as a communications manager is able to support more terminal types than either BTAM or VTAM. Yet from an application perspective, TCAM generally supports only a single application. Quite often TCAM is seen to support a single integrated banking application or perhaps a TSO* environment. Either of these applications, TSO or integrated banking systems, are usually found with a large number of different types of terminals. TCAM also has a MACRO instruction repertoire. One of the TCAM macros causes the generation of a message control program. This program controls the flow of messages through the communications system. The desired TCAM system is the result of a *generation* (GEN) process, which can be invoked when the appropriate parameters have been selected and specified. The same holds true for VTAM. In this way both VTAM and TCAM are distinctly different from BTAM, which is made available through the operating system generation. Relative to BTAM, TCAM has many more facilities. In addition to those mentioned above, TCAM contains enhanced checkpoint and restart facilities, buffer management capabilities, priority message handling, dynamic network modification through operator intervention, and debugging aids. Thus, TCAM appears to be more than an access method. Although it performs actual input/output functions, it also does a great deal more. Calling it an access method can lead to some

---

* TSO—Time Shared Option of the IBM Operating System. TSO is an interactive facility that gives users direct access to selected on-line files. It is often used heavily in application program development.

semantic confusion. If BTAM is an access method, then TCAM is more than just an access method. If TCAM is an access method, then BTAM is less than an access method. The same can be said for the noncommunications access methods. If VSAM is an access method, then BDAM and BSAM are less than access methods; if BDAM and BSAM are access methods, then VSAM is more than an access method.

VTAM

With the next access method, this semantic confusion is compounded further. Virtual Telecommunication Access Method (VTAM) has capabilities far greater than BTAM and in several ways is even more complex than TCAM. To use the term access method in describing VTAM is either totally invalid or implies that the term *access method* has evolved with the technology to the point where it has an entirely new meaning.

VTAM is a component of SNA. As such it is a manager of a communication system network that is composed of nodes and links. *Nodes* are the addressable points in a communications system, that is the terminals, the application programs, the communications controllers, the terminal controllers, and the computers. *Links* are the paths like communications lines and computer system channels used in transferring data between nodes. VTAM is the mechanism which allocates the system resources, establishes logical paths of links among nodes when a connection is required, and terminates those paths when the connection is no longer needed.

VTAM, like TCAM, goes through a generation (GEN) process. Since VTAM is a more elaborate product, the generation process is more involved. The skills of trained technicians are required to perform the GEN and to test the facilities of the system after the GEN to determine that they are working. It is tedious and time consuming work, because simulating the hundreds of different combinations of events that can occur in a computer network is a difficult task.

VTAM is something of a companion to VSAM. Within the SNA strategy, it seems as if IBM intends that these two access methods take care of everything with VSAM interfacing applications to file and data bases and VTAM interfacing applications to communications networks. VTAM is able to interface application and the network because it figuratively "owns" the network. It coordinates and controls the sharing of system resources. In the schematic in Figure 10.5, a VTAM environment is pictured. The picture shows a rather simplistic VTAM environment with three applications: IMS, a data base management system;

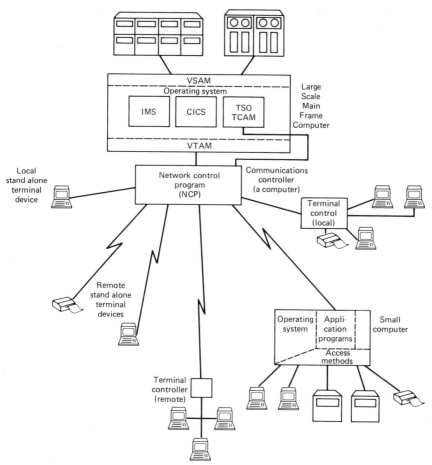

Figure 10.5 VTAM/VSAM schematic.

CICS, a file management system; and TSO/TCAM, an interactive facility supporting a large number or terminal device types. A significant portion of the network management facilities of VTAM is located in the large scale main frame computer. That which is new and different is something called the *network control program* (NCP). As with most IBM products each new announcement comes complete with new language and new acronyms. NCP is actually the BTAM type functions taken out of the main frame computer and installed in a small computer, sometimes called a *front end*. The functions that were performed by BTAM in smaller or pre-VTAM configurations are off-loaded, so to speak, into a smaller computer whose sole function is performing the BTAM type functions of line control, polling, addressing, sending, receiving, and limited error detection and correction. This frees up the large scale computer to do other work.

The implementation of VTAM offers a potential advantage, the ability to access multiple applications with single terminal devices. In a BTAM environment lines and terminals are dedicated to the applications to which they are assigned. The only way to change line and terminal assignments is to do a partial "GEN" of the system. As pointed out earlier, this is time consuming. In a VTAM environment, it is possible for terminals and lines in the network to have access to multiple applications, even if the applications are on more than one computer. Early versions of VTAM did not have multicomputer capabilities. Newer versions have. In case you do not have enough buzz words, a few more can be added. There are *advanced communication facility* (ACF) and *multiple systems network facility* (MSNF). These are the enhancements to VTAM which are GEN options that facilitate cross-computer interaction in a VTAM environment.

When it is in operation, VTAM has two major elements, the network manager and the application program interface. Through the network manager, an operation can: bring about logical (via software) connecting and disconnecting of terminals from applications, display on a terminal device the status of the network, initiate restarts when necessary, and perform other system management functions. The application program interface is the vehicle by which application programs are able to interact with the terminals in the network. Macro instructions are included in the application to bring about the acquisition, reading, writing, and checking of data from the terminal to which it is connected.

VTAM, like so many other sophisticated generalized software products, has significant potential. For instance, since terminal devices in a network can be used by more than one application, thus reducing the number of terminals needed, there is a potential saving in terminal device and in communications line costs. Yet sophisticated software also presents difficulties. VTAM is complex, and consequently the learning time for the technicians who must support it is rather long. It is a process of attending classes, applying what has been learned, attending more classes, applying that knowledge, and so on. Another difficulty is that of coordination. Although an installed VTAM can boast of a communication network with a high degree of flexibility, getting it installed in the first place can be taxing. All of the nodes and links in the network have to be identified very specifically to VTAM as well as to the other software elements, such as IMS, CICS, and TSO, that are going to use them. In many cases while this specification is taking place, changes are being made to the network itself. The changes are in the form of additions and deletions of nodes, reconfigurations of terminal groups, introductions of new types of equipment, and changes in application requirements. Trying to specify precisely and test a network configuration that is changing during the specification process can be difficult and time consuming. Perhaps the biggest difficulty of all, one which applies not only to VTAM, but to all sophisticated software products, is the accommodation necessary to get the product working in a particular organization's operating environment. For instance, VTAM appears in its best light when discussed in the context of a single computer environment. When multiple computers are introduced, the complexity of the installation process increases. VTAM also looks more promising when the group installing it and the group using it are part of the same functional organization. In other words, VTAM may realize its potential more quickly in a centralized organization than it would in a decentralized organization.

To sum up, the software products known as access methods have evolved to a point where they are significantly more comprehensive in function than they were a few years ago. Comparing BTAM and VTAM or BSAM and VSAM functionally is like comparing a Ford pickup with a Peterbilt 18-wheeler or comparing a DC3 with a Boeing 747. There are functional similarities, but the functional capabilities are significantly different. An access method has been defined recently as a technique for moving data between main storage and input/output devices. All the AMs do that, but some do a lot more. That definition of access method is inadequate for VSAM and VTAM.

Commercial Data Processing and Management Information Systems (MIS)

Part 3 concludes this survey of the fundamentals of commercial data processing. Included is a historical overview that describes how computers came to be used ever more extensively in commercial data processing. There is a description of how computer applications are developed, from analysis and design through implementation. A look at word processing, electronic mail, and the "office of the future" wraps up some loose ends while describing some of the most characteristic contemporary commercial computer applications. The final chapter states where we are and what some of the options are.

chapter 11

Historical Perspective

Data processing of one kind or another has been going on for centuries. Recorded history itself is a form of data processing. Data become information in that they have to be recorded, manipulated, and presented in such a way as to be useful to those who manage the resources that are represented by the data. The historian uses information about the past to interpret what has happened. The merchant uses information about sales, receipts, and expenditures to determine his profit.

The ability to mass-produce recorded data began with the printing press, invented in 1456 by Johann Gutenberg. The Mazarin Bible is believed to have been the first book printed in Europe utilizing a mechanical printer, although movable type, made from molds of individual characters, was used in Korea prior to this. The late 18th and early 19th century saw the beginnings of the Industrial Revolution and entrance into the age of the machine. During this time Charles Babbage recognized that scientific methods could be applied to industrial and commercial management. It is generally accepted that Babbage provided the specifications for the building of an analytical calculating machine as early as 1832.

It was the U.S. Census Bureau in the 1880s that put into use the first automatic data processing equipment. The Hollerith code was a method of recording data so that it could be punched into cards. Although the card methodology had been used earlier for the control of looms, the Census Bureau application is generally acknowledged as the first real data processing application.

During the 1900s, more sophisticated equipment was developed for the processing of data on cards. Machines to punch holes in cards, machines for sorting cards, and machines that read cards and transferred the data recorded on the cards to printed data on continuous form paper were all developed and improved.

During World War II, the first working computer was built. It was called the MARK I and was developed at Harvard by Howard Aiken and some friends. It was put together from standard automatic data processing machine parts.

The first all-electronic computer (ENIAC) was put into operation in 1946. A number of other machines were assembled, but not until 1951 were they considered commercial computers. Each of the machines was one of a kind and all were used by either the government or universities.

The original ideas, together with backing of the U.S. Government, led to the production of computers on a commercial basis. A few companies began to produce computers such as Sperry Rand, Univac, IBM, and the Computer Research Corporation. The earliest of the computers were purchased by the U.S. Government, but by 1953 computers were being sold to commercial concerns.

Although computers have been around since the 1940s, their use in commercial applications did not begin until the late 1950s. Even at that time their impact was less than monumental. In the early 1960s, significant advances in computer peripheral equipment, primarily the introduction of magnetic tape and disk, greatly increased the application of computer technology to commercial systems. However, the real turning point in the commitment to commercial data processing on computers came in the period 1964–1966. The IBM announcement and subsequent delivery of the 360 series of computers that had multiprogramming capabilities marked the actual beginning of the computer technology that is now an integral part of business institutions and government.

The IBM announcement and introduction of *multiprogramming*, i.e. the concurrent processing of several tasks within a single computer, did not mean that IBM was the first to do it. However, when IBM announces something, that means it has arrived for mass consumption. That fact bothers some people, but it is a fact. In any event, multiprogramming computers required something called an *operating system*, itself a computer program, to act as kind of a traffic cop to see that the various computer resources were allocated to the right tasks at the right times. The original operating systems were primitive and occasionally did not work according to specifications. However, in time their capabilities, performance, and reliability improved. Concurrently advances were taking place in related technologies like teleprocessing, time sharing and online systems.

Prior to the 360 announcement, business organizations, governmental agencies, and institutions had made substantial investments in what came to be known as second generation computer hardware and software. Second generation is a rather imprecise term used to describe computer configurations of the preoperating system genre; those which generally made extensive use of magnetic tape. The 360 announcement and subsequent deliveries of 360 computers made all second generation equipment obsolescent. IBM was not the only manufacturer of computer equipment to offer multiprocessing capabilities. Other manufacturers did the same. The computer users in business, government, and institutions, responding to the massive marketing effort of IBM and other vendors, soon found themselves in the throes of a major conversion effort that in some cases is still incomplete. Some 15 years later, some of the most up-to-date computer systems contain emulation features that enable the user to run totally obsolete programs that for some reason were never converted. Yet for the most part, the conversion was made. The expense was high. The lesson learned by both user and manufacturer was "Never again!" It became an unwritten law that all future technological advances would have to be evolutionary and not revolutionary.

During the early and middle 1960s, when contemporary computer technology was in its infancy, there was a tendency to try to get as many applications as possible "onto the computer." Prior to the manifestation of the difficulties encountered with the second generation computer to third generation computer conversions, the value of computers in improving operations in areas like payroll, general ledger, budgets, and related finance, accounting, and other applications, was recognized. Although a great deal of attention was given to controlling these systems from an accounting and finance point of view, much less attention was given to controlling them from a computer operations point of view. Application after application was hastily put "onto the computer." When computer resources became insufficient to handle the work, a period of soul searching was followed by a decision to get additional resources, in other words to get additional computer hardware. It was during this time that the phenomenon known as *application maintenance* or *program maintenance* also developed as a factor to be reckoned with. As program after program was written, compiled, tested, and turned over to production status, two things became manifest. First, there were times when the programs did not work. Second, there were times when, although the programs worked, the recipient of what they produced decided that he wanted to change or modify what he was receiving. In both of these instances, programmers were required to "apply the fixes," or to make the changes. The programmers necessary for this activity reduced the number of programmers available to write new programs.

So, by the mid-1960s, the fledgling commercial data processing profession found itself in a somewhat chaotic situation. Computer programming was looked upon as wizardry by the uninitiated. This was partly the fault of the "computer people" themselves who had developed an elitist attitude that is often associated with groups that are, for whatever the reason, set apart. It was also partially the fault of the uninitiated, who either out of a feeling of intimidation or expediency tried to get too much done too quickly with the new computer technology.

When the term Management Information Systems (MIS) was first used is not really important. However, it began to surface in much of the "leading edge" literature in the middle and late 1960s. Originally used to define a concept and later on to describe a function, MIS arose out of the near chaos of this period of time. Business was good, there was still a lot of money around, the optimism of the '60s still dominated. Lessons had been learned. Computers had become an integral part of business and government. They were costing a lot of money. Therefore "management" was beginning to notice. What better way to get greater attention from "management" than to give them management information systems?

Armed with this new concept, together with the potential of newer, more capable computers, groups of individuals often made up of computer manufacturers' representatives, bright and aggressive managers, and executives and perceptive "computer people" were inspired to forge ahead. They were successful not only in business but in government, in education, in medicine, in law enforcement, and in other areas as well.

The decade of the 1970s opened with a tremendous growth in the computer industry. Large mainframe computers with the ability to run several jobs concurrently were commonplace. Online systems, containing man-machine interactive capabilities that processed inquiries and updates within a few seconds were being developed and installed. There were problems, but nothing like those of the early '60s. Justifications for more computer equipment were simple. The basis for most was something called an *opportunity cost*. Presentations, developed by collaboration among the computer manufacturers representatives, the perceptive computer people, and the bright aggressive managers justified computers, not on the traditional cost reduction basis, but rather on the basis of opportunity. It was a sophisticated version of: "This is one opportunity that you cannot afford to pass up." It was effective and possibly even valid, until about 1973–1974. In addition to the economic downturn, another factor made the whole process questionable.

To set the scene: one factor that had helped make the multiprogram-

ming, large-scale, mainframe computer attractive had been the central-
ization of processing in centrally controlled data centers. Technological,
financial, and political arguments had been used to convince management that this method of computer usage was viable. These centralized
computer data centers required substantial numbers of people to run
them—systems software programmers, computer operators, input/out-
put clerks, and data center managers. In addition, staff functions
supporting these data centers also developed. Included in most staffs
were systems analysts, systems designers, and application programmers. On larger staffs there were equipment planners, consultants to
help data center users develop applications to run in a data center
environment, education coordinators to help keep both data center users
and data center technicians up to date in training and education, and
other functions deemed necessary to support a large-scale centralized
computer operation. It was the formation of this organization that
brought about MIS as a function as well as a concept. This organization
became known as the Management Information Systems function, or
simply MIS.

While all this was taking place, other computer technology was
appearing. Small computers, i.e. relatively small, were being introduced
by manufacturers other than IBM. Some marketing genius developed
the term "minicomputer," which in many ways was an adequate
description. Minicomputers were relatively small in size, price, and
processing capabilities when compared to the large mainframes
installed in most data centers. Their appeal was based on economics and
control. The vendors of these small computers marketed them on the
basis that many jobs being run on the large mainframes could be run on
"minis" at less cost to the user. These vendors also pointed out that the
user of a "mini" would have more control over his application than he
had when it was run in a large corporate data center. There was some
merit to both of these observations. Yet, from another point of view,
minicomputers represented a technological "giant step" backwards. In
processing power they were generally on a par with computers that had
been used in the early 1960s. These first minicomputers were made by
companies like Digital Equipment Corporation and The Data General
Corporation and carried names like PDP-8 and NOVA. These names
began to fly around in the MIS community and stories proliferated
describing how these lilliputian PDPs and NOVAs were going to undo
the Gulliver 360s and the soon-to-be-announced 370s.

Although the minicomputers were indeed smaller and less expensive
than mainframes, their use in commercial applications exposed several
drawbacks. First, it was only the computer that was "mini" in size and

price. The peripheral equipment was "mini" in neither price nor size. Line printers, CRTs, tapes, and disks were basically the same size and price as those used on large mainframes. Those peripherals that were less expensive, like teletypes and tape cassettes, were inferior in speed and performance. Floppy disks or diskettes had not yet become available and were not used in great quantity until the mid-1970s.

Another shortcoming concerned software. Whereas the large mainframe computers were supported by high-level language compilers, operating systems, communications monitors, and access methods, minicomputers initially had little software support beyond a one-for-one mnemonic language assembler. An individual who decided to try to use a minicomputer in a commercial application often found that programmer/analysts who had developed business systems on PDP-8s were extremely rare. This was because small computers had originally been designed and built by engineers for engineering applications. Manufacturers had not envisioned commercial applications.

Another difficulty in applying minicomputers to commercial application was that in many cases computer manufacturers did not manufacture peripherals. Peripheral manufacturers were most often completely different companies. Engineers had no problem with this. The required interfaces enabling a brand-X computer to work with a brand Y peripheral were made by the engineers themselves. The commercial user, on the other hand, did not know how to make interfaces and therefore he had to hire somebody who could, or find some one who had made them and purchase them. Needless to say, early pioneers in the application of minicomputers to commercial systems had "lots of arrows sticking in their wagons."

The result was the emergence of a new type of business enterprise. Groups of individuals with a combination of business acumen, engineering expertise, and computer programming skills formed companies that specialized in developing complete computer systems. These organizations would use their talent to purchase equipment from several different manufacturers, build or buy the required interfaces, design software systems, either generalized or tailored to a specific set of specifications, write, test, and debug the programs, and turn over to a customer a completely working computer system. These systems were often referred to as *turnkey systems*. Some worked, some did not. The organizations developing turnkey systems came to be known as OEMs, the initials OEM standing for Original Equipment Manufacturer. It was actually something of a misnomer, because although they fabricated complete systems using equipment from various manufacturers, in fact they manufactured nothing. The actual OEMs were the companies which manufactured the equipment that made up the components of the turnkey system.

While OEMs were beginning to make their presence felt, IBM announced the 370s and virtual storage. The same thing was true of virtual storage as had been true of operating systems. IBM was not the first with "virtual"; others already had it available. In fact, many other manufacturers had it before IBM. But, as in the past, when IBM announced it, then it had arrived. Virtual storage was examined in Chapter four. Basically it is a combination of hardware and software that gives the illusion of an expansion of the amount of computer storage available on a computer. This is accomplished by a combination of software technique and peripheral storage in the form of disk or drum storage devices. For example a 4-megabyte (megabyte = 1,024,000 positions of computer storage) computer can be given the illusion of being a 12-megabyte or even a 16-megabyte machine. Through the use of the software technique or paging algorithm, modules or programs are transferred into computer storage from auxiliary storage devices.

In addition to "minis," virtual storage, OEMs, and MIS, two other developments were taking place. Teleprocessing was advancing from the "leading edge" category of technology into the commonplace. At approximately the same time, the technology of data bases was entering into the leading edge category. During the late 1960s, data base systems and Data Base Management Systems (DBMS) were being developed by several software groups. The concept was sound, and the technology, primarily the software, worked. Yet it was limited largely by inadequacy of the then existing hardware. Although the data base systems and the DBMS performed, they did so only with relatively small data bases. The arrival of computers with greater processing power, together with disk storage devices with capacity for holding billions of characters of data, plus the virtual storage technology, made possible the support of large-scale data base systems. The increased reliability of teleprocessing hardware and software made possible the interfacing of data base systems with data communications systems.

During the early 1970s, while all these developments were "boiling and bubbling just below the surface," many MIS organizations were being directed by management to consolidate their activities and to cut costs. There were some economic and political uncertainties in national and world activities at that time and businessmen were cautious. However, the technological potential of data bases, telecommunications, *distributed processing* (the interfacing of minicomputers with large mainframes, usually including a teleprocessing network), and the so called "office of the future" idea could not be suppressed.

During the late 1970s, something of a technology explosion took place. Data base systems were installed and they worked. Minicomputers were being used all over the place. Telecommunications systems were to be found in virtually every organization of significant size. All kinds of spin-off technology that made use of this technology were being used. Computer time-sharing systems abounded. Corporations whose primary function was the sale of computer time sharing were found to be doing a large volume of business. Other organizations which offered computer related services like consulting, application and systems programming, nontime-sharing computer time, input operations, and so on, also found business lucrative. The consolidation that management had put on MIS within the organization had simply motivated groups and departments to go elsewhere for their computer or MIS needs. Management, realizing this, removed the constraints and allowed MIS departments to expand again. And expand they did.

One other development arising out of this technology explosion was the *microcomputer*. These computers, smaller than ever, were something like a rerun of the minicomputer scenario of the early 1970s. Their performance was roughly equivalent to that of the early minis. Yet their sizes and prices were smaller than anything yet developed. They suffered from some of the same limitations of the early minis, yet at the same time they had many other uses. Although the term *minicomputer* had been a sort of marketing phenomenon, the term *microcomputer* was actually very descriptive. Micros were indeed very small. They found their way into pocket calculators, wrist watches, and were even used as parts of larger computers. Channel processors, for example, were often microprocessors.

In the meantime, the distinction between minicomputers and nonminicomputers had become rather blurred. Minis had been developed to the point where their processing capabilities were equal to the lower end of the large mainframe lines. The manufacturers of these so-called minis had developed software that was competitive with that of the large mainframe manufacturers. The large mainframe manufacturers themselves began to build and market small computers, but they did not call them "minis."

Also in the late 1970s, a number of organizations recognized that with the advances in computer capabilities, it was possible to manipulate words as well as data. There was a concurrent development from several different organizations, a spin-off technology known as *word processing*, which has a text processing facility. The only curious part of that technology is the question of why it took so long to arrive. The initial equipment that was intended exclusively for word processing arrived in the early 1970s. However, advances were slow, and significant breakthroughs did not come until the late 1970s.

So, as of this writing, here we are. Computers come in all sizes, but all are computers. Peripherals come in all sizes too, but basically they are the same. A large disk storage device stores data much the same way as a small one. Teleprocessing equipment continues to improve in reliability and performance, although the modems of 1970 are functionally the same as the modems of 1980. Computer and teleprocessing equipment hold great potential. Software and systems increase that potential. The technology is here. How that potential is realized depends on what existing organizations do with it. Existing organizations include MIS departments, entire corporations, upper management, data centers, users with their own minis, the "office of the future crowd," and the other functional groups within business, government, and institutions. Computers in their simplest forms or in their most sophisticated are merely tools. It is the use to which they are put that determines their effectiveness or harmfulness. In the other chapters, a more detailed examination of the potential has been presented. The most recent developments of the past several years, that is, data base systems, teleprocessing and distributed systems, have been discussed. Word processing and "office of the future" are discussed in Chapter 13.

chapter 12

The Process of
Systems Analysis
Through Implementation

The primary emphasis of most of this book has been on computers, computer equipment and computer software. This is consistent with the main thrust of the book, which is to inform you about the essentials of computers. However, the chapters on teleprocessing, computer networks, and distributed processing were prefaced by a comment that these technologies would merely be surveyed, since their subject matter is of sufficient size and depth to warrant books in themselves. The same could be said for the disciplines of systems analysis, systems design, project development, and systems implementation. Not only does the subject matter for systems analysis, design and the like make up a large body of material, but it is also dynamic material that is constantly expanding and changing. Yet a book such as this would be incomplete without at least a survey of these disciplines. And so, in this chapter we discuss four processes generally performed to get an application "onto a computer." These four processes I will call:

1 Systems analysis.
2 Systems design.
3 Development.
4 Implementation.

SYSTEMS ANALYSIS

One of the first steps in analysis is determination of need. Basic questions such as "What are we doing now and can we do it better?" or "Can we expand our activities profitably by instituting a new system?"

are asked. Need can be expressed in many ways at many levels within an organization. We'll not go into that here, except to comment that a request for a system should be carefully evaluated relative to the position in the hierarchy of the individual making the request. There are cases where systems have been started only to see the individual who initiated them move on to another position. The system, when completed, does not give the initial requester's replacement what he or she needs, and the system is either scrapped or goes into a perpetual state of modification.

Once a valid need has been determined, a feasibility study is begun. Part of this study should include the establishment of "GO/NO GO" milestones at several future points. The main objective of the feasibility study is determination of whether such a needed or suggested system is worth having (what are the consequences?) and if it can be justified economically. If at one of the "GO/NO GO" points during the feasibility study, a serious question of the worth or economic justification of the system comes up, a conscious GO or NO GO decision should be made. This decision can be made by an individual in the case of a relatively small systems request, or by a steering committee in the case of a relatively large systems request.* As the last milestones are approached, a detailed systems analysis can commence. This detailed analysis is a data gathering, question asking, and suggestion making expedition. System outputs are determined and available inputs are researched. The analysis includes the fundamental determination of whether the desired outputs can be produced by getting and manipulating the available inputs. At this point, let's assume the existence of sufficient computer resources to get the job done. Without this, another elaborate analysis would have to be gone through to evaluate and select equipment, select and prepare a site, train programmers and operators, establish equipment installation dates, and so on. So, assuming available computer resources, the next step in the analysis process is the creation of detailed report or display layouts, or both. Systems specifications should also be prepared that explain how each item that appears on a report or a display is derived and from what it is derived. Input specifications explain where input comes from and how it is to be used in the system. Any algorithms, formulas, or calculations should be clearly defined. The overall logic of the system should be specified by either a flow diagram or a decision table. A data flow chart should be prepared to show how data flows through the system.

*This scenario ignores completely the factor of face saving political considerations that often interfere with rational "GO/NO GO" decisions based on mere facts.

Also in the initial analysis, some attention should be given to whatever conversion processes from existing systems may be necessary. If overlooked, the conversion processes may turn out to be extremely costly and time consuming later in the project development. The actual impact of conversion activity takes place during the development and implementation phases, but the conversion activity must be anticipated in the analysis phase, and specifics must be planned for in the design phase. Conversions of record formats from old to new, writing a program to get the data from the old files into the new ones, and making sure that it is correct are examples of conversion processes. Retraining of people may also be necessary. This too is a conversion consideration.

Contemporary systems analysis includes techniques that stress breaking down big jobs into a number of smaller tasks. Good systems analysis has always done this. On the contemporary scene we see jargon like *top down design* and *structured analysis and system specifications.* These are merely new terms that are used to describe sound analysis techniques that have been used for years. Only recently have they been given names. Skill in systems analysis is made up largely of a combination of common sense and a detailed knowledge of the application being analyzed. In the analysis of a large system, familiarity with the internal politics of an organization is a definite plus.

Just prior to the completion of analysis, before beginning design, a useful tool can be applied to keep management apprised of what will be involved in the project and how things are progressing. This tool is called a *GANTT chart.* It is basically a graphic representation of project activities and their estimated durations. GANTT charts appear in many variations and are illustrated here in Figure 12.1. Original estimates are shown as heavy dark lines, revisions are shown with thin solid lines, and progress is shown with a broken line.

SYSTEMS DESIGN

The design phase of a project involves specifying how resources, either on hand or to be obtained, are to be applied to put together an operational system that will produce desired results. The analysis phase produced "what we want to do," the design phase produces "how we're going to do it." The design of a system can be relatively simple in those cases where only a few computer programs are required and existing resources are available. A few basic design considerations are addressed by one or two individuals. Certain things essential to large, elaborate

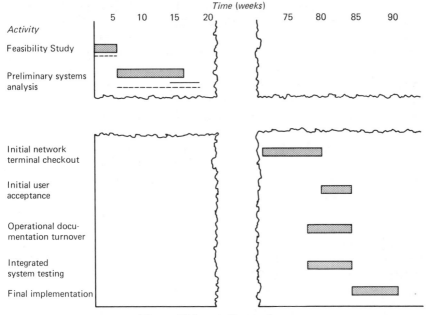

Figure 12.1 A Gantt chart.

systems, such as program specifications, flow charts, and the like are often not even needed. Programming can begin, testing and debugging can be completed rather quickly, and the small system can be made operational. There is a disadvantage to be considered when systems are developed in such a fashion. Although much time can be saved by not preparing program specifications, flow charts, and other support documentation, it is quite probable that in a few years a chaotic situation may develop. An organization may find itself with hundreds of undocumented programs, operational inefficiencies, monumental systems and programming maintenance efforts, and a significant amount of redundant data. This situation is wasteful but not catastrophic. Many computer users have chosen to go this route, but they would probably not admit it in public.

On the other hand, if organizations attempt to develop major systems in such a fashion, catastrophe may well develop. In major systems design, the talents of several types of individuals are usually required. A major data processing system probably has an on-line portion that requires teleprocessing expertise. It may very likely use data base technology. If it is to run in a large-scale computer, it probably will run in a centralized data center and therefore need to run together with other systems under the control of an operating system. In a major system, documentation efforts most likely include the entering of descriptive information into a data dictionary system. Each of these different functions requires a separate technical expertise. All of them may be required to make the system a reality. Since the technicians providing these skills may be using their skills on other projects at the same time, they do not have the vested interest in the success of the project that the system designer has.

One way to deal with this situation is to set up a project team. A project team could be composed of several individuals, one or more from each of the disciplines involved with the system's design and subsequent development and implementation. There could be a representative from the design team, an application programming manager, a data base administrator, a computer operations representative, and a systems software support manager, for instance. Overall direction of the team's activities should be set and monitored by the end user of the system together with a high level MIS manager, or by a steering committee made up of several management representatives.

The project team, once constituted, should remain in existence until the project is completed and the system implemented. The purpose of the project team in the design phase is to reach agreement on the facilities to be used to develop and implement the system. In the development process the project team should monitor progress and provide a forum for the members to report progress and to resolve differences of a technical or procedural nature. Major differences should be left to the steering committee, the user, or to MIS management. In the implementation phase, the project team meets more frequently, and last-minute operational considerations are worked out as the new system goes "live."

In the designing of new systems, the project team decides on the hardware and software configurations to be used. Traffic volumes and operational run times are estimated more concretely than they were during the analysis phase. Terminal devices are selected. The number of devices on a single TP line is established. Design specifications for the terminal network are prepared. A data base/data communication systems software product like CICS or IMS is chosen to support the system (if one of these types of systems is needed). After this, work begins on the specifications of files or data bases. Fields, segments, and records are defined. In those environments with data dictionaries, the field, segment, and file specifications are entered into the data dictionary's files or data bases. The entire system is broken down into a number of separate task elements. Some of these become online transactions;

others become batch processes. Each of the task elements is a separate program, and specifications are prepared for all of them. There are most likely several analysts and designers on the project, and all of this work is going on simultaneously. Periodic project team meetings monitor the progress and keep the various activities in synchronization. At some point, the design specifications are virtually complete and the transition is made into the development phase. This point is usually difficult to discern for several reasons. First, it is actually not a point in time, but more like a period of time. A conscious decision on the part of some individual or group is not made. The transition just happens. There are some who would deny this, but it does often happen that way. Secondly, there may be anywhere from about six to about 15 simultaneous activities taking place. Maybe one third of the activities are totally involved with the system while the other two thirds are supporting the system as well as supporting a few other systems. That some of the individuals or groups involved in the activities connected with system design may get ahead of others and slip into development work is not surprising. Furthermore, the distinction between what constitutes design work and what constitutes development work is not always crystal clear. What sometimes constitutes design work for an application programmer is looked upon as development work by a systems programmer. For example, terminal devices and data base subschema specifications are design work to an application analyst, but they are development work to a systems software programmer when going through a data base/data communications system generation process. In any event, at some point or during some period of time, the project goes from the design phase to the development phase.

DEVELOPMENT

When the members of the project team become aware that the specifications are nearly complete, software and hardware have been selected, and most differences have been resolved, the development phase can begin. As the transition to the development phase takes place, the managers on the project should prepare schedules for the tasks under their jurisdiction. The application programming manager, for example, has to divide up the programming tasks according to the number of programmers available. Assignments have to be made with specific programs given to specific programmers. The programmers, together with the managers, have to make estimates and establish target dates.

During this estimating process major adjustments may be made to the GANTT charts. With more concrete specifications now available, some of the earlier estimates that may have been little more than educated guesses can be improved. Some estimates may be shortened, but it is more likely that during this second estimating process the original projections made during preliminary analysis will be shown to have been somewhat optimistic.

Once the schedules have been set and agreed upon by the members of the project team and the steering committee, the actual work on building the system can begin. An analogy may clarify the distinction between analysis, design, development, and implementation. Think of it as putting up a building. The complexity, time needed, and cost are all variable, depending upon the size and appearance of the building. The analysis phase is like the architect's work; the design phase is like engineering. The development phase is like construction, and the implementation phase is like a shakedown, the first cycle of running, getting everything operational.

Building the system involves a number of detailed tasks performed by individuals possessing a variety of technical skills. Individual application programmers write the programs to perform the functions required by the system. These programmers interact with systems software programmers of different types. The systems software programmers generally are not as involved with the systems as are the application programmers. In fact, the systems software programmers are probably involved in a supporting role for several systems at the same time. They are also involved in maintaining, supporting, and enhancing the systems' software environment in which they labor. Systems software support is required in the areas of operating system, access methods, data base systems, data communications systems, interactive computing facilities, and in overall performance measurement and performance improvement (tuning) of the computer configuration. The software programmers' activity is critical to computer systems; without it everything could wind down quickly and stop. It is like the television industry. You sit down to watch your TV for an evening. You might watch three or four shows and the late news. Totally transparent to you are the individual technicians performing functions, both prior to and during the time that you are watching your TV. You don't see them, but they're there. The same thing can be said for systems software programmers.

In addition to systems software programmers and application programmers there are individuals who specify data base, file, field, record, and network terminal particulars. These individuals, commonly known as *data base administrators* and *data communications administrators*, are responsible for defining fields, records, files, data elements, data bases, and terminals in terms of their attributes and characteristics. They describe these entities in terms of lengths, type of information (alphabetical, numerical, or coded), media on which the data are stored, quantities, and names. For example, a typical record might be defined as an *inventory master record*. Specifications might include the fact that there are 7,247 such records, each record is 846 positions (bytes) long, and they are to be stored on IBM 3350 DASD. The records are hierarchical, and there are 16 data elements (segments) in each record. Additional information about each segment, fields within segments, keys, and information type are also specified by the data base administrator. The data communications administrators specify similar detailed information about terminals. There are currently available systems software interfaces that have the potential to take a message format written in unedited form by an application program and reformat it so that it can be displayed in edited form on a specific device. They also have the potential to take messages in edited form from a specific device and reformat it into unedited form for use by an application program. Notice the word potential. This type of software package has the potential. It is the data communications administrator that enables the interfaces to realize their potential by specifying terminal device characteristics and attributes and relating specific terminal devices to specific transaction programs that produce messages for the devices.

Most of the information prepared by data base administrators and data communications administrators should be entered into data dictionary files or data bases if they are available. As of this writing, data dictionary systems are in their infancy, yet, there is every reason to believe that they will soon advance to the point where data dictionary systems will be a "front end" to all systems development. They will become a centralized repository for all kinds of information. Data dictionary data bases will contain information not only on files, records, fields, elements, and so forth, but also on terminals, network configurations, hardware, programs, data processing standards, and individual names for everything from program responsibility to report distribution.

Another task that must be performed is the creation of meaningful test data. This job should be performed by the analyst. Although there are generators available which can generate test data, they are usually not sophisticated enough to create meaningful test data—the kind with which a user who knows nothing about computers or systems can be shown that the system being designed and developed for him or her is doing what it is supposed to. The analyst is the best person to perform this task. The analyst is most familiar with the user's requirements and can develop test data that appear to be the "real thing" to the user. A test data generator may be used together with the analysts' data to increase the volumes, if the analyst feels that it is appropriate. Test data creation should start early in the development phase because it is a tedious, dull, and time consuming job.

The first of two final areas to be examined under development in this survey is *documentation*. This term evokes the spectrum of reactions whenever it is heard. MIS managers and users believe that there can't be too much. Programmers respond to documentation with questions like "Doctor Who?" or "Documentation? You mean like the Documentation of Independence?" Always a sore point, some type of *operational* documentation is essential if a system is ever to work.

Documentation is made easier by the use of a data dictionary. Modifications and maintenance are simplified. However, initial creation of documentation is still the same basic chore it always was. Modifying and maintaining information that is stored in the computer and that is available online through a CRT is a vast improvement to making up new record layouts and retyping program specifications that are on paper.

Operational documentation includes operator instructions on how to run the system. These are usually simple and straightforward in describing normal situations. In many sophisticated operating system environments, jobs start and run to completion virtually unnoticed by the system operators. However, the unusual situation requires documentation. Instructions are required for back out, restart, and recovery situations where programs abnormally terminate (abend) or where computers or computer equipment malfunctions. Balancing instructions are necessary where report output has to be balanced before it is released to the user. Scheduling information is necessary if a system is to run in a centralized environment with other applications. Report distribution information is required so that output can be sent to the department or to the individual who is to receive it. The source of input data should be specified so that an individual or department may be contacted if something out of the ordinary occurs.

Documentation slows down the development process, but if it is not done, "the chickens will come home to roost," eventually. It's an old lament, but if it is recited often enough, it may be given some heed.

The last area to be discussed under development is testing.

There are many schemes for testing. In this survey, three are to be examined. I'll call them:

1   Unit testing.
2   Integrated testing.
3   Systems testing.

Unit Testing is a task performed by an application programmer after a program module has been written and successfully compiled. The programmer should prepare data to test each instruction in the program. In order to facilitate unit testing, it is important that individual program modules be kept relatively small. A 4k program module is relatively simple to test. With the use of higher level languages, the occurrence of a 4K program is not too common. It is difficult to define small in the context of higher level languages. This can be left to the judgment of the project leader or senior application programmer. As a general guideline, a single application program that initial estimates project to be a million bytes should be broken down into several smaller modules if possible. Each of the smaller modules should then be written, compiled, and tested separately. The smaller modules can then be put together and tested as a single program.

Integrated testing consists of combining modules or programs into groups and testing them to see how well they interact with one another. This is necessary to determine whether individual modules or programs affect one another. It is possible for a program to work well in a "stand alone" situation, yet cause a problem when integrated with others. This is especially likely in the online systems where timing is critical. For example, initial design, programming, and unit testing may not show that two critical transactions (each a separate program) in an online system have need for the same resource (say a particular data base), at the same time. When they are run together, contention for resources occurs, slowing down one or the other, or both transactions. Integrated testing highlights such problems. Test data for integrated testing should be put together by the analyst with an assist from the application programmer. Unit test data are usually insufficient and inadequate for integrated testing.

When all detectable problems and conflicts are resolved through integrated testing, *systems testing* should commence. Test data should be put together by the user with a strong assist by the analysts on the project. The results expected from the test should be specified prior to the test. Testing should put some stress on the system. Dollar totals and unit counts should be as meaningful as possible. Volumes should include both peak loads and average loads. Separate tests can be run using each. With online systems volume tests are essential. Although these testing requirements may seem an unreachable ideal, experience has shown that proper testing has significant impact on the system's success.*

IMPLEMENTATION

Operations involvement in a system begins in a small way during the analysis phase. The feasibility of a system does depend on the capability of computer operations to handle it. This factor is sometimes overlooked. After feasibility is confirmed and the analysis phase gives way to design, Operations should also be called upon to provide suggestions. In a centralized data center environment, for instance, the designers are often aware only of their own system and the few others that directly affect it or are affected by it. They can be nearly totally in the dark about the overall impact of their proposed system on others or of the others' impact on theirs. Therefore the observations and suggestions of Operations during the design phase may be instrumental in making the adjustments necessary for the system to run comfortably in the data center environment. Invariably these kinds of adjustments have to be made. It is much easier to make them in the design phase than it is during the development or implementation phases.

During the development phase, Operations begins to become familiar with some of the details of the new system. Programs are compiled and tested using Operation's facilities. Online regions are brought up on Operation's computers and transactions are run through the system. Interpersonal communications channels between the individuals in the Operations department and those on the project team are established. These channels of communication are most important, since it is through them that informal, day-to-day working relationships are made. Cooperation among individuals at the working level can contribute significantly to the success of a system implementation.

During the integrated testing and systems testing phases Operations can become thoroughly familiar with the system. Operational documentation such as scheduling, output distribution, sources of input, balancing instructions, and job control language (JCL) are turned over to Operations. If Operations has been involved from the start, the whole process of system turnover can be a simple, smooth occurrence. If

---

*I worked on the CBS News Election Night systems development effort from 1970 through 1974. In 1972, we developed a thorough testing scheme similar to that described above. The 1970 elections systems had worked, though shakily. In 1972 and in 1974 and on each election night thereafter, the system has worked very well and I believe that the testing scheme has been significantly instrumental in the success of that system.

Operations has not been involved, there are likely to be some surprises. From the application team's and the user's perspective, the system turnover becomes the classical "us and them" confrontation. Systems have been implemented both ways and either way they generally work. But, systems implemented properly, with Operations involvement from the beginning, work more efficiently and malfunctions are resolved more quickly.

The first few cycles of processing are like a shakedown. Cycles here connote days, weeks, months, or whatever. Everything has been done to assure that the system works according to specifications. All that is left is to run it. A few difficulties invariably come up. If the advance work, analysis, design, and development were done properly, the difficulties are usually minor and can be quickly resolved. If major problems occur, the "us and them" syndrome is heightened and the search for scapegoats and the witchhunts begin. All the individuals involved spend the majority of their time preparing defenses, and planning offenses. It all becomes quite unpleasant. Even so, the system generally rolls on.

There may be a subsequent phase after implementation. It could be called the maintenance phase or the modification phase. The difference between the two is one of degree. Maintenance usually refers to the process of making minor changes to a system, such as, adding a report or a display, adding a few new terminals to the application, changing a tax calculation algorithm or altering some entries in tables or lists of items like product codes or discount percentages. Modification implies major changes to a system, such as reconfiguring the applications terminal network by putting in all new equipment, adding some distributed processing capability and removing it from the host or changing input processing from a batch processing function to an online function. Whatever the system, no matter how well designed, developed, and implemented, a maintenance and/or modification phase always follows. The reason is basic. No one is ever satisfied. If you provide a good system, the user immediately gets new ideas on how to make it better. If you provide a mediocre system, the user immediately finds shortcomings and suggests changes to overcome them. If you provide an inadequate system . . .

This chapter has surveyed systems or application analysis, design, development, and implementation in an environment of large-scale, centralized data processing. It has dealt with a complex, involved situation. Yet there is a lesson for all. In the large-scale environment described, the amount of work and coordination is significant, as we have seen. In smaller, less sophisticated environments, some of the particulars just described may be bypassed. But, make no mistake about it, the essential process is the same.

chapter 13

Word Processing, Electronic Mail, and "Office of the Future"

In earlier chapters topics were discussed that implied the use of large-scale mainframe computers. Data base systems and distributed systems generally involve large computers. Smaller computers are making inroads into these fields, but it must be pointed out that what the "smaller" computer makers are building today has the equivalent processing power of a large scale mainframe of only a few years ago. However, the primary impact that small computers are making is not in data base and distributed processing, or in any of the traditional MIS domains. The primary impact is being made in an area almost totally ignored by MIS organizations, the offices themselves. The term "Office of the Future" is seen in magazines and heard in seminar presentations. What is "Office of the Future?"

FUTURE OFFICE?

Office of the future seems to be made up of at least two components, word processing and electronic mail. Both of these components make use of computers and teleprocessing. In fact, an office of the future system bears a striking resemblance to a network. So, it would seem that much of the technology that is used in networking can also be applied to office of the future.

We are sometimes amazed at tremendous growth that has taken place in the computer industry and in MIS organizations in such a short time. Yet even more amazing is the growth has taken place in the word processing component of office of the future in an even shorter period.

A Short History

Prior to the mid 1960s, when IBM introduced the hybrid magnetic tape/selectric typewriter, word processing systems used some of the same kind of equipment that had been used by teletype systems. Paper tapes or rolls with holes punched in them were used to produce repetitive letters. Later in the 1960s computers produced what were known as *computer letters*. High speed line printers were used, and the quality of the letters was substandard. Computer printers were all right for printing reports used within the corporation, but receiving a letter produced that way was almost insulting. To the recipient, it was obvious that the friendly salutation was machine generated and that everyone else on the street was also getting the same letter.

The IBM product of the late 1960s nudged the word processing technology a little closer to integration with computer technology. The substitution of magnetic tape for paper tape made an improvement in the error correction process, in that retyping of a character over an incorrect character was possible without the need for a tape splice. Another benefit was that the magnetic tape cartridges held significantly more data per unit than strips of paper tape. The major disadvantage in this configuration was that the operator was "blind" as far as control characters on the magnetic tape were concerned. The control codes were not visible and could not be typed by the typewriter. Another disadvantage was the severely limited editing capability. Adding or changing a few characters in a document was possible, but the insertion of new words or lines necessitated a recopying of the entire tape with new information being inserted during the copying. This early word processing technology suffered from one of the same limitations as the original sequential batch MIS applications. In order to update a file, the entire file had to be copied.

In the early 1970s, concurrent with the arrival of minicomputers, word processing began to be totally integrated into computers. The first word processing systems were *shared logic*, that is, they were actually general purpose computers that were used for other applications as well. These early systems seem primitive by today's standards, but it wasn't until the mid-1970s that word processing systems came into their own.

WORD PROCESSING

It may be well to develop a definition of *word processing* at this point. As is the case with many of the terms dealt with in this book, there is

some confusion about just what is included in the scope of word processing and what is not. In the context of its treatment here, word processing
describes the creating, displaying, editing and printing of text information, with facilities for functions such as tabulating, justifying, and
formatting. In the mid-1970s equipment configurations became available that could do the things demanded by that definition. The floppy
disk or diskette and the CRT display device, together with enhanced
word processing oriented software, made it all possible. The diskette
devices, together with the CRTs, removed operator "blindness" and
facilitated editing not possible on the sequentially oriented magnetic
tapes and tape cassettes. Also in the mid 1970s, microcomputers became
available and they were less expensive than minis. Contemporary word
processing systems, then, are configured using either a minicomputer or
a microcomputer, diskette storage, CRT displays, and printers.

Functions

To achieve a degree of versatility in a word processing configuration,
the system should contain at least two diskette drives. Two diskettes
working in tandem give the user certain manipulative dexterity, which
is most useful in editing and in inserting and merging activity. Having
at least two diskette drives also provides an emergency facility as well as
a safety feature, in that it allows copying of diskettes for document
backup.

Trace flexibility and dexterity in editing can be realized only by the
use of a CRT device together with adequate software. Manipulation of
lines and paragraphs with a CRT terminal is significantly less cumber-
some than with a typewriter terminal. The software is the key element.
The features to look for are:

- The ability to add and delete words from a line of text without the
  need to retype the entire line.
- The ability to move blocks of sentences or paragraphs of data from
  one place in a document to another.
- The ability to access other documents and to copy portions of those
  documents into the text being developed.
- The ability to search for and to modify particular character strings
  in a document.
- The ability to format documents and to establish left margins.
- The ability to justify right margins.

These features are found in most word processing systems. The CRT device itself usually has function keys or buttons that can be used by the operator to set up these features. There are other features available in some of the more "high powered" word processing systems. These include:

- Automatic pagination.
- Superscripting for footnotes.
- Automatic spacing for diagrams and illustrations.

Equipment

The CRT devices range in size also. In a word processing system, a CRT with a display capacity for a full page of text is the most useful.

Printers are probably the most critical of all the devices in a word processing configuration. Computer printers can produce output at a rate of thousands of lines a minute, but the quality is substandard. Word processing output, of necessity, must be of high quality. If it is not, then the whole justification for word processing is destroyed. Word processing printers must produce documents of electric typewriter quality. Two types of printers are now used to do this, *Selectric terminals* and *daisy wheel* printers. Daisy wheel printers are somewhat faster than Selectrics and their quality is very good. Selectrics are less expensive. Both come with keyboards. Daisy wheel elements are made of either metal alloy or plastic. The metal alloy elements are relatively expensive. The plastic elements have a relatively short life span.

Numbers and Letters

The use of computers in word processing was a little slow in developing. There were several probable reasons. In the early days of data processing, it was seen that the processing of integers and numbers was significantly easier than processing letters and words. At that time, it was. Despite improvements in the quality and capabilities of equipment, the difficulty of processing letters and words had become exaggerated in people's minds and the fact that there were more similarities than differences was overlooked. In addition, numbers have a precision that words cannot convey. Since digital computers themselves are numerically oriented, there may have been an affinity between computers and the processing of numbers. In the data processing community, as one looks back, letters and words were considered a nuisance to be avoided where possible, changed into numeric codes at every opportunity, and dragged into systems only when absolutely necessary. Whatever the situation previously, the second-class status of letters and words in computer processing is now a thing of the past. With current technology, processing of words is no more difficult than processing numbers.

ELECTRONIC MAIL

Whereas the processing of words is now a minor task, the other component of office of the future, namely, *electronic mail*, is an application of computers that parallels networking. The underlying objective of electronic mail seems to be the reduction of memoranda and other paper movement internal to corporations, government agencies, and institutions. Electronic mail applications consist of creating interoffice memoranda on CRT devices and transmitting the memos electronically to individuals that are to see it. Each individual in the system has an electronic "mail box." These individuals can periodically examine the contents of these mail boxes to read their most current correspondence. There can also be a facility within the system to tell the recipients of the correspondence that there is mail in their mail boxes. As the correspondence in the mail boxes is read or aged, it can be transferred to an archival file. It is possible to have an index set up that contains key words of documents in that archival file, so that document can be retrieved if needed.

Other facets to electronic mail are another electronic "box" for telephone messages and an executive calendar to record meetings and appointments. All of these things can be done with computers and CRT devices. The technology is available.

THE POTENTIAL

Bringing all this technology together in an office of the future or a "paperless" office will probably just happen over the next several years. Look back. Five or six years ago, CRTs were just beginning to appear in offices where computer applications had made their use mandatory. Online business systems used them. More recently, CRTs began to appear on the desks of programmers as more interactive facilities were introduced. Programmers using these interactive facilities were able to increase their productivity. Program listings, indispensable to program development, that used to be listed on continuous form paper, are now stored in the computer system. The programmer can work with listings a page at a time using a CRT device. Job control language procedures that used to be kept in a deck of 80-column cards that had to be read into the computer each time the procedure was needed are now also stored in the computer system. Now when a programmer or operator needs them, he or she makes a single entry through a CRT device to invoke the required procedure.

One of the reasons for the increased use of CRTs and computer systems for storing procedures, programs, and other information is the decreasing relative cost of computer equipment. Every indication is that the cost of computer equipment should continue to decrease. The advantages of using computer equipment to store more information should become obvious to more individuals in the future.

Merging Technologies

There seems to be a merging of several different but related technologies. Whether or not it should be called "Office of the Future" or "Future Shock" is the subject of some debate. But it is coming. The equipment is now being put into place, as it is needed. CRT terminal devices occupy many desks in offices occupied by individuals that ten years earlier had thought a CRT was a television set. As cable after cable is strung, and CRT after CRT is put into place, one of the most troublesome tasks in the area of hardware preparation for office of the future is completed. The next steps in making office of the future a reality may be taken by those creative programmers and terminal users who develop ways of communicating with one another using the devices that are currently being put into place. These individuals now share software resources among themselves. Facilities such as the libraries and catalogs mentioned in an earlier chapter are already shared resources. More of this is bound to follow.

In order to illustrate the manner in which word processing and electronic mail are already working their way into MIS organizations, the following narrative is offered.

A Short Story

Once upon a time, there was a large corporate data center that went to great lengths to offer support to its divisional users for their applications. It was a difficult task, and the staff at the data center spent a significant amount of time trying to find ways to improve service to the divisions. As the number of divisional applications grew, the data center resources were stretched to the limit. Divisional MIS groups began to second-guess the data center's ability to perform, and the data center's staff began to second-guess the divisional MIS groups ability to develop an efficient application. There were skirmishes and battles between the groups and some animosities arose. In order to reduce the friction between data center users and data center staff, standards and procedures were developed to which divisional applications had to conform. A number of paper forms were designed that had to be filled out by divisional MIS programmers and analysts. There were a form for scheduling and a form for report distribution. Standard application and program numbers had to be used. There was a form for balancing. An input/output form was required for each batch program. A procedure was established for application turnover. Recovery and restart procedures were required for batch programs and for online transaction programs. These forms and others, together with the standards and procedures, were the start of a process which soon led to what became known as the data center bureaucracy. It is ironic that the data center which provided the latest in computer support for its users had internal systems that were almost totally manual and paper form based. Because of the preoccupation with the day-to-day operating problems of maintaining support for divisional users, little attention was given to systems within the data center itself. As divisional applications continued to grow in both number and sophistication, the data center systems began to show signs of obsolescence. The three-volume Standards Manual, a very good tool when first put together, was soon three years out of date. Only the thoroughness and foresight of its initial developers kept it from being totally useless. There were six large bookcases filled with application documentation. Maintenance in this area was also behind. If there was an similarity between the recovery and restart procedures that were in the documentation in the bookcases and the copies in the operational run book, it was only in those applications that were no longer run.

In this chaotic situation, many errors were made, there was much duplication of effort, and great pains had to be taken to circumvent troublesome and obsolete procedures. One of the biggest headaches was the recovery and restart procedures. A couple of individuals in the data center decided to revise the Standards Manual, writing it on the *computer system* instead of on paper, and make it available to those who needed it. Approximately 200 copies of the old three-volume set had been distributed. In the new arrangement, the only paper needed was a small booklet containing copies of the forms to be used. These forms were referred to by the text written on the computer system.

Concurrent with this, another effort was made to put the recovery and restart procedures on the computer system also. A security scheme was established so the recovery and restart procedures could be read by almost anyone who had a CRT, but could be updated only by the individuals in the Standards and Documentation department at the data center.

As a word processing and electronic mail system it is quite primitive, but it does represent a step toward the office of the future. It eliminates a lot of paper.

While this is all brought about, some attention should be given to security. All facilities cannot be made available to everyone. Control clerks, for example, need access to the payroll balancing and crossfooting procedures, but not to the payroll master file. Security procedures such as a password identification for operators can help to prevent clerks from getting at master files.

SECURITY

There is no security system that is foolproof. If someone can develop a good set of security procedures, someone else can find a way through it or around it. However, that should not discourage the implementation of security procedures. Limited security is better than no security. For instance, an unarmed guard in front of a commercial computer facility is not going to stop a terrorist group from destroying the facility. Yet that guard will certainly be able to keep most unauthorized individuals from entering the facility and doing damage either maliciously or accidentally. However, the likelihood of a terrorist group attacking a commercial computer facility is somewhat less likely than that of some unauthorized person causing malicious or accidental damage. Unarmed guards are used in almost all computer facilities and are instrumental in preventing everything from petty thievery to computer outages resulting from an action such as an unauthorized person's throwing a switch on a disk storage control unit. Limited computer security, mostly in the form of software, while it cannot stop a deranged systems software programmer, can inhibit most mere mortals from causing trouble where they shouldn't.

Some easy-to-install basic security procedures are: *password security*, *terminal security*, and *transaction security*. Password security is probably the most common. Each individual must have an *identifier* in order to have access to a software facility. This identifier can be as simple as his name or as complex as some code consisting of a combination of numbers and letters that is changed on a periodic basis. In order to help keep passwords confidential, a feature associated with password security inhibits the display of the password. When the user keys it in on the device keyboard, it does not appear on the display screen. Although these schemes are far from foolproof, they are better than nothing at all.

In more sophisticated telecommunications networks, the potential exists for every terminal to have access to virtually every software facility in the computer. The purpose of this global accessability is to offer flexibility and to minimize the number of terminals needed in the network. In many cases, this flexibility is valuable, but it also must be weighed against unauthorized or accidental use of certain facilities. Therefore, when the network terminal specifications are put into the computer, selected terminals can be assigned to a specific facility. In order for a terminal to have access to a facility, it must be specified as part of that facility's network. Usually a list of valid terminal devices is associated with each facility. If a terminal name is not in the table, it cannot have access to the facility.

In many software systems, transactions are given names. *Transaction names* are also kept in a list associated with particular facilities. Transaction names can be correlated with terminal device names, so that certain transactions can be entered on only certain devices. Unless an individual has the knowledge and the wherewithall to enter a new transaction name onto the list of valid transactions, that individual cannot access files or data bases by merely writing a program.

These are a sample of available software security. More sophisticated procedures as well as a host of external security measures can be applied as needs warrant. Caution is advised; too much security will create a computerized bureaucracy.

IT'S TIME

Office of the future is virtually upon us. The hardware or equipment is already available, much of it already in place. The software is another matter. Software is potential. Software can only perform according to the specifications set by individuals. Some software is completely developed internally by the individuals of an organization and it should closely reflect the judgment of those individuals. Internally developed software is very rare in today's large scale mainframe environment. However, a variation of this kind of development is still done by vendors of *small business systems*. These small business systems are similar to the turnkey systems developed by OEMs in the mid 1970s. These types are small, computer based systems, and the software is a customized set of application programs using the facilities of a standard operating system that comes with the computer. Most of the applications are variations of "boiler plate" commercial applications like accounts payable, order entry, payroll, and accounting systems. Some of these systems are developed with word processing capabilities. They are often marketed by the local distributer of an equipment manufacturer. It is the distributor's responsibility to tailor the software to the purchaser's specifications. The complexity of the application specifications determines the price of these small systems.

In most large-scale mainframe environments, software products are purchased. Within these products there is a provision for the purchaser or user to enter parameters to tailor the product to the purchaser's particular environment. Generalized software limits flexibility to some degree, but the software environment still reflects the judgments of the user of the product. It is the individual's selection of parameters that determines what software actually does. Although application programming is still heavily used in this type of environment, there is a trend toward more generalized software to replace even that. The declining cost of the machine resources as opposed to the increasing cost of people gives impetus to this trend.

Office of the future is only a portion of the future, and that future is already here. Under the control of computers in several places, are the technologies and applications of:

- MIS.
- Video graphics.
- Word processing.
- Data processing.
- Video-assisted instruction.
- Electronic mail.
- Data bases.
- Communications networks.
- Optical character recognition (OCR).
- Artificial voice.
- Electronic funds transfer.
- Universal product code.
- Point of sale recording.
- Data entry.
- Computer programming itself.

The list could continue. Computers are into everything. It's time!

chapter 14

The 1980s, Where We Are

In the last several chapters, some basic computer concepts with an overview of their commercial application have been presented. It is not these concepts that make computer technology so awesome. Computers and computer systems can be understood by virtually anyone on a conceptual plane. This does not mean, however, that everyone can become a "computer expert." There are reasons for this. First of all, it's a long way from understanding how an automobile works to becoming an automotive engineer, an automobile manufacturer, or an automobile mechanic. Most of us, over the years, have learned some basic things about our automobiles. We have learned how to do basic repair work or at least how to deal with an automobile mechanic so that we can understand what he is doing. Only a few of us are automotive engineers and even fewer are automobile manufacturers.

In the case of computers, in addition to manufacturers and engineers, with whom we seldom come in contact, we have to deal with salesmen and two types of technicians. These technicians are quite different from one another, both in skill and, in most cases, in temperament. One type is known as a field engineer. It is this type of technician that repairs or modifies equipment. His equivalent in the automotive field is the automobile mechanic. The second type is the computer programmer. His equivalent is the automotive engineer.

Both these technical skills are becoming more specialized as the sophistication and potential of computer equipment increase. At one end of the scale, field engineers are less frequently required as equipment repair becomes the responsibility of the user. In some of the more recently manufactured computer systems, diagnostic equipment is included. The user is able to diagnose a problem, determine the component causing the problem, order a replacement, and fix it himself. At the other end, the field engineering function is utilized in the repair and maintenance of the more sophisticated equipment. In the case of computer programming, sophistication in software has made it more frequently possible for the user of the computer to do his own programming. High level languages like BASIC and APL have made the computer the tool of the financial analyst, the market researcher, the engineer, and the statistician who can write programs without the services of an application programmer. Other developments continue to make the computer available to users without the need for application programmers. However, programmers are still required to support the software itself, but they function in environments where they generally do not interact with users. They usually either work for a manufacturer of computers, or for a software developer who then sells the software, already tested and workable to the user. One other place where programmers are found is in large corporate, university, or governmental data centers where they support multiprogramming, time-sharing, data base systems environments and other software resources that are used by many users concurrently.

So, in one sense, understanding computers is relatively simple. Yet some sophisticated technology is still needed to support a computer environment. Field engineering and computer programming are still with us. The complexion of these skills is changing, in that both are becoming more technically sophisticated and more transparent as far as the user of computers is concerned. Yet, although everything seemingly becomes simpler for the computer user, he must become more discerning, as the applications to which he wishes to put the computer are themselves becoming very sophisticated. The potential computer user has at his disposal sophisticated and in some ways, easy-to-use tools that he can apply to meet some of his needs. However, these tools when used in sufficient quantity can be quite costly. The potential user is advised to be aware that the sophistication of his own application is also a factor in the complexities often associated with computer systems.

Many of us marvelled at the fact that we, in the United States, put men on the moon. Computers were a significant part of the effort required for that accomplishment. Many of the techniques we now use were developed in the space program. However, there are few users of computers that can afford the amounts of money required to finance a space program like NASA's.

Unknown to most potential users of computers is the inherent complexity of their own applications. Quite often a user is shown a "canned software package" that will solve his problems. Upon closer examination, the user sees that it looks "pretty good." "The package only needs a couple of 'minor changes' to fit my needs." Although these packages have been applied in many areas with reasonable success, there have been many other instances where the work on "minor changes" has dragged on for months and even years, causing cost overruns far beyond original estimates. More often than not, it isn't that the package was inadequate, but rather that the user's underestimation or misunderstanding of the complexities of his own application.

In addition to application complexities, the technical specifics to be dealt with vary depending on whether the instrument chosen is a microcomputer, a minicomputer, or a large scale mainframe computer. As shown earlier, the distinction between these types of computers can be blurred. Yet there are some generalizations that can be made. Although there are exceptions to these generalizations, they are on the whole accurate.

Smaller computers, when used in nonturnkey applications, that is, when completely tested and debugged software is not part of the system, generally require a staff of technicians that thoroughly understand the specific computer being used. In those cases where a turnkey application is to be implemented the technicians need to be sufficient to maintain, support, and enhance the system, unless the purchaser of the system is convinced that the application will never require maintenance, support, or enhancement. If the purchaser of such a system is willing to rely on the vendor for maintenance, support, and enhancement, there is no need for any technical support.

If a user elects to put his application on a large-scale computer, he has basically two options. He can put it up in a time-sharing environment, either "in-house" if it is available, or by using "outside services" of a time-sharing firm. As an alternative, he can develop an application from scratch, using systems analysts and programmers, which he can hire or acquire from contractors or from in-house MIS departments. As a general rule, the time-sharing applications require less development time, but are more costly to run on a sustained basis. The development of applications using analysts and programmers generally takes longer to get implemented, but once installed it is less costly to run. Time-sharing is quite useful in handling one-time jobs and certain types of ad hoc requests where the amount of data needed is either relatively small or has to be stored for only a short time. The more conventional type of application development is clearly more cost effective for applications which have to be run on a scheduled basis, day after day or week after week.

Dealing with application development in a mainframe environment involves several factors other than application complexities. There are technical and political complexities peculiar to large mainframe environments. These include sharing computer resources with other users and a certain loss of control of an application, such as having to make adjustments because of large mainframe scheduling realities. Although running applications in a large mainframe computer in some corporate data center frees the user from a number of headaches, like elaborate scheduling and the costs of air conditioning and other facilities, he is subject to the failures of software elements over which he has no control. Operating systems, data base management systems, and access methods are all necessary in a large corporate data center in order to make it cost effective. The user reaps the benefits of this software in the form of reduced costs, but at the same time he is penalized when they fail, as they occasionally do.

A contemporary development that affects all aspects, mini and micro as well as large mainframe computing, is the introduction of microprogramming. The use of *boards* or *chips* that contain program modules is a technological development that introduces the potential for substantial cost reduction in computer systems. The *boards* or *chips* are electronic components that contain executable programs already tested and debugged. The components contain what once was software. The cost of producing these components continues to fall. As they become less expensive the potential cost savings may spur many organizations to make the required changes in their ways of doing things and adapt to the canned approach contained in these components. As we now see "accounts receivable" software packages, we shall soon see "accounts receivable" chips.

These chips and boards are also used for other computer-related functions such as tape and disk read-and-write operations, and the transfer of data between computers and teleprocessing control units. The use of chips or boards for these functions makes the repair of computers significantly less time consuming.

Technologically, computer systems are becoming much more simple for individuals to deal with. Although the technology is sophisticated, most of it continues to become more transparent to the user. Two current examples of this are word processing and small business systems. Most contemporary word processing systems are made up of a computer, some CRTs, some auxiliary storage devices, tape or disk, and some high quality printers. The "software" in the system is quite often not really software, but some boards or chips. Small business systems are made up of basically the same components, but are used for different functions, business applications like accounts receivable, order entry, or payroll. Quite often, boards or chips contain pieces of these applications.

So, in conclusion, computer systems are not mysterious black boxes, but rather a set of boxes or components, each with a specific function. The functions of each component are usually quite straightforward;

printers print, and tape and disk storage units hold relatively large quantities of data. Computers themselves hold relatively small amounts of data which they process during a given interval of time. Involved with computers and commercial applications are two groups; MIS, largely data center and large-scale computer oriented, and the office of the future advocates, mostly small computer and local processing oriented. Despite a lot of politics, a merger of the two groups is inevitable. The technology is virtually identical. The differences are a combination of myth and shadow. Networking is going to bring everything together. Data processing and word processing are not different technologies, but merely slightly different versions of the same technology. The technology is available and largely in place. Can the sociological and psychological adjustments be made? That question I leave to others. I hope that this book can help some individuals to make the necessary adjustments.

Appendices

A Contemporary System

The following is a description of the CBS News Election Night computer systems. It reflects the system that was used beginning in 1968 and though modified in some way every two years, it continued to be used through 1976. Although no longer in use, this particular system employed virtually every facet of the computer and related technologies described in this book. For its time, it was a "leading edge" technology system. It was replaced in 1978 with a redesigned system. Yet because of its sophistication, it serves very well as an illustration of computer systems within the scope of this book.

The purpose of this appendix is to present both the functional description and the chronology of the real-time computer system. Although the system described is unique, it contains all the ingredients of a typical computer system in today's sophisticated environment. This system was until 1976 the CBS News Election Night System. In actuality, it was not merely one system, but five separate systems. These systems were integrated in varying degrees with one another, but had been developed separately, and each was a distinct system unto itself. One of the systems was a batch system that was run prior to Election Night; the other four systems were real-time systems used on Election Night. These four systems provided information to CBS News correspondents, editorial personnel, and management on a real-time basis on Election Night.

The presentation which follows is an overview of the Election Night Broadcast, looked at from an EDP point of view. EDP plays a very large part in the broadcast, but is not the whole story. Other divisions of CBS get very involved with the broadcast in several other ways. As far as the Election Night Broadcast is concerned, the CBS News Division is responsible for producing the broadcast. The CBS Television Network Division supplies the facilities such as the Broadcast Studio, Control Rooms, and other space used as computer rooms. The Corporate Group of CBS also contributes to the Election effort. The CBS Corporate Data

Center allows the Election Unit to use its computers both for testing, and during the Election Night Broadcast. The Systems Programming Group within the data center provides the Election Unit application programming staff with technical support. The Corporate Facilities Group renders the necessary facilities support in other locations besides those provided by the Television Network Division. Also included within the Corporate Facilities group is a centralized telecommunications group which services the whole of CBS in the teleprocessing and communication area. This group provides the Election Unit with the teleprocessing equipment and acts as an interface with the Telephone Company.

Before we get into the systems, it may be useful to explain what is done in covering an election race. Basically, a race is reported on three levels. First, CBS News reports and displays the continuing unofficial vote count throughout the evening, as it is amassed and counted at the precinct, county, and state level. Second, based on the computer projection systems, returns from a carefully selected set of precincts are used to estimate the outcome of a contest, long before the unofficial returns have reached meaningful totals. And third, analysis of the vote is provided by breaking it down into significant demographic components.

All of this activity on Election Night involved complex operations that obviously require computers. The projection system, for example, involves the use of historical data in combination with current data from the sample precincts, and since there are as many as 3500 precincts nationwide, the data-handling problem is one that makes computers mandatory. The instantaneous tabulation of the returns for demographic analysis, the various summary requirements, would be impossible without computers.

This had been the case since 1962, when CBS News first used projections and analysis. From a systems and programming point of view, it was comparatively easy then. Because of the growing public and business interest in computers, IBM supplied CBS News with all the necessary hardware and software in return for the promotional benefits it derived from Election Night. The projection and analysis system was handled by Louis Harris. This arrangement continued through 1966. But in 1967, the situation changed drastically. CBS management decided it wanted in-house capability and responsibility for the projections and analysis, so that a department was set up within the CBS News Division to handle all of the research, statistical work, systems design, and data bank development necessary to do the job. At the same time, IBM got more realistic about the promotional benefits of elections as against cash expenditures, and the new department had to take on the programming responsibilities for the first time. The 1968 system, to keep it brief, ran on Election Night, with some difficulties.

In 1970, IBM got out of the free hardware game. The department was left to its own resources. The decision was made to use the existing computer facilities at the CBS Data Center. This decision carried with it the concurrent commitment to teleprocessing, since the broadcast studio was two miles from the data center. All the previous systems had been installed at the Broadcast Center, which houses the broadcast studio. The decision to use the CBS data center was made for the sake of economy, since renting large-scale computers was and still is expensive. The decision paid off, because the prime CBS Election System worked very well on Election Night. So in 1970, the 1968 system, known as the Vote Profile Analysis (VPA) system, was modified for teleprocessing and used again, and was very successful, encountering only a few minor problems during the evening.

Also in 1970, development of a second system was attempted. This system, of which more will be said below, was to support the VPA system, but failed in 1970. It just never got off the ground.

In 1972, VPA was modified again and used with complete success. The second system, which had failed in 1970, was completely redone in 1972, and it also ran well. The newest breakthrough in 1972 was the interfacing of a manually operated electronic character generator with a computer. This was also a success.

The year 1974 saw the VPA system, virtually intact, being used again. Modifications had to be made for new technology (equipment), but the original 1968 design, with the 1970 addition for teleprocessing, was still the same. The new system, known as the County Return Estimator (CORE) system, having been thoroughly tested in 1972, was redone much more economically in a time-sharing environment in 1974. The Electronic Character Generator System, used for CBS estimate graphic displays in 1972, was expanded to include vote count displays in 1974.

Large-scale election broadcasts are done on the CBS Network every two years and it takes two years to prepare for them. The department of CBS News that handles this task has a small permanent staff which grows in increments to about 300, exclusive of field reporters, on election night. The permanent staff is sufficient to handle the work for about 10 months and then, in September of the year preceding the election broadcast, the increases in staff begin. It is also at this time that the computer equipment is ordered. In addition to using the computer equipment already installed at the CBS Data Center, additional computers and peripheral equipment are required for system testing and for use on Election Night in support of the broadcast.

As stated above, through 1976 five systems were used by CBS news for elections. They were called the Data Bank system, the Vote Profile Analysis (VPA) system, the County Return Estimator (CORE) system, the VPA Backup system, and the Display system. Four of these systems; VPA, CORE, VPA backup, and the Display were online systems; the other was a batch system. Of the five systems, four were used on Election Night, the fifth, the Data Bank system, was used in the months preceding Election Night. The four systems in use on Election Night interacted with one another. For development, and on Election Night in 1972, four systems used IBM computers, the Display system utilized a digital equipment minicomputer. The VPA system ran in two IBM 370/155s each with 2 million bytes of memory. The CORE system and the VPA Backup system cohabited in two IBM 370/145s, each with a quarter million bytes of memory. The Data Bank system also used an IBM 370/155.

In 1972, the IBM 370/155 computers housing the VPA system were those located at the CBS Data Center. The same arrangement was in effect in 1974. The 370/145s used in 1972 had been located in the CBS Broadcast Center. In 1972, the statistical methodology of CORE system had proven valid, and a time-sharing facility had been used successfully in backing up this system. The system had worked. The methodology had been good and the time-sharing backup had performed well. In 1974, the decision was made, for reasons of economy, to employ time-sharing for the CORE system. The digital equipment minicomputers, a PDP8 in 1972, and the larger PDP11 for the expanded system in 1974, were located in the CBS Broadcast Center. An overall schematic of three systems and their relation to one another appears in Figure A.1. The VPA back-up system is not shown, as it replaced the VPA system in the event that it failed. Otherwise, the VPA backup system was virtually idle, although it was kept up to date.

Before we get into a detailed description of the systems, let's digress to define some of the language of election coverage. Following are some of the terms used by CBS News.

Vote Profile Analysis—was the system by which the sample vote was recorded, stored, and used in computations. The results of these computations were used in system output in the form of estimates and analysis. The estimates were referred to as CBS News Estimates.

News Election Service—(NES) was and still is the five-member (CBS, NBC, ABC, UPI, and AP) pool that reports unofficial returns throughout the nation. These unofficial returns were often referred to as "raw vote."

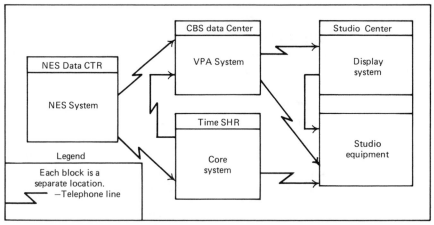

Figure A.1   Schematic of CBS News Election System (1972).

Sample Precincts—were the basis for CBS News Estimates. An estimate was based on the returns from sample precincts throughout a state that taken together reflected state voting patterns as a whole. Estimates were not made until actual returns were in from some or all of these sample precincts. A CBS News term, SVU, used to signify sample precincts, is defined later.

VPA Status—was the description of the status of a race. Under the VPA system a number of descriptions was possible. Correspondents used terms such as "close," "leading," "winner," to indicate the status of a race.

In addition to the correspondents reporting the information supplied to them on the display devices and printers, there were, until 1974, a number of boards and displays containing the vote returns from the NES, the estimated percentages from the VPA system, as well as summary information, such as "total Senate seats won by party." These boards were used for "on air" purposes. Illustrations of two of these displays are seen in Figure A.2 and A.3. Beginning in 1974, the vote returns and VPA estimates were put on air by means of an electronic character generator. The system for doing this is described in detail later on.

In addition to the display devices and boards within the studio, there was a network of private lines with telephones distributed among locations within the studio, in control rooms, at the data center computer room and at remote sites so that operational communications could be expedited during rehearsals and the Election Night Broadcast. An internal teletype network also existed within the studio to insure that

VIRGINIA	
SENATE	25%

SCOTT (REP.)	50%
1,226,639	
SPONG (DEM.)	40%
1,981,311	
HENDERSON (IND.)	10%
245,327	

Figure A.2   A raw vote display.

CBS NEWS ESTIMATE
VIRGINIA
SENATE

SCOTT (REP.)	53%
SPONG (DEM.)	45%
HENDERSON (IND.)	2%

Figure A.3   A CBS News Estimate display.

editorial information was sent to correspondents, producers, posting editors, and other personnel from a single source, on hard copy, at the same time.

A description of the various systems follows.

The Data Bank System—was centered around the Master Data Bank, a disk file containing historical and constant data which were accumulated prior to Election Night. The actual data bases (minifiles) used on Election Night were essentially subsets of the data bank. The data bank, which resided on a single disk pack, was made up of six distinct files or *data sets*, each of which contained records of a particular type for the entire nation.

The six data sets and the type of data associated with each were:

1   NATION—nationwide and regional data. It contained one national record and four Regional records.

2 STATE—state-wide data. There were 51 of these.

3 COUNTY—data applicable to individual counties. There were approximately 3500 of these.

4 CD—data applicable to individual Congressional Districts. There were 435 of these.

5 STRAT—data resulting from grouping or stratifying precincts (SVU) into party vote and geographic strata.

6 SVU—data obtained from the Smallest Voting Units (SVU) that exist. Across the nation they were variously called "precincts," "election districts," "wards," and so forth. Hence the use of the single terms "SVU". There were about 5000 of these.

Some of the information for the data bank was available from public records, for example, county vote returns. Other information had to be obtained locally. The Field Operations staff sent representatives into localities within states to obtain these data. The data, once obtained, were microfilmed and keypunched into cards. The county, state, and national data were fairly straightforward and, after some minor editing, were entered into the data bank. As a general rule, Congressional district data was also straightforward, but occasionally, because of reapportionment, boundary change processing was necessary.

The SVU data presented the greatest difficulty in preparation. Voting information was gathered from every SVU within a state every two years. Sample selection was a two step process. First, a preliminary sample was selected and after some analysis a second sample of 150 SVUs was selected. The selection of this sample, which was based partly on size, was under the guidance of the Statistical Research Group of the Election Unit, since statistical validity of this process was critical to the accuracy of the Election Night estimates. A sample SVU selected in 1970 could have been different than the same SVU in 1972, because of a boundary change, so boundary change processing was run to compensate.

The process of the Data Bank system is as follows:

1 Maintenance Program

This program provided all of the functions needed to create, update, and delete records. In addition, it did further editing of input data, provided protection against accidental destruction of certain data, and produced the following types of output:

History Logtape—a cumulative file on tape of images of every card input to the maintenance program and not rejected by it. This tape could itself be used as input to the program and hence served as a backup in case of destruction of the master file.

Transaction Log—a printed list of every input data card in the order in which the cards were processed. Each entry consisted of a formatted card image followed by a message indicating whether the data on the card were accepted or rejected by the program. In the latter case, the message usually indicated the reason for rejection.

Deletion/Creation Report—a log similar in format to the transaction log, but pertaining to those input cards whose specific function was the creation or deletion of records, rather than updating. A disposition message always indicated exactly what actions were taken by the program.

State Summary Report—a two-page report that summarized the current status of the master file on a state-by-state basis. It was produced after all input cards had been processed.

Data Bank Maintenance Printout—a complete printout of each record in the data bank which was updated in the current run, produced in the order in which the records were processed.

2 Presort

The maintenance program described above was designed so as to accept input cards in any order and to process them correctly. However, a great deal of efficiency was gained by having the input grouped in a specific way. This sort was able to put the input in sequence to achieve that efficiency.

3 Data Bank Printout Program

This program provided the facility to print out the contents of the entire data bank. In addition, through the use of control cards, selected portions only were able to be printed out. The formats of all printed records were identical to those produced during maintenance program runs.

4 General Selection Algorithm

Stratified SVUs by party vote according to prescribed criteria and selected the Election Night subset of SVUs. The Election Night data base (minifile) for the VPA system used on an average 75 SVUs for each state, not 150 as in the original sample. The selected SVUs were flagged in the data bank itself, and were made ready for use by the Data Base Generator programs. The selection of SVUs for the minifile was also based partly on size.

5   Data Base Generators

Election Night subsets of the data bank appropriate for each Election Night System (VPA, VPA Backup, and CORE System) were produced. The VPA Election Night data base (minifile) made use of data in all files of the data bank, except the county file. The minifile, when it was generated, also had space allocated for current data when they were entered on Election Night. The VPA Backup data base was also created from these files, but used substantially fewer data. The county file was used by the CORE Data Base Generator to create a data base for the CORE system.

The VPA System—the VPA system was originally written for the 1968 elections. It was written for two 1 million byte IBM 360/65s under one of the earliest versions of IBM's operating system, OS 360 PCP*, which at the time was the best option available. The VPA system had its own executive which, in a sense, gave it some of the capabilities of a multiprogramming system.† In 1970, in order to use the CBS Corporate Data Center computers, which were remotely located from the Broadcast Studio, teleprocessing was added to the system. The system was then run in an OS/MVT‡ environment on a half-million byte IBM 360/65 with 1 million bytes of large capacity storage (LCS), backed up by a half-million byte IBM 360/50 also, with 1 million bytes of LCS. Although using some of the features of MVT, the system remained essentially a PCP system with its own executive controlling the multiprogramming.

In 1972 and 1974, the system remained essentially the same except that the computers used were two IBM 370/155s. The input portion of the system used CRTs. Field reporters, with minimal training, numbering 3500 in a Presidential election year (2500 in a non-Presidential year), telephoned race results from their SVUs on Election Night. There were over 100 CRT operators taking these calls. Within the VPA

---

*An original unsophisticated version of the operating system which essentially permitted the execution of one job at a time in the computer.

†Multiprogramming—the capability of executing more than one program concurrently in one computer.

‡MVT—A later version of the operating system which allows concurrent execution of a number of jobs in the computer. As jobs end, new jobs can be brought into computer storage in those areas of storage no longer needed by completed jobs.

system's software, there is a comprehensive editing function that enabled most input to be completely validated while SVU reporters were still on the phone. Once the information was validated, it was stored in the minifile, available for subsequent computations for VPA estimates. Other input came from NES. The VPA system contained programs enabling it to receive and tabulate the "raw vote" data that were sent over telephone lines by NES. Once the data were validated and accepted, they too were stored in the minifile and became available for various computations in combination with VPA data and the historical data from the SVUs within that state.

On the output side, virtually all output was remote. There were about 75 CRT terminals in the broadcast studio, and a number of remote printers located in a room next to the studio. The CRTs were utilized by the correspondents and their producers, as well as other personnel in the studio, for two purposes. They carried a selection of displays of data and they were used as the instrument to request these displays and hard copy reports as well. The CRTs in the decision area of the studio were used for inputs for certain types of editorial decisions, such as win estimates. More specifically, although the computations of the system indicate status, a conscious entry was made by the decision team (a group of statisticians and CBS News executives) for each race where a winner was projected.

Some of the displays on the CRTs were generated on a time cycle basis by the computer, so that the displays were updated without any action by the user. In 1972, the bulk of these "fixed screens" were used to display Presidential race status information and electoral vote totals. In 1974, they were used to display Senate and Governor race status information and summary data. As stated above, prior to 1974, only VPA data were displayed on the CRTs. IBM 2260s, which had a 480-character display capability in a 40 x 12 format, were able to fill the need quite well. The raw vote totals were posted manually to Digital Display Units (DDUs), located atop the walls of the studio set. These DDUs were used for on-air displays of raw votes and were used as references by correspondents. The graphic display system, which is explained later, subsequently replaced the DDUs as on-air displays.

The VPA Election Night system was a single job that had three main parts, called, in the language of EDP, tasks and subtasks. The job was a hierarchy, with the main task called the root task and the two subtasks called the teleprocessor and the processor. The root task existed to provide a communication area common to both subtasks, and to start (initiate) and end (terminate) the job. It merely started up, brought in (attached) the two subtasks, and waited to end (close) the job at the end of the night. The teleprocessor ran in a higher priority than the processor and was interrupt-driven. The processor ran in the lowest priority and was driven by its own executive, which scheduled all the other sections as required. The teleprocessor interrupted the processor, never the reverse. Stated another way, whenever the teleprocessor portion of the system had something to do, the resources of the computer were turned over to the teleprocessor programs. When the teleprocessor had nothing to do, the processor got control of the resources of the computer. The interrupt-driven concept meant that if the processor was doing something, and the teleprocessor got something to do, say that someone in the studio requested a display on his CRT, the processor was interrupted, and the teleprocessor took over. When the teleprocessor was finished, and if it had no other requests to handle, control was given back to the processor task, and it commenced operation at the point where it had been interrupted. The processor was composed essentially of four parts.

1 Executive.
2 Edit Update.
3 Computations (State Race Estimate,* Analysis and Congressional).
4 Reports and Screens.

A brief description of two types of transactions will help explain how the system worked.

First, vote input: a field reporter, one of many, called in from an SVU somewhere in the United States. The call went through a switchboard to a CRT operator who was wearing a telephone headset. Indicative data and vote data were entered via the CRT in numerically coded form. The executive program transferred the coded input from the CRT into the computer memory. The executive program then called the edit and update program which validated the format of the coded input and then by referring to the minifile translated the coded input into a message.

The message was passed back through the executive program to the CRT screen. This all took place within seconds and the CRT operator then verified with the field reporter, who was still on the phone, that the input was correct. If the field reporter and the CRT operator confirm

---

*A state race is a race on which an entire state votes. These races are Presidential, Senatorial, and gubernatorial, but not the House of Representatives.

that the data displayed on the screen were correct, the CRT operator, by depressing a function key on the CRT keyboard, entered the data into the minifile, where they became available for computations. Occasionally the correctness of the data displayed on the CRT screen was not confirmed. In such cases, a function key is depressed and the screen was cleared. The field reporter and the CRT operator then started over by reentering the coded input. Most of the time the second attempt was successful. In those cases where the second attempt also failed, the call from the field reporter was transferred to a control desk for further attempts at correction.

Second, remote requesting from the studio: the "Decision Team" in the studio decided to examine the detailed status of a race. A current computation was desired. A coded request was entered via a CRT. The teleprocessor carried the request to the data center computer and posted an electronic flag in computer memory. The executive recognized this flag and passed the request to the edit and update program. The edit and update programs edited the request and passed control to the decision report generator. The decision report generator in this case called the state race computation routine, which computed this state race using data in the minifile and then assembled the report and passed control back to the executive. The executive posted an electronic flag in computer memory for the teleprocessor. The teleprocessor, when ready, carried the report back to the studio.

An additional feature of the system worth mentioning is the decision management function. Computations, in addition to being invoked when a decision report was requested by the decision team in the studio, were also done for all state races on a cyclical basis. The computational algorithms, although they never determined whether a race has been won, did determine status for state races. This status, together with estimated percentages and other criteria, were used to form an ordered list which was updated and displayed every minute on a fixed screen CRT in the Decision Area of the studio. This function helped a busy Decision Team determine which races were probably the most ready to be called. As stated above, all win calls for state races were conscious entries into the system via CRT by the Decision Team.

The scope of the VPA system can be best shown by a presentation of its various outputs. There are a number of reports and displays that could be requested or which were generated by the system. The system was both management and information oriented. The management portion of the system supported the Decision Team in its efforts to estimate the outcome of the races. It also provided up-to-the-minute status of the input situation. The information portion of the system provided the CBS News correspondents with the latest data in both summary and detailed format. Correspondents, producers, and other personnel had CRTs with keyboards with which they could request reports and displays.

Examples of some reports:

1 Decision Report—a state race report containing estimators which were prepared by the computations of the system. These were the reports that were used in assisting the Decision Team in estimating the winner of state races.

2 Decision Management Report—a national report which contained a list of all state races in alphabetical order. This list provided the Decision Team with the status of all state races.

3 Congressional District Detail Report—a national report which listed historical and current votes and percentages and other statistical information on the 435 Congressional Districts. It printed these data ordered by state within regions.

4 National, Regional, and State Analysis Reports—a breakdown of voting results into groups, such as ethnic background, geographic area, income, education, and so forth. These reports were based on the stratified SVUs mentioned in data bank.

Some examples of displays:

1 Posting Display—a national display used by those who posted summary information on display boards.

2 House Summary Display—a regional display that showed the status of house races in terms of the number elected and leading by party.

3 Senator/Governor Recap Display—a national display that showed the summaries of Senator and gubernatorial races that are won, leading, and undecided within regions by party.

4 Senator/Governor by Regional Display—a regional display that showed status and in some cases estimated percentages of total vote by party for Senate and Governor races on a state-by-state basis. There was also a Presidential equivalent of this display, which was automatically generated once a minute by this system.

In 1972, the VPA system ran on two computers. In prime mode, it ran on an IBM 370/155 computer with 2 million bytes of storage. It also ran at the same time in backup mode on another IBM 370/155.

The CRTs and printers, remote as well as local, were wired to the computers through switches. In this way, if one machine failed, the equipment could be switched to the second machine. The second computer was kept up to date by reading in data from cards that were being punched by the prime computer.

In 1974, a new concept was tried. The practice of running the VPA system in two machines dated back to 1968 when hardware and software were less reliable. In 1974, in order to introduce some economies into the election system, a methodology was established which provided backup and redundancy at less cost. It was called a "gracefully degraded VPA system." The prime system ran on one IBM 370/155, while the gracefully degraded system occupied the second IBM 370/155.

The peripheral hardware was still switchable, since it was possible to run both prime and backup systems in either computer. A checkpoint/restart procedure developed in 1972 made this possible. In the event of a catastrophic hardware failure, the prime system was to be moved from the first machine to the second machine, at which time it would either overlay or cohabit in the second computer with the "gracefully degraded VPA system." Overlay or cohabitation would depend on the situation at the time of failure. The systems were designed to do either, and a management decision made at the time was to determine which alternative was to be taken. The situation never arose.

The Core System—The County Return Estimator System (CORE) was one which handled the vote input on a county and Congressional District level rather than at the SVU level. Before describing the CORE system, a more detailed description of the News Election Service (NES) processing is in order.

NES was and still is a consortium of the three networks (CBS, NBC, and ABC) and the two wire services (AP and UPI) that takes on the nationwide responsibility to collect, aggregate, and distribute the unofficial vote returns on Election Night. NES hired and trained approximately 100,000 precinct reporters and 3500 county reporters for this purpose. They used computers to tabulate and to transmit the vote data.

NES transmitted to its members in two ways; one, by regular teletype circuits for display by the members, the other by a high speed teletype circuit, which contained votes by counties within state races, for special computation by the members. The VPA system did its projections on the basis of returns from sample precincts, or SVUs as they were called by CBS News. The CORE system on the other hand, estimated race results based on returns from counties. The reasons for developing the county system were to provide a means of confirming the estimates made via the VPA system and also to assist in estimating results that were not able to be determined with the VPA system when all the SVUs had reported. This condition arose on very close races. An important distinction existed between the CORE and the VPA system. The CORE system was a management system only. It did not, in any direct way, supply information to correspondents, nor was its output used directly for display purposes.

The County Return Estimator (CORE) system as originally designed in 1972, resided in a quarter-million byte IBM 370/145. The system was in essentially two parts; the front end, which captured the data from the NES input lines, logged it, edited it, and updated the system's files; and the back end, which consisted of the statistical calculations and the report generators. In 1972, the system was designed in this manner to allow the option of having either the CORE back end or a third-level VPA backup system, described later, in the computer. There were two IBM 370/145s, and the entire CORE system occupied one, while the CORE front end and the third-level VPA backup occupied the other.

The purpose of the CORE system was two-fold; to provide additional estimators to the Decision Team to assist them in estimating race results, and to supply the VPA system with additional information on state races and House races.

From a technical viewpoint, the CORE system bore some resemblance to the VPA system. It is a multiprogramming system. Since it was designed four years later, it used the facilities of the IBM operating systems to a greater extent than the VPA system. The system a main task which attached the other subtasks, the Line Termination task, the Move and Edit task, the Quality Control task, and either the CORE computations and Reports task or the entire VPA Backup system.

Briefly, a description of the tasks is as follows:

1 The Line Termination task had the responsibility of getting the data from the lines into the line buffers in memory. The line buffers were set up to handle physical as opposed to logical transmissions. The logical records were variable in length, with a maximum length of 56 characters. The maximum size of a physical transmission block was 200 characters. Stated another way, a record of voter information about a county or a Congressional district was a maximum 56 characters long. As many complete records of voter data as could fit

in a 200-character block would be sent as one message. The up-to-56 character blocks were logical records. The up-to-200 character blocks were physical records.

2   The Move and Edit task got the data from the line buffers to tape buffers for logging and to process buffers where the data were acted upon by the Quality Control task. As the data were moved from the line buffers, they were then handled in logical records. Records were placed in the logging buffers in physical blocks. Actual writes to tape occurred on both buffer full conditions and timing considerations. Logical records that were candidate votes by county were placed in the process buffer until a complete state race (all counties for that race and state) was accumulated. A preliminary edit was also performed on the data by this task.

3   The Quality Control task came into play when a complete state race was in a process buffer. The Quality Control task brought in from disk the historical and master information for that state race. This information was contained on a data base which was put together from the county file portion of the data bank. Data saved from prior transmission cycles were also used together with the historical and master information to perform a rigid quality control and to execute some basic computations.

4   The Computations and Reports task was responsible for calculations of all state races for producing the outputs required by the system users. These reports included a decision report issued by the system on request and a Decision Management report issued every five minutes, along with a Congressional District report issued on request. The Decision Management report was similar to the Decision Management display in the VPA system in that it listed in order of importance (based on internal computations) the state races requiring attention by the Decision Team. Cards were punched containing estimates for state races. These cards were transmitted over off-line card transmitters to the CBS Data Center. These estimates were read into the VPA system and were selectively integrated with the VPA estimates. In some cases, based on the judgment of the Decision Team, the CORE estimate stood by itself. Although the correspondents did not know which estimate had been used, they were given the estimate, whatever its source, for editorial use.

Although the CORE system in no way approached the information capabilities of the VPA system, it did provide information to the VPA system, as just shown. Also, in addition to the county tables, Senatorial races were also sent. These data passed through the CORE system and a status (leading, elected, or undecided) was assigned to each race. This information was also punched into cards by the CORE system and read into the off-line remote card readers for transmission to the data center for entry into the VPA system. These data helped a great deal in producing the CBS News House estimate and other House reports. In 1974, the House data was taken directly into the VPA system and the algorithm was performed in the VPA system.

Also in 1972, a great deal of time, effort, and money went into the CORE system to determine the validity of the statistical methodology. A CORE backup system was developed which was a stripped down version. This backup system was used in a time-sharing environment. In 1974, the decision was made to enhance the time-sharing version of the CORE system, for the sake of simplicity and economy.

The VPA Backup System (Gracefully Degraded VPA)

The VPA backup system was designed to be a software backup. It was to provide a limited repertoire of reports and also data for the critical screens in the studio as well as to the minicomputer which drove the graphic display system.

Input to the system was furnished on cards, from the VPA prime system or, if the VPA prime was down, from a keypunching operation. These cards punched from the VPA prime system were to be images of all input except report and display requests. All vote input and decision input had to get to the backup system to keep it up to date. The calculation portions of this system were less complicated than those in the prime system, and the entire system was designed and written by a different group of programmer analysts. Output requests were made from a central location in the studio. Part of the request code was a location code for the requester, which was received and stored by the system and then was printed on the output report to facilitate distribution.

If the VPA prime system was down, the calls would continue to come into the CRT operators. However, when the CRTs were inoperative, the CRT operators were to code the information onto an input form. The forms were to be sent to keypunch. The punched cards were to be read into the card reader on the backup computer. The cards were to be held, so that when VPA prime came back up, they were to be input to VPA prime to catch up the system. A shortcoming of the backup system was the fact that the input was to be keypunched. The on-line editing and validation that took place with the CRT operation were sacrificed when a fallback to keypunching was required.

The VPA backup system could produce limited output, so that the most important type of information got to the correspondents. But the backup system was significantly slower than the prime system. If it became the only source of VPA information for the studio when many reporters were calling in their returns, the timeliness of the information would suffer, falling further and further behind what could be achieved with the prime system in operation.

The Display System—the Display system was first designed in 1972 to display on-air the VPA status information for each race. The VPA prime system transmitted the status information to the display system at the same time as it was transmitting to the fixed screens in the studio.

The Display system was originally designed around a PDP8 computer using VIDIFONT displays as the output devices and communicating with a remote IBM 370 computer to receive the election estimate information. The system was designed to be automatic with operator involvement required only to request a display or to perform certain tasks in the event of hardware failures. In the 1972 version, the sequence of calling displays to the on-air monitor was controlled by a small terminal keyboard associated with a CRT display unit. The CRT display was used primarily to give immediate feedback to the operator as to which state and race has been called up. This allowed for correction of errors before the results were displayed. The CRT display was also used to give the operator system messages and to allow preview of the data without disturbing the on-air monitor. To guard against the possibility of operator errors' causing the displays to change, the system had inputs from the on-air control to inhibit update of any display that was currently on-air.

Enough hardware redundancy was built into the system to guard against the loss of a VIDIFONT, the lost of a command keyboard or CRT, or the failure of any hardware module in the system. Failure of the transmission line from the IBM 370 was compensated for by a manual update routine which used a teletype.

In 1974, the enhancement of the display system was the single biggest modification to the election effort. In 1972, it had been used only for VPA status displays. In 1974, it was used for all raw vote displays as well as for VPA status displays. The entire sweep of display boards around the studio was no longer necessary. This represented a big dollar savings in studio costs.

The system in 1974 used two PDP/11 computers. The operation was duplexed. All information, with raw vote and VPA status, was transmitted from the VPA prime system (or the gracefully degraded system) to the display system. The Display system also took in data from the NES lines, in the event that, should VPA system go down completely, the display system would at least have the current raw vote.

The peripherals attached to the PDP/11 included CRTs and keyboards, a printer, a card reader, floppy disk, teletypewriters, and line adapters for teleprocessing. Twenty-eight thousand positions of memory allowed the system and files to be completely resident in the computer memory. The system was basically simple. It merely received and stored the most current raw vote and VPA status information. When these data were requested for a particular state race, they were displayed on a CRT. When the control room director was ready, he asked for the data, the CRT/keyboard operator depressed a key, and the information was passed to the VIDIFONT interface, which formatted and displayed the TV compatible image on an on-air monitor in the control room. When the director was ready, the image was shifted to on-air.

In conclusion—although the election systems were very sophisticated in some respects, they were only when they had to be. Simplicity was sought in system design and operation. For example, the use of off-line card readers to get data from one location to another. There are more sophisticated ways of doing that job, but it was judged that sophistication was unnecessary in this case.

The above describes the role of computers in the production of the CBS News Election Night Broadcast. They represented a significant part, similar in magnitude to setting up the studio and remote location operations. However, a host of resources of the CBS Television Network Division and the CBS News Division were called upon to provide up-to-date in-depth information to the viewing public for this most important news story. In many situations, computers are integral, but other resources are always required to make any system successful.

ASCII and EBCDIC Characters

Appendix B.1 ASCII Characters

Row	Bits	Col.							
		Control Characters		Graphic Characters					
		0	1	2	3	4	5	6	7
		000	001	010	011	100	101	110	111
0	0000	NUL	DLE	SP	0	@	P		p
1	0001	SOH	DC1	!	1	A	Q	a	q
2	0010	STX	DC2	''	2	B	R	b	r
3	0011	ETX	DC3	#	3	C	S	c	s
4	0100	EOT	DC4	$	4	D	T	d	t·
5	0101	ENQ	NAK	%	5	E	U	e	u
6	0110	ACK	SYN	&	6	F	V	f	v
7	0111	BEL	ETB	'	7	G	W	g	w
8	1000	BS	CAN	(	8	H	X	h	x
9	1001	HT	EM	)	9	I	Y	i	y
10	1010	LF	SUB	*	:	J	Z	j	z
11	1011	VT	ESC	+	;	K	[	k	{
12	1100	FF	FS	,	<	L	`	l	¦
13	1101	CR	GS	−	=	M	]	m	}
14	1110	SO	RS	°	>	N	^	n	~
15	1111	SI	US	/	?	O	—	o	DEL

Appendix B.2 EBCDIC Characters

bits 0 and 1 →	0 0				0 1				1 0				1 1			
bits 2 and 3 →	00	01	10	11	00	01	10	11	00	01	10	11	00	01	10	11
bits 4,5,6,7 0000	NUL		DS		SP	&	-									0
0001			SOS				/		a	j			A	J		1
0010			FS						b	k	s		B	K	S	2
0011		TM							c	l	t		C	L	T	3
0100	PF	RES	BYP	PN					d	m	u		D	M	U	4
0101	HT	NL	LF	RS					e	n	v		E	N	V	5
0110	LC	BS	EOB	UC					f	o	w		F	O	W	6
0111	DL	IL	PRE	EOT					g	p	x		G	P	X	7
1000									h	q	y		H	Q	Y	8
1001									i	r	z		I	R	Z	9
1010		CC	SM		¢	!	|	:								
1011					.	$	,	#								
1100					<	*	%	@								
1101					(	)	_	'								
1110					+	;	>	=								
1111	CU1	CU2	CU3		|	¬	?	"								

Facilities Engineering Rule of Thumb

An often overlooked, but potentially troublesome aspect of EDP is the physical planning of an EDP facility. A great deal could be written and has been written about the subject, but experience is the best teacher. It is usually the "little things" that get you in trouble in the area of facilities operations, things like no convenience outlet for the adding machines, no carriage tapes for the line printers, or no pencils for the clerks. Less frequently, one underestimates the "big things" like total electrical power required, total space required, or total air conditioning requirements. The reason for this is that when budgets are being prepared, the "big things" are usually fairly well known ahead of time and can be carefully planned for. Here are a few items that often help in shortstopping questions that come up regarding facilities work:

1 Rule of thumb to determine approximate airconditioning requirements:
   A:

$$\frac{\text{BTU per hour}}{12,000} = \text{tons of air conditioning}$$

or the more conservative
   B:

$$\frac{\text{BTU per hour}}{12,500} = \text{tons of air conditioning}$$

2 Determination of power functions:
   A Single phase:

$$KVA = \frac{\text{volts} \times \text{amps}}{1000}$$

B Three phase:
$$KVA = \frac{\text{volts} \times \text{amps} \times 1.73}{1000}$$

3 Conversion to metric. A factor of 254 applied to inches results in metric measures:
A 1 inch (in.) = 25.4 millimeters (mm)
B 1 m = 0.03937 in.
C 1 in. = 2.54 centimeters (cm)
D 1 cm = 0.3937 in.

A factor of 0.304801 applied to feet results in meters
A 1 foot (ft) = 0.304801 meter (m)
B 1 m = 3.280829 f.
C 1 in. = 0.0254 m
D 1 m = 39.37 in.

Square inches and square feet
A 1 in.^{2} = 6.45163 cm^2
B 1 cm^2 = 0.1549 in.^{2}
C 1 ft^2 = 0.0929034 m^2
D 1 m^2 = 10.76 ft^2

Pounds to kilograms
A 1 pound = 0.453592 kilogram (kg)
B 1 kg = 2.205 lb

Temperature: Degrees centigrade & Fahrenheit
A Temp (°C) + 17.78 × 1.8 = Temp (°F)
B Temp (°F) − 32 × .05556 = Temp (°C)

Programming Language Example— Mnemonics

In order to show what a mnemonic instruction set looks like, a list of mnemonic operation codes is presented. The "op codes", as they are called, are a partial list of the instruction set of the PDP 11/40 computer. The list is only partial, since the meaning of many of the instructions would be lost on those readers not familiar with the specific computer which uses the instructions. The actual number of instructions in the PDP 11/40s repertoire is 66. Twenty-four are listed here. Each mnemonic instruction generates one machine instruction when assembled.

Op code	Meaning
ADD	Add
BEQ	Branch if equal
BGE	Branch if greater than or equal
BGT	Branch if greater than
BHI	Branch if higher
BHIS	Branch if higher or the same
BLT	Branch if less than
BLE	Branch if less than or equal
BLO	Branch if lower
BLOS	Branch if lower than or the same
BMI	Branch if minus
BNE	Branch if not equal
BPL	Branch if plus
BR	Branch (unconditional)
CLR	Clear
CMP	Compare
DEC	Decrement

DIV	Divide
HALT	Halt
INC	Increment
JMP	Jump
JSR	Jump to subroutine
MOV	Move
MUL	Multiply
NEG	Negate
NOP	No operation
RTS	Return from subroutine
SOB	Subtract one and branch
SUB	Subtract

When mnemonic instructions (op codes) are being written by the programmer, they have what are called operands associated with them. Operands are written symbolically by programmers, but they are assembled into storage addresses in the same process (assembly) that puts mnemonic op codes into machine language instructions. For example, a programmer might write:

ADD GROSS,YTD

Assembled this instruction would look like:

06ssdd

06 is the PDP 11/40 machine language instruction for ADD, ss (source) is the address of GROSS and dd (destination) is the address of YTD.

Programming Language Example— COBOL

This discussion is offered to provide a contrast to the mnemonic instruction set of Appendix D. What appear here are some basic COBOL statements. COBOL is an acronym for Common Business Oriented Language. COBOL allows the use of many English language words, at the discretion of the programmer. However, some words are reserved for specific functions by COBOL itself, and cannot be used by the programmer except in the syntax established by COBOL. Currently there are many versions of COBOL in use (ANS COBOL, COBOL E, COBOL F, to name a few). Because there are many COBOL compilers, the effectiveness of one of the basic objectives of the COBOL language is minimized, that is, the ability to transfer a program from one machine to another by merely recompiling it. Since a number of compilers exist, this transfer generally requires that modifications be made to COBOL programs before they can be recompiled to run on a machine other than the one for which the program was originally written.

Following are some of the most basic COBOL statements. The purpose here is not to provide a complete COBOL repertoire, but rather to give the reader a feel for the kind of statement found in high level languages.

Input/Output Statements

READ "file name." Read a record from the file indicated by "file name."

WRITE "record name." Write a record "record name" to the file set up for it.

ACCEPT "data name." Data are read in from a low speed I/O device and stored in a location specified by "data name."

DISPLAY "data name." Data from the location specified by "data name" are read out to a low-speed I/O device.

Data Transfer Statements

MOVE "data name 1" TO "data name 2." Move the data in the location specified by "data name 1" to the location specified by "data name 2."

Arithmetic Statements

ADD "data name 1" AND "data name 2" GIVING "data name 3." Add the data in the location specified by "data name 1" to the data in the location specified by "data name 2" and store the sum in the location specified by "data name 3."

SUBTRACT "data name 1" FROM "data name 2" GIVING "data name 3." Subtract the data in the location specified by "data name 1" from the data in the location specified by "data name 2" and store the remainder in the location specified by "data name 3."

MULTIPLY "data name 1" BY "data name 2" GIVING "data name 3." Multiply the data in the location specified by "data name 1" by the data in the location specified by "data name 2" and store the product in the location specified by "data name 3."

DIVIDE "data name 1" INTO "data name 2" GIVING "data name 3." Divide the data in the location specified by "data name 1" into the data in the location specified by "data name 2" and store the quotient in the location specified by "data name 3."

ROUNDED. When attached to an arithmetic instruction, this statement results in the right most retained digit of an arithmetic operation being increased by one, if the last discarded digit is five or greater.

Sequence Control Statements

GO TO "procedure name." Proceed to the first instruction at the location specified by "procedure name" and execute it.

IF "conditional expression" THEN "imperative statement" OTHERWISE "statement." If the "conditional statement" is true, execute the "imperative statement." If not true, execute the "statement."

PERFORM "procedure name." Proceed to the series of instructions specified by "procedure name." When finished return to the statement following the PERFORM statement.

PERFORM "procedure name" UNTIL "conditional expression." Execute the series of instructions specified by "procedure name" repeatedly as long as the "conditional expression" is false. When it is true, proceed to the statement following the PERFORM statement.

Processor Control Statements

OPEN INPUT "file name 1, ...file name n", OUTPUT "file name 11, ...file name nn." Housekeeping instructions that prepare the input and output files for use.

CLOSE INPUT "file name 1, ...file name n", OUTPUT "file name 11, ...file name nn." Wrap up instructions that remove the files from accessibility by the processor.

STOP RUN. Indicate to the processor that the program has processed all the data, finished the job, and no longer needs the resources of the computer.

The statements shown here are basic. The words in capitals are reserved by COBOL and have fixed uses. Those in small letters are parameters or variables and the programmer gives them actual names. For example:

Instead of: OPEN INPUT "file name 1, file name 2," OUTPUT, "file name 3."

one might see: OPEN INPUT "INVENTORY MASTER, TRANSACTION," OUTPUT "UPDATED INVENTORY MASTER."

Instead of: MULTIPLY "data name" BY "data name 2" GIVING "data name 3."

one might see: MULTIPLY "TOTAL HOURS" BY "HOURLY RATE" GIVING "GROSS PAY."

Each COBOL statement generates a number of machine instructions when it is compiled.

Glossary

Glossary

This is a limited glossary. One limitation is intentional. The other is beyond control. In constructing this glossary, terms that have been in use for a substantial period of time have been for the most part intentionally left out. It is not the purpose of this glossary to redo what has already been done, and done well.

Today a multitude of terms, words, phrases, acronyms, and initials confound the uninitiated. The list of terms continues to grow, with new ones added on almost a daily basis. This phenomenon creates an uncontrollable limitation in preparing this glossary. It is regretable, but new "buzz words" appear in the interval of time which occurs between the writing of a book and its publication and distribution. Perhaps, in the future, books will be on-line to both author and reader, and this situation can be remedied.

This glossary is different from most. Although it is less comprehensive in the quantity of terms covered, it is somewhat more qualitative in the definitions of the terms that are covered.

Access method A method (software) of transferring data between main memory and the control unit of a peripheral device. The access method activates the necessary hardware that brings about the actual transfer of data. Access methods employ techniques and use other hardware to compensate for the speed differential between computer memory and control units. Access methods abound and can bring about sequential data transfers, direct access data transfers, teleprocessing data transfers, and queued data transfers. As newer access methods are introduced, they are found to be very elaborate and have many functions in addition to their ability to transfer data.

Access time A term that can describe several types of activity. It is used to define the amount of time it takes to get an instruction or a unit of data from computer memory to the processing unit of a computer. It has also been defined as the amount of time it takes to get a unit of data from a direct access storage device to computer memory.

ACK Acknowledgment. An ACK is an affirmative acknowledgement control character that a receiver sends to a transmitter following a successful transmission of data.

Acoustic coupler A device that can be connected to a telephone handset. It serves as a converter between the analog electronic signals of communications equipment and the digital electronic signals of electronic data processing equipment. Acoustic couplers are generally found as part of portable communications terminals that can communicate with computers over a public telephone network. The schematic in Figure G.1 illustrates.

ACU Automatic Calling Unit. A device that allows a business machine to make dial calls on a telephone network.

Address The term is used to define either a specific location in computer memory, a specific location on a direct access storage device, or a relative location. The third address is one which indicates a specific location relative to some reference point, say the beginning of a data set or file. However, since the data set or file itself can be completely relocated from time to time, there is no location or address in an absolute sense.

A/D Analog to Digital converter. An interface device that handles conversions of natural parameters (analogs), such as temperature displacement and magnetic field strength, to digital form.

ADP Automatic Data Processing.

ALC Assembler Language Coding. The name of the mnemonic programming language of the IBM 360, 370 and 303X lines of computers. Also called ALP and BAL.

ALGOL Algorithmic Language or Algebraic Oriented Language. A high-level language whose expressions and statements take the form of algebraic formulas or algorithms.

ALP Assembler Language Programming. See ALC.

Alternate routing The practice of providing a secondary communica-

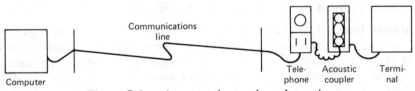

Figure G.1   An acoustic coupler schematic.

tions path (line) that can be available when the primary path is not available.

ALU   Arithmetic and Logic Unit. The ALU is that part of the processing unit that performs arithmetic (additions, subtractions, multiplications, etc.) and logic (ANDs, ORs, and exclusive ORs) operations.

AM   Amplitude Modulation. The process of changing the value of a signal by varying the amplitude (fluctuation of the wave) of the signal. See Carrier.

Analog   Can be applied as an adjective to nouns such as: data, transmission, and computer. Analog means that which is continuously available (often expressed as a wave), as opposed to that which is discreetly variable (often expressed as pulses). Analog data are often graphically represented as a sine curve as seen in Figure G.2.

APAR   Authorized Program Analysis Report. An IBM acronym. The APAR is a procedure that is followed when reporting problems that arise with IBM supported software. When a "fix" for the reported problem is returned, it is sometimes referred to as an APAR.

APL   A Programming Language. A high-level programming language. It is used interactively. Its statements use mathematical notation, and the language is a favorite among mathematicians and statisticians.

ASCII   American Standard Code for Information Interchange. A seven bit, plus an eighth bit for parity, code established in an attempt to standardize data representation. There is a chart of all ASCII characters in Appendix B.1.

ASR   Automatic Send/Receive. A description of a teletype device that can receive information on "hard copy" paper or on paper tape as well as having the ability to send information by way of a keyboard or a paper-tape reader. Devices like this are being replaced for by more up-to-date terminal devices.

Asynchronous   The exact meaning of this term is largely determined by the context in which it is found. When used in the context of communications (teleprocessing), it describes a method of data trans-

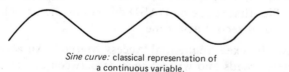

Sine curve: classical representation of
a continuous variable.

Figure G.2   Continuous variable, sine curve representing an analog signal.

mission. In asynchronous transmission, characters are sent one at a time, with each character bounded by start/stop symbols. When used in the context of computer processing, the term describes a method of concurrent task processing by the computer. When two program modules are being executed concurrently in a computer and they do not have impact on one another, they are said to be running asynchronously.

Audit Trail A means of identifying the actions taken upon a file or a data base by data moving step by step through a processing cycle. It provides a method for checking or tracking output back to its original form. The audit trail is useful in pinpointing where an error has taken place.

Autopolling A contraction for automatic polling. Polling is a process whereby terminals in a computer network are scanned periodically to determine whether they are ready to send information. Autopolling is a combination of hardware and software that polls the terminals in a computer network. It is automatic in the sense that an individual programmer does not have to concern himself with terminal polling when writing a program. It is something to look for when evaluating "front end" systems.

BAL Basic Assembler Language. See ALC.

BASIC Beginners All-Purpose Symbolic Instruction Code. A high-level programming language, approximating business English, that is used in an interactive computer environment. It is a favorite among financial analysts.

Baud For all practical purposes, it is the measure of the speed at which data travels over a communications line. For example, a 1200 baud line is one that commonly supports data transmission at a rate of 1200 bits per second (bps). In reality, baud is not necessarily the same as bits per second, but it is commonly accepted as such.

BCD Binary Coded Decimal. A four-bit coding structure that is also known as the 8 4 2 1 system.

BDAM Basic Direct Access Method (IBM). An access method that transfers (reads and writes) records between computer memory and direct access files that reside on DASD devices in an unblocked fashion, that is, one logical record at a time.

BISAM Basic Indexed Sequential Access Method. An access method which transfers (reads and writes) records between computer memory and indexed sequential files that reside on DASD devices in an unblocked fashion, that is, one logical record at a time.

Bisynch Short for binary synchronous. It is the most commonly known synchronous data transmission protocol. Through the 1970s, most devices found on computer networks used it.

Bit The smallest piece of data recognizable to a computer. The term bit is a contraction for binary digit.

Bootstrapping A bootstrap is a small initialization computer program that is used to load another program and to start up an inactive computer.

BSAM Basic Sequential Access Method. An access method which transfers (reads and writes) records between computer memory and sequential files that reside on DASD or magnetic tape devices in an unblocked fashion, that is, one logical record at a time.

BSC Binary Synchronous Communications (IBM). The IBM supported communications protocol used in communication networks during most of the 1970s. See bisynch.

BTAM Basic Telecommunications Access Method. An access method that transfers (reads and writes) records between computer memory and telecommunications control units, one record at a time.

Buffer A term that has more than one meaning. In hardware, it is a component that compensates for the different rates at which data are transmitted from one component to another. Software buffers perform a similar function, but are located in computer memory. One type of hardware buffer is that which is used to compensate between computer memory and a tape drive. Computer memory moves data at electronic speeds while a tape drive moves data at mechanical speeds, which are significantly slower. Rather than tie up the computer as data are moved bit by bit from a tape drive to computer memory, a buffer is put between the two. While the tape drive fills up the buffer, the computer memory does other work. When the buffer becomes full, the computer memory pauses in its work and empties the buffer. Software buffers are like staging areas where pools of data are kept, with individual data records selected when needed. Software buffers are used to handle blocked records, that is, where one physical record contains more than one logical record. The buffer is used to hold the block of several logical records, and they are selected one at a time from the buffer as needed.

Bug An error in a program, or a malfunctioning piece of hardware. Bugs can manifest themselves in many different ways. Those that manifest themselves most quickly cause the least damage, but they are not necessarily the easiest to find or to fix.

Bus A hardware component to which can be connected several components making up a computer configuration. A bus is like a channel across which data can flow from one component to another. See Figure G.4c.

Byte An electronic data processing term that is used to describe one position or one character of information, made up of eight bits. A character of data or a position of computer storage of the eight-bit variety is called a byte of data or a byte of memory.

Carrier This term has two meanings. A common carrier is a communications company that provides communications lines and services. Included are firms like AT&T, local Bell companies, Western Union, and Comsat. Carrier is also used to describe the signal that is continuously present on a communications line. It is that signal that can be modulated by amplitude (width), by frequency (time), and by phase (angle or degree) to alter data communications. Figure G.3 illustrates (a) carrier, (b) amplitude modulation, (c) frequency modulation, and (d) phase modulation.

Channel A channel is a path on which data travel. In the data communications area, a channel refers to a communications line, often a telephone line. In the computer hardware area, a channel is the equipment and cable that interconnect computers (processing unit and memory) to peripheral devices. Computer channels are of two basic types, high speed and low speed. High speed channels are used for tape

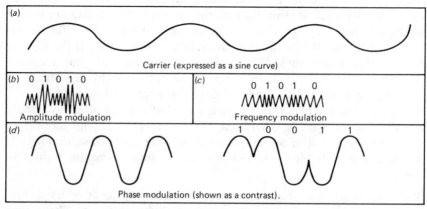

Figure G.3 Representations of carrier, amplitude modulation, frequency modulation, and phase modulation.

and disk devices, while low speed are used for printers and CRTs. Interleaving of data from different devices on channels is made possible by subchannels. Actually, channels are made up of a number of distinct physical wires. The different wires are different subchannels. Figure G.4 illustrates channels and buses.

Checkpoint   A point during the execution of a program where significant data are recorded, usually for the purpose of restarting the program. The purpose of a checkpoint is to reduce the amount of rerun time required for a long-running program that malfunctions. For example, suppose a program is scheduled to run for 14 hours. Without a

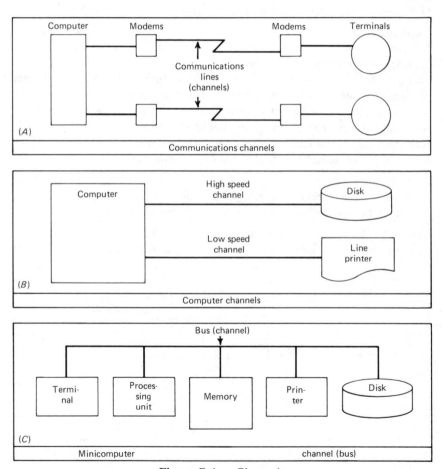

Figure G.4   Channels.

checkpoint, if the program malfunctioned after 13 hours, it would have to be restarted at the beginning; the 13 hours already run would be a total waste. With a checkpoint, taken, say every 15 minutes, the greatest amount of rerun time would be 15 minutes.

CICS Customer Information Control System (IBM). A data base/ data communications software package that provides an interface between a computer network and an application's data bases and programs.

COM Computer Output Microfilm. An equipment configuration that is able to produce on microfilm what is normally on printed output. The data that are recorded on the reel of microfilm come from an output reel of magnetic tape produced by a computer.

Concentrator A device (maybe a computer) that can provide interfacing between many low speed communications lines and one or more high speed communications lines. The purpose of the device is to lend economy to a communication network by reducing the number of lines needed between remote terminals and the computer. Concentrators can send a block (a number of messages from the many terminals) when requested by the computer. They can send individual messages to the terminals after deblocking the concentrated messages sent from the computer. The schematic in Figure G.5 illustrates.

Conditioning A service provided by common carriers (e.g., telephone company). The service, through the use of additional equipment, enhances the quality of communications lines for data transmission.

Console Usually the main input/output device by which individuals can interact with a computer. The device used for a console is generally

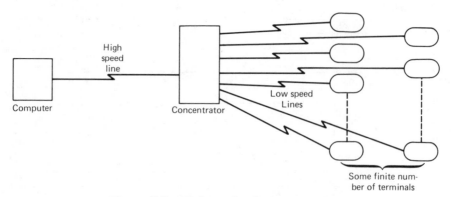

Figure G.5   Schematic of a concentrator.

a CRT with a keyboard or a typewriter terminal. A console, as the main input/output device, often has some privileged capabilities not available to other terminal devices that can interact with the computer.

Control character A configuration of bits (a character) that when found in a specific context has a specific meaning or purpose. For example, there is a specific configuration of bits for a start of text (STX) character, that tells the equipment being used that text is going to be transmitted and that all data following the STX character are text; until an end of text character (ETX) is encountered. The ETX is another specific bit configuration.

Conversational A type of processing where an individual at a terminal device has a "conversation" with the computer. The individual at the terminal enters some data, the computer responds; the individual responds to the computer's response, and so on, until the conversation is terminated.

CPU Central Processing Unit. The CPU is that part of a computer that contains the arithmetic, logic, and control functions. For practical purposes, it is everything except computer storage (memory) and input/output.

CPU time The amount of time actually used by the processing unit to complete a job. This is different from actual elapsed time, since the processor is not always working on the job. During input/output processing in a multiprogramming computer, the processer is not working on the job; it is doing some other tasks. It is very likely that during I/O operations for one job, the processor is working on another job.

Cycle This term ranks as one of the all-time greats in the "buzz word" category. In the world of EDP, there are several different types of cycles. Basically, a cycle is an interval of time required to complete an event. Examples: an instruction cycle is the interval of time required by a processing unit to execute an instruction; a memory cycle is the amount of time required to fetch a piece of data from memory and get it into the processor; a processing cycle refers to the interval of time between the processings of a job. For instance, a payroll might get processed once a week; that payroll job would be said to be on a weekly cycle.

DAA Direct Access Arrangement. Equipment provided by a common carrier that permits attachment of terminal equipment to the common carrier network.

D/A   Digital to Analog converter. An interface device that converts digital impulses into analog or natural parameters such as: magnetic field strength, temperature, or displacement.

DASD   Direct Access Storage Device. Those computer peripherals upon which information is commonly stored so that individual items can be accessed directly. Magnetic disks and magnetic drums are examples.

Data base   A collection of data elements within records within files that have relationships with other elements within other records within other files. Pointers are used to establish interrelationships among data elements that transcend file boundaries.

Data base management system   A collection of programs that can store, manipulate, and retrieve data elements that make up a data base.

Data dictionary   A collection of files or a data base and a system of programs. The files or data base hold descriptive information about an organization's data. The system of programs permit the storage, manipulation, and retrieval of that information. The scope of data dictionaries is widening to include descriptions of other organizational assets in addition to the data asset. Those other assets include terminals and computer equipment.

Data set   At one time, a modem was sometimes known as a data set. This use of the term seems to be less frequent today. In the area of software, files and arrays of data are called data sets.

DBMS   See Data base management system.

DCB   Data Control Block. A function of a compiled (executable) computer program that contains information about data upon which the program is to operate. The programmer, when originally writing the program, establishes a DCB for every data set or file that the program is going to reference when it is executing. The DCB, like the rest of the program, is originally coded in source statements and compiled into the program. The DCB is commonly called a control block.

DCTL   Direct Coupled Transistor Logic. A method of coupling transistors in an integrated circuit configuration.

DD Statement   Data Definition or Define Data Statement (IBM). A job-control language statement. The concept behind the DD statement is to define the properties of a set of data (a file) to a program during its execution. The properties typically include such information as the number of records in the data set, the number of characters in the individual records in the data set, the type of storage device on which the data set is stored, and how long the data set is to be kept before it can be destroyed (scratched). This list is not exhaustive, but serves to illustrate the kind of information provided on DD statements.

DDCMP Digital Data Communications Protocol (DEC). See protocol.

DDD Direct Distance Dialing. A service which allows a subscriber to call other subscribers outside his area without the assistance of an operator.

DD/D Data Dictionary/Directory (IBM). A data dictionary, data directory software package.

DEC Pronounced "deck," the term is an acronym for the Digital Equipment Corporation of Maynard, Massachusetts. DEC is the maker of PDP computers and other computer equipment.

Delimiter A character that is used as a separator or an organizer of data. The most common example of this is the space or blank character that is used to separate words in ordinary prose. Others that are often used in the EDP community are commas, semicolons, or dashes.

Dial up A function within a teleprocessing control unit or a front end computer that enables a computer system to call up a remote terminal over the switched line telephone network. It is also possible to have a dial-up facility where the terminal calls up the computer. Terminals with acoustic couplers are used with ordinary telephones.

Direct line A direct communication link between two devices. It is direct in a logical sense only. From the common carrier perspective, it is a service. It is not a physical connection with a dedicated circuit. If traffic on the line is expected to be heavy, a direct line service is generally less expensive on a monthly basis than is a dial-up facility. Modems are required on both ends of a direct line arrangement.

DMA Direct Memory Addressing (Access). A facility that allows data to pass in and out of memory without passing through the processing unit.

DOS Disk Operating System. A smaller, simpler operating system than OS or MVS, having fewer facilities and less sophistication. It is generally used on smaller machines.

Duplex The name given to simultaneous two-way transmission over a communications line.

EAM Electronic Accounting Machine. There are two uses for the term. EAM equipment refers to electromechanical equipment such as card sorters, collators reproducers, and tabulators, also sometimes called unit record equipment. Since there are still some 80-column cards in use, the peripherals that read them into computers are also known as EAM equipment.

EBCDIC Extended Binary Coded Decimal Interchange Code (IBM). An eight-bit code that allows up to 256 different bit configurations. See the appendix B 2.

EDP Electronic Data Processing.

ENQ Enquiry. A communications control character used to elicit a response from a remote station for identification.

EOT End of Transmission. A communications control character that indicates the completion of a transmission. A transmission may contain one or more messages. The EOT character resets all stations to control mode. That is, to a status of awaiting a poll by local operation.

ETX End of Text. A communications control character that terminates a string of characters transmitted as an entity and started with a STX character. See STX below.

EXCP Execute Channel Program. The input/output instructions of an access method. The EXCP instructions are those which bring about data transfer between computer and peripherals. These instructions are usually generated from macro instruction statements of an access method. In some cases it is possible to write the instructions without an access method.

FAX Facsimile. An equipment configuration that facilitates the transmission of images over a common carrier network.

FCC Federal Communications Commission.

FDP Field Developed Program (IBM). The term covers a range of software products marketed by IBM that can be licensed to a customer. They may have interfaces enabling them to interact with other software products.

FIFO First in, first out. A concept with application in inventory (stock rotation), in list theory (a push-up list), and in other areas. Basically it means: first come, first served.

FM Frequency Modulation. The process of changing the value represented by a signal by varying the frequency of the signal. See Carrier.

Front end A configuration of equipment (usually a computer with or without peripherals) and software that performs tasks that are in communications based systems. The size of the front end depends to a great degree on the size and complexity of the network and the number of applications in the host computer(s). Front-end software includes tasks such as the following: line control, message handling, transmission error control, and the polling of terminals. A front end can run in size and complexity all the way from a single small computer up to a configuration of equipment that includes several computers of varying sizes. See Figure G.6 for a schematic.

GIGO   Garbage in, garbage out. A process that has been known to be more efficient when converted to computers.

Glich   Same as a bug. An error condition either in hardware or in software that causes a malfunction.

Half duplex   The name given to nonsimultaneous two-way data transmission over a communications line.

HASP   An acronym for Houston Automatic Spooling Program. It is a software "front end" for use on IBM 360 and 370 computers that efficiently handles local and remote batch input and output. In more advanced shops (late 370 and 303X with VS software) it has been replaced by another piece of software called Job Entry Subsystem or more simply, JES.

Host   The term host has several uses:
Host computer implies a primary or controlling computer in a multiple-computer operation.
Host system implies a system to which a communications system

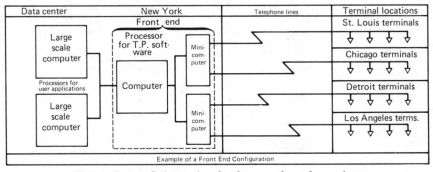

Figure G.6   Schematic of a front end configuration.

is connected and with which the system can communicate.

Host processor is the processor that houses VTAM in a VTAM telecommunications system.

For practical purposes, a host is usually a large-scale computer that is given work by satellite equipment. The large-scale computer usually exercises a degree of control over the satellite equipment.

IC   Integrated Circuit. An integrated circuit is composed of multiple transistor, resistor, and diode structures on semiconductor wafers. Integrated circuits are able to perform functions that at one time required several discrete electronic components.

IMS   Information Management System (IBM). A data base management system software package that provides the facilities for storing and retrieving information from hierarchically structured files and data bases.

IMS/VS   Information Management System/Virtual Storage (IBM). A data base/data communications system software package that provides the facilities for storing and retrieving data from hierarchically structured files and data bases in a communications environment.

Indexing   A programming technique whereby an instruction can be modified by a factor called an index. Depending upon the specific function to be performed, the index can be used to control several iterations of the same group of instructions. For example, suppose an individual wanted to compare a value (a part number) to a list of values (part numbers) in order to determine a corresponding value (price), using a table such as the one below.

Part Number	Price	Item in List
64 7286	4.00	1
64 9123	.83	2
64 9947	3.98	3
65 0042	7.23	4
65 0192	4.40	5
•	•	•
•	•	•
•	•	•
•	•	•
•	•	•
67 9413	1.79	74
67 9902	.43	75

An individual writing a program without indexing would have to write 75 compare instructions, each followed by an instruction telling the computer what to do if an equal compare takes place. Using indexing, the programmer writes one instruction setting the index to 0. The programmer then writes an instruction comparing the index to 75. An instruction is then written telling the computer what to do if the index is equal to 75. The next instruction tells the computer to compare the part number being sought with the first part number in the list modified by the index. The next instruction indicates what should be done if the values are equal. The next instruction adds a 1 to the index and the last instruction of this series directs the computer to go back to the instruction that compares the index to 75. This example shows how to loop through a table of values seeking a match by using seven instructions instead of 150. It is one of many ways to use indexing.

Intelligent terminal   A terminal device that is able to do more than send and receive data. The range of intelligent terminals is very broad. For a terminal device to have intelligence merely means that it is a computer.

Interactive   An adjective describing the ability to interact with a computer. Facilities like TSO for programmers and APL and BASIC provide interactive services for computer users.

Interface   Generically, an interface is a common interconnection between two components or functions that do not normally interact. In the case of hardware, it can be a piece of equipment. In the case of software, it can be a common area of computer storage or some common instructions shared by two or more programs. In the realm of minicomputers, the term interface is used to describe the circuit board that is necessary to attach a particular peripheral device to the minicomputer. Figure 6.7 conveys the concept.

Interrupt   A function of computer hardware that allows the processing of a set of instructions to be discontinued and control passed to another set of instructions. It is this interrupt hardware that enables operating systems to function. There are several types of interrupts. Some of the better known are: input/output (I/O interrupts), machine failure (machine check interrupts), invalid data or instructions (program check interrupts), and manual intervention (external interrupts). For example, suppose a console operator wishes to know how long a specific job has been executing in the computer. The operator keys in a request through a console device. The program that is currently executing is interrupted, a time-keeping program is invoked, the response to the

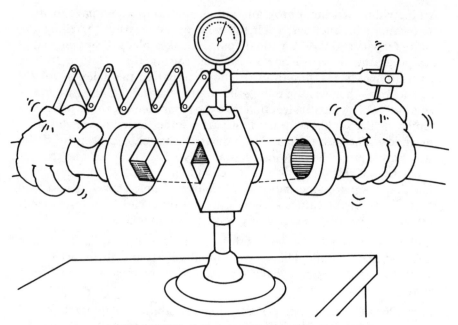

Figure G.7   Concept of an interface.

request is generated and sent back to the console, and control is returned to the program that was interrupted. In actuality, in an operating system environment, several programs are going concurrently and interrupts are being constantly generated for inputs and outputs.

I/O   Input/Output. An acronym used to signify the transfer of data between computer storage and peripheral devices.

IPL   Inital Program Loader. A procedure by which the initial portion of an operating system or of some other program is loaded into computer memory.

IUP   Installed User Program. The term refers to a range of program products developed by users of IBM equipment and marketed by IBM.

JCL   Job Control Language. A language that is used to give job and data information to the operating system. A group of JCL statements, called a PROC (short for procedure), accompany each program as it is readied for execution by the computer's operating system. There are six basic types of JCL statements: Job, Execute, Data Definition, Delimiter, Null, and Command. The first three are the most familiar.

JES   Job Entry Subsystem. A software subsystem (part of the operating system) that is used to route batch input and output through computer systems in a multiprogramming environment.

K   An expression signifying a unit of memory size. It refers to 1024 positions of computer memory. For example, a 28K memory contains 28,672 positions of memory.

Leased line   See Direct line.

LIFO   Last in, first out. A technique employed in queuing theory. A push-down list has the most recently added item removed first. It is the antithesis of FIFO.

LSI   Large Scale Integration. This is component miniaturization technology. LSI usually refers to a piece of semiconductor containing hundreds of transistors.

Macro   A macro is a single programming language statement that when compiled results in a series of machine language instructions. Macros are often developed by programmers themselves for programming routines that must be used over and over again in an installation.

Main line: A programming technique whereby the logic of file and/or transaction handling is coded into a program module called a main line. The actual processing of the data from the files and the transactions is done by subroutines that are called according to logical determinations made by the main line.

MES   Miscellaneous Equipment Specification (IBM). Refers to the request for parts that are required to modify a piece of equipment that is already installed, and also to the parts themselves.

Message switching   A process of receiving and holding messages until an outgoing channel is ready for them, and the retransmitting of the messages. Entire computer configurations have been dedicated to this task when the quantity of messages and the complexity of the network demanded it.

MFT   Multiprogramming with a Fixed number of Tasks (IBM). A version of the IBM operating system that supports the concurrent execution of multiple programs of fixed number and size. MFT has been made obsolescent by virtual storage (VS) operating systems.

MICR Magnetic Ink Character Recognition. MICR is a facility by which a machine can recognize characters that have been written with special magnetic ink. A common example of this technology is seen on personal checks and deposit slips.

Microcomputer A very small computer, usually contained on one or a few semiconductor chips.

Microprocessor A piece of hardware that houses the computing parts of a computer on one circuit board or in one set of integrated circuits. It is an integral part of a microcomputer, but does not contain the I/O interfaces and memory unit. Microprocessors have been hailed as "computers on a chip."

Microprogramming The process by which a microprogrammable processor, that is, a processor whose instruction set is not fixed, is programmed. Simply stated, microprogramming is programming hardware.

Microsecond Millionth of a second.

Millisecond Thousandth of a second.

Minicomputer Difficult to define precisely. The definition seems to evolve. A minicomputer, in general terms, is mini in price and size. Until the late 1970s, minis were also small in terms of word length and memory size. The cost of a mini is difficult to use as a criterion because of the changing nature of minis themselves and the economic climate. The only concrete portion of a definition is that a mini is a general purpose, programmable digital computer.

MIS Management Information Systems (Services). When originally coined, the term was intended to describe comprehensive computerized management information systems. Later on, the term came to be applied to the organizations that developed those systems.

Modem Acronym for modulation/demodulation. A modem is a hardware device that interfaces telephone lines and computer equipment. This is shown schematically in Figure G. 8. A signal on a telephone line is analog and a signal on computer line is digital.

Module Simply described, a module is a part or a component. It can refer to a section of a program, a piece of hardware such as an integrated circuit board, or a peripheral device that is part of a computer system configuration.

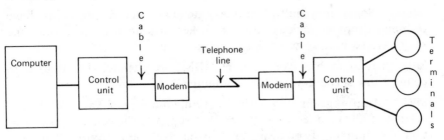

Figure G.8   Schematic of modems and their use.

MOS   Metal Oxide Semiconductor. A product of semiconductor technology that, although somewhat slower than LSI bipolar, is significantly less expensive.

MPX   Multiplexor.

MSI   Medium Scale Integration. Integrated circuitry that contains about ten transistors on one piece of semiconductor.

MTBF   Mean Time Between Failures. An indication of reliability.

MTTR   Mean Time Till Repaired. An indication of field engineering performance. "How long after I find it broken does it take to get it fixed?"

Multidrop   See multipoint.

Multiplexor   A mixer, of which there are many types. It can be a device that divides one path into several. Devices for doing this exist in both the computer and the telephone disciplines. In the telephone discipline, multiplexing can be done by dividing a transmission channel into several smaller channels, either by splitting frequency bands of the channel into smaller frequencies (frequency division multiplexing) or by using one channel to act as several channels on an intermittent basis (time division multiplexing). Computers have what are called multiplexor channels. One of these channels can have several smaller channels called subchannels.

Multiprocessing   Simultaneous processing by two or more processing units that are sharing a common memory and peripheral devices.

Multiprogramming   Concurrent processing of several programs by one processing unit, often giving the impression of simultaneous processing.

Multipoint   Describes a communications line to which more than one terminal device is attached. Each of the terminals has a unique identification. Sometimes multipoint lines extend across the country and have terminal drops in various cities. In other instances, a multipoint line may have several drops in the same building.

MUX   (byte) multiplexor channel (IBM). A channel that is used to connect low speed devices to a computer.

MVT   Multiprogramming with a Variable number of Tasks (IBM). A version of IBM's operating system that supports the concurrent execution of a number of programs of no fixed size, the limitation being the amount of computer storage available for processing. MVT has been made obsolescent by virtual storage (VS) operating systems.

NAK   Negative Acknowledgment. A communications control character transmitted by a receiving station indicating a "not ready" condition or indicating that a transmission was not correctly received and that a retransmission is required.

NCP   Network Control Program (IBM). A set of computer programs that reside in a front end computer. NCP controls the activity of the computer network. The activity includes the establishing and breaking of logical connections, interfacing the network and host computer(s), transmission error checking, and handling.

Nanosecond   Billionth of a second.

Network   Generically, a network is an interconnected group of nodes. Nodes can be computers and peripheral devices. The connectors between the nodes can be telephone lines or some of the more exotic links such as satellites or microwaves.

Noise   Spurious interference on a communications line. Because of the precision required in data transmission, noise is troublesome. Noise can be reduced by the addition of hardware to the line by the carrier (telephone company). Modems also filter out some noise.

Null modem   (Modem bypass) A piece of equipment that simulates a modem. There are many types of terminal devices that are normally used in a remote environment. If for test purposes or for some other reason, such a device was to be set up locally, a pair of null modems would be substituted and a telephone line would not be needed. Yet the simulated arrangement would appear to be a remote set up to the computer software.

OCR   Optical Character Recognition. A process of recognizing characters or numbers in printed form through the use of photoelectric technology. Also known as optical scanning.

OEM Original Equipment Manufacturer. The term is used to describe the process of obtaining pieces of equipment from various manufacturers and configuring them as a single entity and then marketing the configuration to a third party. In addition "OEMing" firms also include software, as they market the entire package. These types of systems are called "turnkey systems."

On-line/off-line In a sense these terms are complementary. Devices are said to be on-line or off-line. Operations are said to take place on-line or off-line. Simply stated, on-line means under the control of a computer and off-line means not under control of a computer.

OP Code Op code is a term that describes the action portion of a programming statement. For example, ADD, MOVE, READ, WRITE, COMPARE, and LOAD are action statements. An Op code is the equivalent of an English language verb.

OS Operating System. An operating system is a collection of programs that controls the execution of other programs. It handles such tasks as scheduling, allocation of resources, input and output, data management, and related services.

PABX Private Automatic Branch Exchange. An exchange (a group of telephone numbers) that is privately controlled, but that is able to place and receive telephone calls from the public telephone network.

Paging A type of segmentation where software and data are modularized into modules of a specific size. These parts are read into computer storage from peripheral devices as they are needed. The parts are known as pages.

Parity Parity is a coding mechanism that is used to check data for accuracy as they are moved from device to device. Parity can be odd or even. For example, in EBCDIC, the bit configuration 000100110 is odd. To make it even, the last bit, reserved for parity use is changed to a "1." It does not change the character but in even parity, the bit configuration is 000100111. In real situations, parity is determined by the type of equipment in use.

Patch (Zap) A method for modifying a program in its load form without recompiling it. The practice of patching programs should be restricted to emergencies, and recompilations should be done at the first possible opportunity.

PAX Private Automatic Exchange. A dial telephone exchange, the use of which is restricted to the organization using it. It is connected to a public telephone network for incoming and outgoing calls.

Payback   This term refers to the estimated time required for a proposed system to pay for itself. Based on estimates, a small formula can be used to let management decide if a proposal is economically feasible. The formula is:

$$\frac{\text{Implementation costs}}{\text{Annual Savings}} = \text{Payback}$$

Annual savings are the difference between what it currently costs to do the job and the estimated cost of the proposed way of doing it. Implementation costs are the estimated costs of systems design, programming test time, and other start up costs.

PBX   Private Branch Exchange. A manually operated exchange, operated by the organization using it. It is connected to a public telephone network for incoming and outgoing calls.

PDP   Programmed Data Processor. PDP is a term that refers to a line of computers from the Digital Equipment Corporation of Maynard, Massachusetts. There are PDP8s, PDP11s, and PDP10s. Within the lines there are types, PDP11/35, PDP11/40, and so forth.

Picosecond   Trillionth of a second.

Polling   A process by which a computer system inquires to see if a terminal has any transactions to send. The computer system commonly accomplishes this by going through a list of terminals that are supported by the system and making inquiries on a time basis. It is not uncommon for multiple terminals in a system to be polled once a second.

Power   When applied to a computer, this term usually refers to the speed at which instructions can be fetched from memory to the processor and the speed at which data can be moved from one memory location to another. In the broadest sense, it defines the amount of work that a configuration of computer equipment can put out. It does not refer to electrical power.

PROM   Programmable Read-Only Memory. Read-only memory has programs "frozen" onto it when it is produced. With programmable ROM, modules of ROM can be replaced. For example, imagine a 16K module of ROM made up of eight 2K modules. A modification could be made to one of the 2K modules by remanufacturing (reprogramming) it. In this sense ROM becomes PROM.

Protocol   A formalized set of conventions used for the establishment and maintenance of contact between two communicating devices. Some commonly known protocols are IBM's Binary Synchronous (Bisynch), and the Synchronous Data Link Control (SDLC) and DEC's Digital Data Communication Message Protocol (DDCMP). Some of the functions of a protocol are: error checking and recovery procedures, synchronization of sending and receiving stations, and controlling of the transfer of data.

QISAM Queued Indexed Sequential Access Method (IBM). An access method that transfers (gets and puts) records between computer memory and indexed sequential files located on direct-access storage devices. In the queued methodology as opposed to the basic, records are moved in blocks, that is, there may be more than one logical record in each physical record.

Queueing The process of putting something in a line to wait. A job queue is established for jobs as they await the allocation of computer resources for their execution. Transactions are queued up in a telecommunications environment awaiting the arrival into computer memory of the program modules that are necessary for the processing of individual transactions.

QSAM Queued Sequential Access Method (IBM). An access method that transfers (gets and puts) records between computer memory and sequential files located on peripheral devices. Records are moved in blocks, that is to say, they are moved in groups of two or more records.

RAM Random Access Memory. A computer memory that allows access to any of its locations. It is the most common type of computer memory.

RCTL Resistor Capacitor Transistor Logic. A method of combining resistors, capacitors, and transistors in an integrated circuit configuration.

Register Register is a word that describes a hardware device where data are held for specific uses. The uses depend on the function of the register. There are several different kinds of registers—address registers, general purpose registers, instruction registers, and accumulators.

Remote This term has more than one meaning. One describes a site or a terminal that is located at a place other than where the computer is located. A remote terminal, for example, refers to a terminal that interacts with a computer over communications lines since it is located at a site remote from the computer site. Remote is also used to describe program testing that takes place when the programmer is not present.

Resource   A term that is used to refer to a component of a computer configuration. Memory, processing unit, disk storage, printers, tape drives, and control units are considered resources. So too, are programs, access methods, and other software. In large data centers, billing for the computer resources used is often based on resource utilization.

Response time   There is some debate about what actually constitutes response time. Basically, it is the elapsed time from when an entry is made from a terminal device until a response is received back on that terminal.

RJE   Remote Job Entry. A method of processing batch jobs on a terminal device that is generally, but not necessarily, located at a site remote from the computer site. The terminal often has a card reader, a CRT, or both, and a printer in its configuration. The software to accommodate the RJE devices is located in the computer. The HASP or JES software packages contain RJE modules, and they have widespread use. The schematic in Figure G.9 illustrates.

ROM   Read Only Memory. A memory module that is manufactured with its use predefined and included. This kind of memory can be read from but not written to. It is not programmable in the traditional sense. See PROM for the exception.

RPG   Report Program Generator. A high-level language, with a compiler that is intended primarily as a vehicle for quickly producing programs that access data from data bases or files and for providing listings or summaries of those data in tabular or formatted reports.

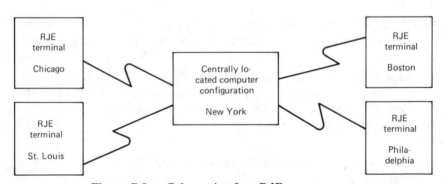

Figure G.9   Schematic of an RJE arrangement.

RPQ Request for Price Quotation (IBM). The term RPQ has come to mean more than a mere price quotation request. It has come to mean a feature that is not normally supported but that will be furnished for a price.

RTL Resistor Transistor Logic. A method of combining resistors and transistors in an integrated circuit configuration.

SDLC Synchronous Data Link Control (IBM). A synchronous data transmission technique (protocol) that is a uniform way of transferring data between computers and remote terminals.

Semiconductor A substance whose electronic conductivity is intermediate between an insulator and a metal, at normal temperatures. Semiconductor technology has been able to produce in great quantity electronic components that are nearly microscopic in size. They have also been produced very economically and under many different subtechnologies within semiconductor technology. There is, therefore, a proliferation of terms describing semiconductor modules.

Session Software that establishes relationships between two separate units that are to communicate with one another. The units are said to be having a session for the purpose of: (1) establishing the format of the information that is to be exchanged, (2) establishing operating protocols, (3) binding the required resources, and (4) protecting the integrity of the union.

SLT Solid Logic Technology. A broad term for solid-state electronics technology.

SNA System Network Architecture (IBM). SNA is a collection of hardware and software products that addresses the world of computer networks. Its aim is the standardization of equipment and software in computer network environments.

Source The term has two meanings. When seen in the context of programming, it indicates a computer program in the form that it was originally coded by a programmer. The source program may exist on coding sheets, on a deck of 80-column cards, or may reside on a DASD desvice. A program in its uncompiled state is called a source program or more simply source. The term is also used to describe input to a computer system as that input exists in its original form. Documents such as time cards or invoices, before they are put into computer-recognizable form, are called source documents or source.

Spooling A resource optimization technique, where output reports, for example, are stored on disk, and printed out as resources become available. If all printed reports had to be printed as they were being produced by computer programs, the speed at which jobs producing them could be executed by the computer would be governed by the speed and quantity of printers available and their speed. Spooling output reports to disk is significantly faster and allows the computer to get other jobs done more quickly, because the printers are not governing the computer speed. The reports are printed from the spool when resources become available.

SRL System Reference Library (IBM). This term refers to the technical manuals published by IBM.

SSI Small Scale Integrated. The smallest integrated circuit package, roughly between one and 10 transistors, on one semiconductor wafer.

Statement An expression or an instruction of a computer program. It is analogous to a phrase, clause, or sentence in the English language. Programs written in high-level languages (languages closer to the problem than the machine) often have statements in them that bear close resemblance to English language statements.

Structured programming A programming technique. Although the technique has been known for some time, its current applications are being presented as a standardization and simplification tool. The technique embraces the concept of writing completely self-contained program modules. Each module is written and subsequently executed without branching to another module. Unfortunately, although structured programming is the best way to write programs from a program simplicity and program maintenance perspective, the technique is already suffocating under a mountain of technical jargon which belies its simplicity.

STX Start of Text. A communications control character that precedes a string of characters transmitted as an entity. The string is terminated by an ETX character. See ETX.

Subroutine A program module that handles a specific task or group of tasks within the framework of a larger program or group of programs.

Supervisor A program within an operating system that can interrupt and alter work flowing through a computer.

SVC Supervisor Call. An instruction from a program language set that is used to give control of the computer's resources to a module within the operating system, known as the supervisor. The SVC is used in an application at the point in that program where a task that must be done is the responsibility of the operating system rather than of the application program.

Synchronous A term that indicates that two systems are in step with one another. The word is often seen in the context of synchronous transmission, which describes a method of transmitting data at a fixed rate with sending and receiving stations synchronized with one another.

Syntax The conventions governing the formation of programming statements. Just as proper syntax makes for easy reading of the English language, so too, proper syntax is required for statements are that are to be read and compiled by a computer. Stated another way, just as incorrect syntax in the English language hinders or destroys effective communication between individuals, so too, incorrect syntax in writing programming statements can make programming statements uncompilable or can lead to compilations that are incorrect.

System This term can refer to either a combination of hardware, a combination of software, or a combination of both. A computer equipment configuration of processing unit, memory, and peripherals is referred to as a system. A collection of related computer programs that work in tandem with one another or in sequence one after another for the purpose of doing a specific job is called a system. A complex computer configuration consisting of many pieces of equipment and a number of computer programs for executing several jobs is also known as a system.

Switched line The normal type of telephone connections between two points that is established when needed.

Task A unit of work. When an operating system is cranked up and applications begin running under the operating system, many units of work are required for the application programs to complete what they have to do. These units of work are system services performed by the operating system for the application and are called tasks. These tasks include activities that range from the small and quick to the large and long of duration. For example, getting a record for an application program is a task. Such a task is relatively small and quick. Invoking a data base/data communications system and letting it provide services to applications using it for 12 hours is also a task. Tasks sometimes delegate subactivities within themselves to other tasks called subtasks.

TCAM   TeleCommunications Access Method (IBM). An access method used to transfer records between computer memory and remote terminals and local peripheral devices. This method is a successor to the earlier BTAM access method and is an interface between a single application and many different terminal devices. See VTAM.

TCU   Teleprocessing Control Unit. A hardware device that sends and receives data over communication lines. Recent technological advances have given more capabilities to TCUs. Most TCUs now are computers, often called front ends.

TELEX   Has two uses. TELEX is a telegraph service provided by Western Union. It is also the name of a company that manufactures and markets a range of computer peripherals.

Thrashing   This word aptly describes what takes place in a paging environment when the reading of pages of software from auxiliary storage is taking place with such frequency that the overall performance of the system is degraded.

Time-sharing   An interactive or conversational method of working on a computer. In a time-sharing environment, a number of typewriter or CRT terminals are given access to a centrally located computer. The software (an operating system option) allocates intervals of time to each of the terminals on a regular basis. The terminals may or may not be located in the same location as the computer. Time-sharing can exist in a communications or in a noncommunications environment. In a hypothetical time-sharing facility, pictured schematically in Figure G.10, there might be six terminals attached to a computer. Out of each minute (60 seconds), each user might be given a time slice of 10 seconds of CPU time. Since the CPU is significantly faster than the terminal, it appears to the user that he has the whole CPU. In reality, time-sharing

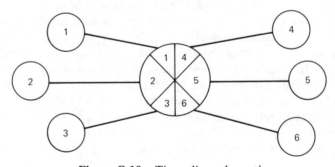

Figure G.10   Time slice schematic.

facilities support many more than six devices. Installations supporting hundreds of terminals are not unheard of. Some corporations have as their sole purpose the providing of time-sharing services. These enterprises house a computer at a central site and have customers at various sites to whom they sell time.

Trace A tool to assist programmers in "debugging" their programs. The trace function itself is a program that records events that take place in the step-by-step execution of a program.

Transparency The use of a piece of equipment or a feature or a module for the purpose of enhancing a system or a process, the application of which is undiscernable to users of the system or process. Replacing several small TCUs with a single large TCU for the sake of economy should, barring an unforeseen difficulty, be undiscernable or *transparent* to users of the system. In terms of software, making a transition from one release of an operating system to another should, barring unforeseen difficulties, be transparent to system users.

Trunk In the communications field, a trunk is the main line of a telephone system.

TTL Transistor, Transistor Logic. An integrated circuit made up only of transistors, no diodes, capacitors, or resistors. Such circuits can be produced less expensively than mixed transistor, diode, and capacitor integrated circuits.

TTY Teletype equipment.

TWX Teletypewriter exchange service. An AT&T service in which a typewriter station is connected to a service that resides in a central office, to which are connected other teletypewriter stations in the same service. The facility services both the United States and Canada.

UNIBUS Together with PDP and DEC, a registered trademark of the Digital Equipment Corporation. A unibus is a single asynchronous, high-speed bus structure shared by the PDP/11 processor, memory, and peripheral devices.

Utilities These are programs that are often used in a computer environment. They include programs such as sorts, merges, copiers, reorganizers, restart and recovery programs, and formatters. They are often provided by hardware and software vendors as enhancements of their products. They can also be produced (written) by software vendors and by in-house programmers. Utilities are generalized programs that can be made to perform particular functions by specifying parameters. For example, specifying parameters to a generalized sort program, indicates to the sort the keys on which the file is to be sorted.

Virtual storage   A technique in which auxiliary storage is used to provide a depth of memory that is not actually present in the computer. For example, a computer may have 2 million bytes of memory, but it is possible through operating-system technology for users to treat it as an 8 million byte machine. In a virtual storage environment, the computer's operating system contains a paging algorithm. Within a virtual storage computer, modules are a specific size. The algorithm keeps track of the most frequently used modules. The operating system, together with the algorithm, keeps the most frequently used modules in main memory; the rest reside on peripheral storage till needed. The modules of fixed size are called pages. The process of bringing the needed modules into main memory as they are needed is called paging.

VS   Virtual Storage. Addressable storage that appears to be real but isn't. Also a contemporary version of IBM's operating system. It is called OS/VS or MVS.

VSAM   Virtual Storage Access Method (IBM). An access method for handling both direct and sequential data sets. More elaborate than earlier access methods like SAM and BDAM, VSAM it also catalogs and manages data sets.

VTAM   Virtual Teleprocessing Access Method (IBM). A teleprocessing access method that interfaces between a computer network and several applications. The number of terminal devices that are supported is limited to SNA devices.

WATS   Wide Area Telephone Service. A telephone service that allows calls to be made to or from a zone for a flat monthly rate rather than be billed on a per-call basis.

Index